Guidance and Counselling

Guidance and Counselling

Asha K. Kinra
Associate Professor
Department of Psychology
Jai Narain Vyas University, Jodhpur

Pearson

ISBN 9788131715277

First Impression, *2008*
Sixteenth Impression, 2023
Seventeenth Impression, 2024

Published by Pearson India Education Services Pvt. Ltd, CIN: U72200TN2005PTC057128.

Head Office: 1st Floor, Berger Tower, Plot No. C-001A/2, Sector 16B, Noida - 201 301, Uttar Pradesh, India.
Registered Office: Featherlite, 'The Address' 5th Floor, Survey No 203/10B, 200 Ft MMRD Road, Zamin Pallavaram, Chennai – 600 044.
Website: in.pearson.com; Email: companysecretary.india@pearson.com

Printed in India at Repro India Limited

Dedicated to the memory of
my loving mother

Contents

Preface

Guidance and Counselling caters to the requirements of postgraduate students of psychology and education as well as those pursuing their diploma course in educational and vocational counselling. This book will also serve as an elementary guide to future psychologists.

An individual faces numerous problems during his lifetime but the nature and extent of their problems differ. These problems can be solved through proper guidance. This is usually provided through various services, or by teachers and parents. However, teachers and parents are not equipped to provide adequate guidance; therefore, the help of qualified and trained counsellors is required. This book focuses on the nature of guidance and its relationship with education, the counselling process, counsellors' skills, and group counselling, and concludes by discussing the latest trends in this field.

Suggestions for the improvement of this book will be gratefully acknowledged.

I am indebted to H. R. Jaggi for his valuable assistance in preparing and editing the manuscript.

I am also grateful to numerous publishers and authors whose works have been extensively quoted. Finally, my thanks to K. K. Kinra for all the necessary support and encouragement.

Asha K. Kinra

1

Guidance

An Introduction

Life in today's modern world is becoming increasingly complex with science and technology pervading in almost every sphere of our lives. In order to adapt modern life, we depend on others' advice and guidance to a large extent. Even in ancient times, when life was relatively simple, people turned to their elders for advice in their struggle to adapt to their environment. It is clear that the need for guidance has always existed in human societies. However, from a psychological point of view, the empirical need for guidance and counseling for an individual—in different stages and spheres of their life—has been recognized only since the last two centuries. This recognition has led to the rise of guidance and counseling services as a scientifically organized profession since the early twentieth century. Earlier, assistance provided by any experienced person could be called guidance, now the assistance provided by a professional counselor is called guidance. It is clear that the concept of guidance has undergone a lot of changes. Let us now discuss in detail what guidance means.

What is Guidance?

Before we proceed to define guidance, an important fact must be kept in mind: Guidance does not focus on the problems of individuals but on their strengths and abilities to solve their problems independently. In other words, guidance assists individuals in unravelling their potential, abilities and interests, and on this basis, enables them to solve their own problems. In the case of guidance to young people, one of the chief aims of any guidance programme is to promote all-round development of the individual. We can say that guidance is a process or a tool that enables an individual to discover the ways to recognize his/her inherent strengths. Also, it is clear that as every individual is different, the guidance needed by different individuals will vary considerably.

The United States Office of Education (1918) defines guidance as 'the process of acquainting the individual with the various ways, including special training, in which he may discover his natural endowments so that he makes a living to his own best advantage and that of the society'.

Guidance should not be equated with providing directives to an individual. It does not mean thrusting of somebody's views on others or someone taking decisions for others. It is crucial that individuals take their own decisions. Keeping these very views in mind, Crow and Crow (1962) maintain that 'guidance is an assistance provided by a competent counselor to an individual of any age to help him direct his life, develop his own point of view, make his own decisions and carry his own burdens'. Similarly, according to J. Jones (1934), '[to] guide means to indicate, to point out, [and to] show the way. It means more than to assist'. Traxler (1966) describes the main objective of guidance 'to assist each youngster in such a way that he can recognize his capacity and strengths, and after building on them can integrate them into his life values and aims, and to ultimately enable him to steer his own path'. John, Stefflre and Stewart (1971) define guidance as follows.

> Guidance is the help given by one person to another in making choices and adjustments and in solving problems. Guidance aims at aiding the recipient in growing in his independence and the ability to be responsible for himself. It is a service that is universal—not confined to the school or the family. It is found in all spheres of life—in the home, in business and industry, in government, in social life, in hospitals and in prisons; indeed, it is present wherever there are people who need help and wherever there are people who can help.

Based on the foregoing definitions, we can define guidance as follows.

(a) An integrated, organized and creative process, which is useful and applicable to all spheres of life.
(b) A process aimed at ensuring the all-round development of the recipients so that they can solve their problems themselves.
(c) It aids the process of self-discovery in the recipients, and helps them to develop their own personality, point of view and a unique way of handling problems.
(d) Assistance provided by a professional counsellor is an organized, scientific and professional activity.

In the following paragraphs, we will look into the historical development of guidance, and its nature and scope as a professional practice.

Historical Development of Guidance

The roots of guidance lie in the needs felt by every society and their members throughout human history to train and help their young members in leading happy and successful lives. Guidance has developed as an integral part of education, which may be seen as the all-round development of an individual. In fact, vocational guidance grew out of the need to link the education system to the needs of the economy and industries in the early nineteenth century.

Rise of Vocational Guidance

The school system that started in the latter part of the nineteenth century was narrow and limited in its scope, it fulfilled only the scholastic needs of an individual. However, with the industrial development and technological advancement, societies became complex, and therefore, the need for guidance as a part of schooling came to be increasingly felt. With the growing demand in the industry for 'the right person in the right job', vocational guidance emerged as an organized service in education. It rendered vocational help to the youth on the threshold of their career. The cities of Boston and New York were the first to undertake such programmes. The term 'vocational guidance' was coined by Frank Parsons, the Founder–Director of the Vocational Bureau of Boston, Massachusettes in the United States. The Bureau was set up in January 1908 as a civic service house of North Boston, which helped people in choosing their careers and also in adapting to their work environments. Parsons wrote a book called *Choosing a Vocation* in 1909 which is still a valuable outline of the principles of vocational guidance.

The difference between educational guidance and vocational guidance was pointed out by Truman L. Kelley, whose doctorate dissertation entitled *Educational Guidance* was published in 1918. The testing movement was becoming popular in education at that time which helped the guidance movement to make speedy progress.

Guidance Movement in India

The guidance movement in India started off as a branch of research and study at the University of Calcutta in 1938. Soon, Vocational Guidance Bureaus came to be established by private and government agencies, for example, the Batliboi Vocational Guidance Bureau in 1941 and Parsi Panchayat Educational and Vocational Bureau, Bombay in 1947. Dr. H. P. Mehta, Director of the Bureau, provided vocational guidance services to the public of Bombay as well as to the Parsi Community. Dr. Mehta organized several training courses for career masters at his Bureau.

The most important step in this direction was the appointment of the Acharya Narendra Dev Committee by the government of Uttar Pradesh in 1938 to examine the issue of providing vocational guidance in schools. The establishment of the Bureau of Psychology in Allahabad was the direct outcome of the recommendations of Acharya Narendra Dev Committee. The Uttar Pradesh government first took interest in providing educational guidance to school-going children. After encouraging results and increasing demands to extend the service to more people, the government of Uttar Pradesh established five regional Bureaus at Varanasi, Lucknow, Kanpur, Meerut and Bareilly. In 1950, the Institute of Vocational Guidance was set up in Bombay. The Mudaliar Commission was set up by the government of India in 1952 strongly recommended the provision of guidance and counselling services in secondary schools. Based on this recommendation, the State Bureau of Guidance came to be established in the country in the next five years.

The Central Bureau of Educational and Vocational Guidance was established in 1954. Today, it is known as the Department of Educational Psychology and Foundation of Education (DEPFE) in the National Council for Educational Research and Training (NCERT), New Delhi. This department trains guidance personnel through a one-year postgraduate diploma course in guidance and counselling. With effect from the year 2000, the DEPFE also facilitates the training of professional guidance personnel at the regional institutes in Ajmer, Bhopal, Bhubaneswar and Mysore.

Nature of Guidance

As discussed above, guidance is an organized set of services whose objective is to assist an individual's development in consonance with his/her personal and social needs. As life is never static, and people, especially the youth, face new problems in every walk of their lives, guidance must be understood as a continuous process. In this process, the recipients of guidance are helped to understand their own personality and learn to make optimum use of their potential, interests and other capabilities. They try to make adjustments in varying social situations. The recipient individual develops the skill to independently solve problems and make judicious decisions in different situations. Needless to say, guidance helps an individual in adjusting himself in different situations. In today's changing environment, an individual is surrounded by myriad problems.

The chief contribution of guidance for a person is to foster wisdom and insight to tackle his/her problems independently. In this way, guidance helps an individual in planning the future, making important decisions and implementing them.

The scope of guidance cannot be limited to only educational or vocational spheres of life. Guidance is related to every aspect of life. Individual's development is facilitated by both formal and informal guidance. Informal guidance is the one that we receive from friends and relatives whereas formal guidance is received from professional guidance services. Guidance is recognized as an individual assistance. Even when it is imparted as a group activity, guidance provides the right direction for an individual's personal development. Today, guidance is being extensively used in almost every sphere of man's activity. Guidance is not meant for a particular or a special type of individual, rather it is meant for an individual who may need guidance at any stage in his/her life.

All of us receive informal guidance from our elders, and the society in general. However, this kind of guidance is subjective and based on personal experience instead of scientific body of knowledge. This is where professional guidance differs from informal guidance.

Guidance is the job of trained people. Professional guidance involves the use of various well-researched and scientifically tested techniques, methods and skills keeping in view the problems of an individual. In the case of educational guidance, experts, counsellors or school psychologists are needed who are trained to find appropriate solutions to the given problems.

Objectives of Guidance

The process of guidance is an objective-oriented process. The objectives of any guidance programme must be clearly demarcated right at its inception. The main objectives of any vocational or educational guidance programme are as follows.

(a) To make the individual aware of his/her inherent potential, interests, talents and capabilities.
(b) To help the person to develop his/her abilities, interests and skills in a way that he can make a useful contribution to the society according to his capacity.
(c) To assist the person in a balanced physical, mental, emotional and social development in such a way that he/she gets satisfactorily adjusted in his milieu.
(d) To make a person aware of the available educational and vocational opportunities in keeping with his abilities.
(e) To help the person to make correct interpretation of the facts of a given situation.
(f) To help the person become capable of solving problems in changing social situations in such a way that he/she renders maximum good to himself/herself as well as to the society at large.

Guidance programmes are developed and used in various special services in different walks of life. Services like probe and evaluation, consultancy, educational and vocational training and placement and compliance involve guidance programmes. Guidance programmes are, however, used most widely in educational environments, and the technical and conceptual aspects of most guidance programmes conform to it.

Problems of Guidance

On the basis of extensive study of the character of guidance, scholars have put forward various definitions in an attempt to throw light on its wide-ranging nature. However, no single definition can be regarded as final. In the following paragraphs, we will discuss the major debates around the concept of guidance.

Is Guidance a Generalized or a Specialized Service?

As mentioned earlier in this chapter, informal guidance is the one which we receive from our parents, friends and relatives, whereas formal guidance is provided by the guidance service within one's school. Another form of formal guidance is vocational guidance that fulfills a person's professional needs. But the fulfillment of a person's vocational guidance needs is not possible without personality development. Therefore, guidance is both a specialized as well as a generalized service in which teachers, parents and counsellors play a significant role. However, like other services, guidance services too need qualified personnel to implement them satisfactorily. In the process of guidance, everybody's role is important but the focus and responsibility remains of the counsellor. So, guidance must be looked as a service that is both generalized and specialized at the same time.

Is Guidance for a Particular Individual or for All?

Earlier it was held that guidance is needed only for problematic and maladjusted individuals. Because of the usual difficulties of time, space, personnel and budget, etc., most schools limit guidance services to those pupils who come to the counsellor on their own for a solution of their problems, or those who are identified with some problems.

Also, it must be kept in mind that every student comes across problems of their own. Students may be perfectly well adapted in one part of their life, and facing problems in others. There are many facets to the life of a student, and a proper development of an individual may need guidance at some or other stages in life. Therefore, guidance should not only be available to a particular or a special individual but should be available to all.

Is Guidance an Art or a Science?

There is a debate among psychologists on whether guidance is an art or a scientific discipline. Many psychologists believe that it is an art because a counsellor makes use of his/her individual skills, developed over a period of time, for the successful resolution of the problems of recipients.

However, the fact that guidance and counselling are a specialized scientific profession makes it important that the practice, despite the individual variations, should be based on solid scientific grounds. But according to Rogers, the process of guidance is scientific. Every science has a definite objective, and scientists use various tools and techniques to achieve it. Similarly, in the case of a counsellor, he/she uses different methods and techniques to solve the problem.

Is Guidance a Direction or a Developmental Process?

According to many psychologists, guidance means providing direction or guiding. According to this connotation, by guiding an individual you do not develop in him the ability to take his own decisions in an unknown area. Guidance is not forcing your views or formulating decisions, which a person should take for himself/herself. Lastly, guidance is also not taking another person's burden on your shoulders.

If we take guidance in the context of a developmental process, then guidance means assisting an individual to become aware of his/her talents and strengths. This will help him integrate them with his life values and objectives in a way that he can take his own decisions and chart his own direction. In other words, it means more than just assisting or providing direction.

Basic Principles of Guidance

For the successful execution of the process of guidance, the nature of different steps should be relevant for achieving the objectives. Objectives cannot be achieved without understanding the principles of guidance as they play an important role in the operational and practical stages of guidance. Psychologists, however, are not unanimous about the principles of guidance. These principles can be broadly discussed as following.

Guidance is for the Total Development of Personality

Guidance should be related to a student's all-round development. At times, a student does not know as to what his abilities are and what he wants to become? Guidance helps him in discovering his hidden endowments in such a way that all aspects of his personality develop to meet the varied needs of life.

Guidance Service is for Everyone

The main principle of guidance service is that it is meant for everyone. It is believed that an individual may come across problems at any stage in life and to overcome them he needs guidance.

Giving Importance to Individual Differences

It is universally admitted that no two individuals are alike, and even in twins we notice differences. According to this principle, the individual variations are both hereditary and environmental in nature. In the process of guidance, much of variations cannot be overlooked nor should they be. It is due to these variations that we see different impacts on an individuals'. Therefore, it becomes imperative to do a comprehensive study of these individual variations before starting the process of guidance to solve an individual's problems. Only on the basis of these studies, an outline of consultancy should be prepared for helping an individual.

Study of an Individual and Its Evaluation

In order to carry out the guidance programme successfully, it is necessary to supply accurate information to those running the programme. This gives the guidance expert a clear picture of the student's achievements and progress at a glance. This helps the expert to use properly selected and recognized tests. These tests help the counsellor to form a data bank about an individual's achievements, interests, mental abilities, etc. Compilation of all these facts in a well-documented form is essential for guidance.

Guidance Must be a Cooperative Effort

A guidance expert has to perform various tests to arrive at a solution for individual problems. But the expert has to rely on the availability of information from teachers, professors, parents and administration.

Guidance is a Lifelong Process

Guidance is a continuous process. Its need can arise in different situations of an individual's life. With increase in the pace of development, complexities in an individual's life are also increasing. Hence, for the solution of these problems a person may need guidance at any age. A person discovers himself/herself only through this process, learns to make bigger use of his capabilities, interests and other abilities. He keeps trying to adjust himself/herself to various situations and develops the ability to take his own decisions.

In this way, we see that it is a continuous and an active process.

Guidance Promotes Self-Reliance and Inspires Self-Development

The aim of guidance as such is the development of an individual's self-realization, self-reliance and self-development. To achieve this, a guide should assist a youngster in understanding his behaviour and facilitating improvement in it. A guidance expert should not impose his decisions on the subject but should assist him to inculcate an insight to understand and guide himself, so that the student can take his own decisions and start working accordingly.

Guidance Should be Imparted by Trained Personnel

Only qualified and trained personnel can do guidance and consultancy, everyone cannot offer profession guidance. A professional guidance expert is trained in both fundamental and practical elements. The training also includes knowledge of different aspects of psychology, psychological tests, guidance and consultancy techniques as well as peculiar nature of guidance and consultancy.

Guidance as an Integral Part of the Total Educational Process

Guidance services and educational activities are related to each other. Guidance is not the same as direction, but it helps the student in making suitable adjustments while receiving instruction and education. As such it is an integral part of education, the aim of guidance is to achieve the objectives of education. It should be related to the education system in totality.

Importance and Need of Guidance

In the modern age because of a scientific outlook and increase in the pace of development, rapid changes are taking place in social and individual fields. As a consequence, an individual's social, cultural, religious and professional value system is undergoing change. The effect of these changing conditions is most discernible in India because under the Indian democratic set-up different communities, religions and groups coexist. India is as yet counted among the developing nations. After independence, many plans for economic and social development have been made but problems like increase in population, unemployment, low industrial productivity, religious and political rivalries are staring us in the face. The need for guidance services is being felt much more than before. We can look at the guidance services from the following points of views.

From an Individual Point of View

Each human being has his own psychosomatic needs. The satisfaction of these needs and emotions determines his personality. It has become apparent from psychological studies that heredity as well as environment mould an individual's personality. Guidance helps in understanding the kind of environment needed for developing a child's personality.

(a) *The Role of Individual Differences*: It is certain that individuals vary from each other as regards physical, mental, emotional and developmental traits. For this very reason, development of each individual is different. Individual differences are influenced by heredity and environment that is why each individual's mental level, abilities and interests differ, and these determine individual capabilities. Children should be taught keeping these differences in view. This is possible only through guidance services. This service analyzes these differences among children and counsels them regarding their educational and vocational opportunities.

(b) *Personal and Social Development*: For an individual's personal and social development, it is essential for him to gain self-understanding and strike a balance between self and society. Variation has been observed even in the pattern of learning and development of individuals. Every person's process of development is different. Even the ability to learn and opportunities differ from person to person. The primary objective of teaching is the optimum development of a child's personality. It plays an important role in the achievement of this objective. Guidance contributes significantly in creating a proper environment for the development of a child by unravelling his inherited talents.

(c) *Academic Growth*: For the educational advancement of a child, it is essential to remove hurdles in the way of his skill honing. It is therefore important for the teacher to understand his students. He should find out how efficacious are the methods of his teaching. Only then would these methods prove useful for children. Classroom teaching cannot be effective till such time as children's problems, needs, interests and methods of teaching do not relate to their capabilities.

A teacher does not have enough time to teach and at the same time to understand children's problems, needs and capabilities. This effort can be meaningful only if guidance is made an integral part of the process. Students' educational advancement and proper adjustment is possible only if subjects of study are selected keeping in view their interests, capabilities and needs after a thorough understanding of their problems.

(d) *Professional Maturity:* It is very important for an individual to develop attitude and aptitude. Guidance can help in the selection of right subjects in schools and evolving a work culture which is in keeping with the wishes and aptitude of students. It is thus not enough to have only right attitude in the profession. Developing interests, opinions and skills is also important.

From the Educational Point of View

Education should be compulsory for everybody. To this effect, there is also a provision in the Indian Constitution that makes education compulsory and free up to the primary level. Compulsory education implies that each child should be educated in keeping with his ability and intelligence. This can be achieved only through guidance.

Need for guidance in education can be described as below.

(a) *Imparting Education According to Individual Differences*: The main fault with the present system of education is that it is not imparted keeping in view the individual differences among children in the areas of interest, aptitude and ability. The result is waste of a student's energy, time and money. All children are treated at a single level because of which they find education boring. This gives rise to indiscipline and dissatisfaction among children. These very problems can be overcome through guidance.

(b) *Choice of Relevant Curriculum*: With the progress in science and technology, new subjects have come into being. In a number of institutions, a single group of subjects, for example, arts, science or commerce is available. However, in some institutions different subjects are taught.

This being the age of science, for promoting proficiency in computer applications, computer education too has been introduced in many institutions. But one has to keep the individual differences in mind. All children cannot receive the type of education they want. Hence, choice of subjects should be made keeping in view individual differences. This necessitates the need for guidance. A guidance expert makes use of standard tests to help students choose the subjects of his study.

(c) *Increasing Number of Students in Educational Institutions*: Post-independence steps have been taken by the government to emphasize the spread of education. As a result, the number of students has substantially increased. It has become a challenging task, indeed, for a teacher to teach, understand children's problems and provide them correct guidance. For the Nation's progress, it is important that each child should be taught according to his ability, intelligence, capacity and interest, and should be provided vocational training to make him an able, useful and self-sufficient citizen. This objective can be achieved only through guidance.

(d) *The Problem of Indiscipline*: It is a nationwide problem, but now it is casting its shadow on education too. Every other day we witness and hear about incidents of strikes, vandalism and looting in colleges and universities. Because of this indiscipline, education fails to satisfy students fully. For the resolution of these problems, there is a need for guidance services so that students can overcome their problems satisfactorily.

(e) *Problems of Wastage and Stagnation*: Guidance services help to unnest the drop-out rate which is pronounced at the primary level in rural areas. Reasons as varied as poor school management, untrained teachers, tedious educational system, negligence of students because of excessive number of students, low attendance in classes because of rampant practice of private tuitions, inadequate or difficult course content, etc. have contributed to educational waste and stagnation.

This has made the implementation of guidance services at various levels of education impression.

From the Social Point of View

Today society is changing rapidly. Behind this lies the natural tendency of growth, new scientific discoveries, industrialization, mushrooming population, impact of different foreign cultures and the structural changes in the family system. This climate of flux in society is bringing in its train a sea change in individual's religious, social and ethical values. For the security and progress of the nation, it is necessary that each individual be so placed that he can become a useful and an active constituent of society. In this changing social climate, guidance has a vital role to play by giving a proper direction to social development of an individual.

(a) *Acceptance of the Fundamental Worth of the Individual*: The growth of a nation depends on the progress of the individuals who constitute it. A nation that pays proper attention to providing adequate opportunities and facilities for the welfare of its citizens will certainly progress. A society in which adequate opportunities for an individual's progress and exploitation of his talent are non-existent is not capable of producing progressive citizens. Guidance is needed for adequate development of an individual's latent talent in conformity with the social requirements.

(b) *Guidance for Better Family Life*: Family being the basic social unit it is essential to have cordial familial ties. Ideal family relations and good social adjustment within the family lead to good adjustment with the society and keep the individual in a healthy mental state.

It is within the family that adolescents learn to express, restrain and refine their sentiments, thoughts and emotions. It is in the family that an individual inculcates social traits like love, sympathy, brotherhood, etc. Hence, family's environment goes a long way in moulding an individual's mental state. An adverse family environment leads to disturbed mental state, thus promoting juvenile delinquency and maladjustment. Guidance can provide suitable help in ensuring an individual's sound mental health.

(c) *Complexity of Social Demands Arising from Machine Age*: Use of machines in every field is increasing, as a result, less people are needed to do the same job. Guidance makes productive use of this spare manpower and time so that both the individual and the society may benefit.

Further, constant industrial growth is bringing in its wake new techniques and processes at places of work. With emphasis on specialization, the number of professions and their diversity is also increasing. Learning and training have assumed greater significance. Hence, guidance is needed to identify which person is suited for which work.

From the Psychological Point of View

From psychological point of view, the primary aim of education is to achieve the optimum development of an individual's personality. When environmental factors are not conducive to personality development, an individual's growth suffers, giving rise to abnormality as well as mental and emotional instability. It is guidance that can determine the kind of environment needed to meet the psychological requirements for achieving an individual's desirable development.

(a) *For Proper Adjustment*: Adjustment is the basic need of any being. Satisfactory adjustment influences an individual's efficiency, mental state and sociability. If the prevailing environment is not conducive to his needs, he finds it difficult to adjust giving rise to symptoms of inferiority complex, dissatisfaction, frustration, inner conflict and tension. Under these circumstances, an individual feels the need for guidance so that the problems relating to his maladjustment may be addressed and suitably resolved.

(b) *Proper Development of Personality*: The word 'personality' has a very wide connotation. It is a complex of psychosomatic attributes and acquired characteristics. But understanding and gauging personality is not easy as it is a complex of so many attributes. Each attribute has a special significance in a person's life. Guidance service, with the help of trained personnel and different tests and techniques, unravels different attributes and builds a proper to pave way foster proper development of personality.

(c) *For Proper Emotional Development*: Emotional development is an important element of individual's personality. Emotional problems arise due to difficulties in different areas of a person's life. As a result, symptoms of personality disorder and abnormality manifest themselves. Family, school, neighbourhood and community environment influence emotional development. Children who grow up in families where the environment is happy, mutual relations are cordial, parents' attitude towards children is positive, children's sentiments respected and their problems too attended, are emotionally sound and keep their emotions under control. In contrast, in families where environment is not so conducive and has a negative influence on children, their psychological, social and individual needs are not taken care of and their emotional health is impaired. Because of emotional stress, children become aggressive and feel neglected. They do not find interest in any work and cannot concentrate. Maladjustment of children in schools can be attributed to teachers' partial and impersonal behaviour, unhealthy school environment, inadequate course content and unsavoury teaching methods. These emotional problems affect an individual's behaviour and disturb his mental peace. In this kind of problematic situation, if an individual does not get guidance it gives rise to emotional instability causing an imbalanced personality.

From the Political Point of View

Even from the political point of view, there is need for guidance services in the country. There is rampant poverty and unemployment. Due to political instability administrative set up of the country too is not sound. For these reasons, we need guidance services to solve development related problems of the country.

(a) *For Developing Democratic Values*: India is world's largest democracy. Development of a democratic system is possible only if emphasis is laid on the promotion of democratic values, viz. our rights and duties. A citizen will be aware of his rights and obligations only if he is educated. We must elect capable representatives with impartial and selfless motives so that a well-knit government is formed and a strong administrative set-up comes into being. Guidance can prove useful for educating people about these principles.

(b) *For National Security*: Only when the country is secure we will be able to think about the well-being of the people and the country and other niceties. The army or acquisition of arms alone cannot ensure impregnability of borders. The main need is to ensure proper selection of men and officers, strengthening their morale and motivating them in every possible manner so that when time comes they plunge themselves into the cauldron to ensure that the nation lives even if they perish. This can be accomplished only through a well-conceived 'operation guidance'.

(c) *For Promoting National Integration*: A nation's development is inconceivable without the development of its people and society. After the achievement of Independence, our country opted for a democratic system of government. Development of the democratic system is possible only when importance is given to the promotion of democratic values. Since in India people of different religions and communities live together, the spirit of nationalism can be inculcated in them only on the basis of communal harmony. The spirit of national unity has to be generated so that people think of national development and progress before thinking about their individual interests. For the inculcation of these values, guidance services can make valuable contribution.

(d) *For International Understanding*: In the present age with the unprecedented development of means of communication, geographical distance among nations has almost disappeared. This way, for the promotion of a feeling of universal brotherhood, guidance services are needed at different levels. This would lead to world peace and save humanity from the horror of a nuclear holocaust.

Summary

Assistance provided by a professional counsellor to an individual seeking advice for the solution of his problems is called guidance. The tendency to seek guidance has existed in human society since times immemorial. With the passage of time its nature has undergone change. Guidance movement in India started in 1938 at the University of Calcutta. The Central Bureau of Educational and Vocational Guidance was established in 1954. Now this department is known as Department of

Educational Psychology and Foundation of Education as part of National Council of Educational Research and Training.

The focus of guidance is the individual and not his problem. Guidance is not a direction. At the same time, it is not thrusting somebody's views on others. Guidance is also not taking decisions for others. Guidance is, in fact, an integrated, organized and creative process. Chief objective of guidance in today's context is to ensure the all-round development of an individual.

Process of guidance is related to every aspect of life. Guidance helps in recognizing and developing an individual's inherent abilities in such a way that he makes optimum use of his potential. Guidance is an objective-oriented process. In short:

(a) Guidance is for total development of a subject's personality.
(b) Everybody needs guidance.
(c) Guidance recognizes inherent individual differences.
(d) Guidance is based on the study of an individual and its evaluation.
(e) Guidance is a cooperative effort.
(f) Guidance is a lifelong process.
(g) Guidance promotes self-development and inspires self-reliance.
(h) Guidance should be imparted by trained persons with knowledge of human psychology.

2

Understanding the Individual: Testing Techniques

Guidance, like education, is a type of service imparted by one individual to the other. Under no connotation of education can education and guidance be treated separately. Guidance has been regarded as a supplementary function of education. According to this theory, the purpose of education is to relate all educational processes to the developmental needs of a student. Education is successful only when a teacher pays individual attention to all the students. The youth face many problems. For resolving those problems, they need the assistance of an experienced person. The assistance provided to a student by a teacher or a counsellor cannot be effective without an understanding of his individual characteristics, abilities and interests. In India, parents decide their children's future without getting to know their needs and abilities. Every parent wants to make his/her child a doctor, an engineer, a professor, a scientist, *et al.* Such children do not become as useful as they could have because whatever study or work they do is not necessarily in keeping with their interests, potential and abilities. For this reason, most children find education boring and some of them just drop out, or are seen altering their traits. Such individuals need proper guidance, but it is not possible without knowing or understanding the individual.

To understand a person, it is essential to collect and analyze information on different facets of his life. It is on the basis of this information that a guide or a counsellor can decide the type of guidance that might be given to that person. Collecting different types of information about a person is called the study of an individual. It is the pre-condition for his guidance.

Elaborating the study of an individual, Arthur J. Jones (1934) says: 'Assistance in making choices should be based on as thorough an understanding as is possible of the individual, his basic needs and of the real circumstances surrounding his decision.'

On the significance of gathering knowledge about students, Reavis and Judd say: 'To attempt to guide the development of the pupil without an intimate knowledge of his background and the sum total of his experience is to attempt the impossible'.

The nature of each individual's needs is different. Finding a solution to problems without understanding the different facets of an individual is not only difficult, rather it is impossible. Which aspects should be taken into consideration and what kind of information should be collected to study an individual in the process of guidance are some of the pertinent questions in this regard.

Various aspects of life can be understood through scrutiny because in different situations a person behaves differently. This scrutiny can be done by talking to a student's teachers, members of his family and community or his peers. Man is a thinking being. Since he is capable of introspection, he can understand himself better than others will. What is needed is to inculcate in him an insight to understand and form his self-concept according to his needs and abilities.

There is no clear definition of self. Self is subject to constant change but there is also something that gets fundamentally ingrained and retains its core character. Self is constantly influenced by a person's experiences. It is these experiences that determine the direction in which his self will develop.

In the context of study of an individual, self-image or self-concept is the core content that is analyzed. For this investigation, a counsellor uses different types of techniques. These techniques have special significance as regards understanding an individual's self and evaluating his comprehension. Thus, it is clear that comprehensive information about an individual is very significant for a teacher, a counsellor or a guide.

Types of Information Needed

For the study of an individual, it is important to gather information in the following areas.

General Data: This information contains all those elements that are required to establish contact with the subject. It consists of his name, surname, age, sex, birth place, residential address, telephone number, etc.

Physical Data: For the purpose of guidance, physical data have particular significance. In order to study an individual, full information about his diseases, disabilities and accidents should be obtained and recorded in his health check-up docket. Most people have some or other physical shortcoming. A guide must be aware of these shortcomings so that while providing educational or vocational guidance due consideration is given to these shortcomings. For instance, those with eye defects are not suitable for professions of surgeons, aviation, truck driving, etc.

Family and Social Environment: A person's family and social environment influence his personality. This information must specify:

(a) Parents' names.
(b) Parents' occupations.
(c) Parents' educational status.
(d) Parents' religion.
(e) Parents' health.
(f) Parents' birth place and citizenship.
(g) Mother tongue.
(h) Family environment.
(i) Information about other members of his family.
(j) Parents' attitude towards the youth and mutual relations.
(k) Information about the neighbourhood of his family.
(l) Information about the youth's peer group.

School History and Record of Class Work: From school history, we get the complete detail about a student's school- and class-related facts. On the basis of this information, the following aspects of that individual can be ascertained.

(a) What difficulties was the student facing in the school?
(b) What was the teacher's impression about the student?
(c) What subjects did the student study and how did he progress?
(d) The student's interest in extra-curricular activities.
(e) Which different institutions did the student attend and reasons for changing.
(f) The student's rapport with other students, etc.

This information helps the guidance expert or a counsellor in understanding the student and arriving at a conclusion as to how to solve his problems at the earliest.

Mental Abilities: Before giving guidance to an individual, it is essential to have knowledge of his mental abilities. Only after finding out the mental ability or intelligence quotient (IQ) of an individual, a counsellor can offer educational guidance regarding the choice of subjects or vocational guidance on the choice of a career. For gauging mental ability, psychologists have devised various types of intelligence tests.

Interests: In order to impart educational or vocational guidance, it is very essential to know the individual's interests. Interests are related to an individual's feelings or his current mental inclination or propensity. Sometimes an idea about the individual's interests can be obtained from his works or activities. If an individual spends most of his money, time or energy repeatedly on something then that thing or activity is related to his interest. But these techniques are not verifiable. To learn about an individual's interests, psychologists have formulated different types of interest inventories. These are verifiable.

Aptitudes: Every individual is endowed with some ability or the other. Aptitude is the ability that foretells a student's success. In other words, it provides a crystal-ball view of as to what are the possibilities of an individual's success in a particular profession or line of work. These abilities are rooted in the present. To discover an aptitude, we must use verifiable tests. The information forms basis for the type of assistance to be provided to students in the choice of subjects of study or vocations. While counselling a student or an individual about the choice vocational, the counsellor formulates his vocational objectives in keeping with his aptitude.

Educational and Other Achievements: While studying an individual we must have full knowledge of his educational achievements. It must be ascertained as to what type of education an individual is receiving and up to what class has he passed; in which year, what examination, in which subjects and with how many marks has he passed. This information is useful not only for providing guidance to a student in the school, but is also helpful for selection in higher institutions and industrial organizations as well as for preparing submissions for guidance. While studying an individual's educational achievements, we must also pay attention to his aptitude and interests in different subjects. Different types of psychological tests are also carried out for a reliable evaluation of the progress made in different subjects.

Personality: The primary aim of education is to achieve the all-round development of a child's personality. To understand an individual's personality, we must study the coordination of his inherent physical and psychological traits. Anecdotal records can help in properly understanding the personality traits. Personality tests are another tool for understanding an individual's personality.

Information Regarding Adjustment: For giving educational guidance to a student it is very important to know how much can he adjust, how are his relations with his friends, parents, teachers and other students and how does he react in different situations. A student's participation in activities such as plays, sports, etc. provides an index to his adjustability. His activities outside the school provide an index to his social adjustment. This information helps a counsellor in understanding a student's social and emotional problems and providing correct guidance.

Knowledge About Future Plans: For successful guidance, it is essential to gather information about a student's future educational and vocational plans. The youth plans himself or with assistance from his parents, but many a times parents, being illiterate or semi-literate or being too ambitious, decide about their child becoming an engineer or a doctor without giving adequate thought to his abilities or interests. This decision leads to future problems for the child. He becomes a victim of inferiority complex and frustration that is highly damaging for his development. Counsellors can help students in making their future plans according to their abilities, interests and wishes. Information regarding future plans can also be obtained through questionnaires or interviews.

Many types of needed information required for guidance and counselling can be obtained objectively through the standardized psychological tests which are described below.

Intelligence Tests

In day-to-day language, we commonly use the word 'intelligence'. According to ancient Indian philosophy—"The inborn ability to look for the right thing at the right place is intelligence." This word is profusely used in psychology. Psychologists have defined it in so many different ways.

Intelligence is the Ability to Adapt to Changed Circumstances

According to William Stern, 'Intelligence is a general capacity of an individual consciously to adjust his thinking to new requirements. It is general mental adaptability to new problems and conditions of life'.

According to Garrett (1971), 'Intelligence includes the abilities demanded in the solution of problems which require the comprehension and use of symbols'.

According to Terman (1916, 1921), 'Ability to think in terms of abstract ideas defines the degree of an individual's intelligence'.

Impelled by these conflicting definitions the *Journal of Educational Psychology* organized a symposium. In this symposium, various views on the nature and measurement of intelligence were expressed. Sixteen psychologists participated in this symposium. All of them expressed their views. They variously described intelligence as 'the capacity to learn', 'the ability to adjust', 'the ability to do abstract thinking', 'an amalgam of various elements', etc. But all of them were unanimous on the view that intelligence is an extremely complex phenomenon.

Intelligence is an Aggregate of Various Capacities

According to Wechsler (1939), 'Intelligence is the aggregate of global capacity of an individual to act purposefully, to think rationally and to deal effectively with his environment'.

Husband (1949) talks about the different capacities of an intelligent person: 'The intelligent person uses past experience effectively, is able to concentrate and keep his attention focussed for longer periods of time, adjusts in a new and unaccustomed situation rapidly with less confusion and with fewer false moves, shows variability and versatility of response, is able to see distant relationships, can carry on abstract thinking, has a greater capacity of inhibition or delay and is capable of exercising self-criticism'.

Husband's description of an intelligent individual is quite apt. But intelligence cannot be taken to be the sum total of all these attributes. There are as yet different opinions among psychologists intelligence over being a lone factor or an amalgam of various abilities.

Binet (1905) has defined intelligence on the basis of its main functions. He has included three elements in intelligence which are as follows.

(a) The tendency to take and maintain a definite direction.
(b) The capacity to make adaptations for the purpose of attaining a desire.

(c) The power of self-criticism.

Intelligence is, therefore, an extremely complex phenomenon. It is a kind of ability or a combination of abilities which helps an individual to think logically for a longer period, enables him to perform purposeful actions, to make knowledge-based and symbolic attainments, to adjust effectively in changed situations and to take advantage of past experiences.

Life is a series of situations and problems, and adjusting to them is very important. In the absence of scrutiny of the suitability of an objective, adjustment is not possible. The nature of an objective is dependent on its purpose. But for the achievement of an objective, suitable means are also essential. Intelligence thus can be defined as the ability to achieve an objective.

Some facts about intelligence

(a) Intelligence has been accepted to be an inborn ability.
(b) Heredity has significant impact on intelligence.
(c) Sex difference does not influence intelligence.
(d) Development of intelligence is complete by the time of adolescence.
(e) Majority of children have average intelligence.
(f) Intelligence helps man in overcoming difficult and complex situations.
(g) Sharpness and power of intelligence varies in different individuals.
(h) Social, economic and cultural levels influence intelligence.
(i) There is a strong correlation between knowledge and intelligence. Knowledge can be attained with the help of intelligence, but with the help of knowledge significant development of intelligence is not possible.

Theories of Intelligence

In order to understand the nature of intelligence, it is essential to understand the theories of intelligence. Scholars have put forward following theories regarding intelligence.

(a) *Binet Unifactor Theory*: According to this theory, intelligence is a prowess that influences all mental activities, initiates them and coordinates them. These views were first put forward by Frenchman Alfred Binet (1905). This was later corroborated by American scholar like Terman and Stern and as well as by German scholar Ebbinghaus.

According to this theory if an individual is endowed with high level of intelligence, he can attain proficiency and skill in all fields. Binet calls this ability as the ability to make decision. Stern has described it as the ability to make adjustment in new situations whereas according to Terman it is the ability to think.

(b) *Spearman's Two-Factor Theory*: British psychologist Charles Spearman (1904, 1927) propounded this theory on the basis of his research. According to him, intelligence consists of two factors. These two factors are (1) one general factor, and (2) many specific factors.

According to Spearman, general intelligence factor influences the entire gamut of mental activities. This is denoted by 'G' which is believed to be fixed. But man's other specific factors called 'S' are not fixed. Spearman believes that different specific factors are found in different quantities in the same individual at the same time.

$$\text{Intelligence} = G + S1 + S2 + S3, \ldots, Sn.$$

General factor 'G' influences other specific factors 'Sn'.

To what extent does G factor influence Sn factors depends on the extent of correlation between G factor and specifics, or S factors, each being strictly specific to a single activity. Positive correlation between any two functions was thus attributed to the 'G' factor. The more highly the two functions are "saturated" with G, the higher the correlation between them would be. The presence of specifics, on the other hand, tended to lower the correlation between functions.

Later, Spearman modified his Two-Factor Theory and put forward three factors in place of two. Spearman stated that apart from general factor and specific factor there is also a third factor in intelligence. Spearman called this third factor as the cluster factor. According to him, mental abilities reside in clusters. Different specific factors residing in the same cluster have high level of positive inter-relationship.

(c) *Thorndike Multifactor Theory*: This theory was propounded by Thorndike. According to this theory, intelligence consists of many elements and factors. We can describe this view as 'anarchic' because according to it, intelligence is not a specific omnipotent mental process but a grouping or amalgam of many factors. Thorndike held that intelligence consists of a number of innate abilities. These abilities are totally independent of each other. He also believes that intelligence tests evaluate only some general abilities and not the total intelligence. According to this theory, evaluation of an individual's capability in one area does not point to his capability in other areas.

(d) *Group Factor Theory*: Group Factor Theory of intelligence was propounded by Thurstone (1938). This theory is a median between Spearman's Two-Factor Theory and Thorndike's Multifactor Theory. By using factor analysis technique, Thurstone suggested that out of seven factors in intelligence, two or three factors come together to form a group. Seven factors present in intelligence are as under:

(i) Verbal comprehension—V
(ii) Word fluency—W
(iii) Number ability—N
(iv) Space—S
(v) Associative memory—M
(vi) Perceptual speed—P
(vii) Inductive reasoning—I

From this it is apparent that an intelligence is not a single factor but a combination of many basic abilities. Kelley and Cyril Burt too support this theory.

(e) *Sampling Theory*: Sampling theory of intelligence was propounded by Thompson. According to Thompson, when a person performs some function he uses his abilities, for the purpose. But rather than using all his abilities, he tries to perform that function by using just a sample of his ability. For this reason what is evident in that performance is just a sample of that ability rather than the entire ability. We possess a vast reservoir of mental abilities. While doing something we take out just a sample out of that reservoir, and the correlation between these samples is the outcome of free interaction among all the abilities.

(f) *Hierarchical Theory*: Burt (1949), Vernon (1960), Humphreys (1962) and Cattell (1971) propounded the Hierarchical Theory of Intelligence. (See figure 1) Elucidating the nature of intelligence, these scholars attached hierarchical significance to mental abilities. According to them, among all the mental abilities, general mental ability is the most important. Hence, it has been accused the first place. General mental ability is divided into two parts—verbal, educational and practical. These are further sub-divided by the scholars. In this way, they went on sub-dividing the abilities. Each next sub-division was relatively less significant than its previous sub-division.

(g) *Three-dimensional Theory*: This theory was propounded by Guilford (1967, 1988). Guilford and Hoepfner (1971) gave a box-like model called the Structure of Intellect (SI). This model

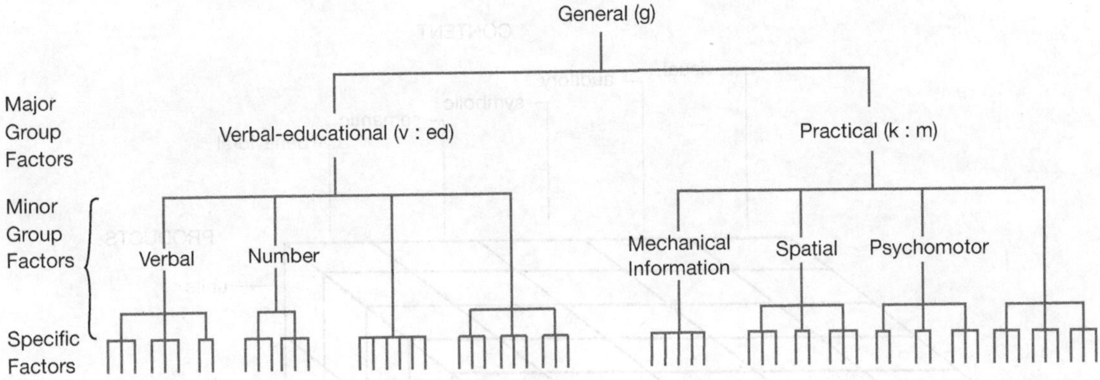

Figure 1: Model of a Hierarchical Organization of Abilities.

classifies intellectual abilities into three dimensions—operations, content and product. This classification includes 6 × 5 × 6 categories. There are 180 cells in the model and each cell represents one ability or factor. Some cells contain more than one factor. Each factor is described in terms of all three dimensions. (See figure 2)

With the help of the above-mentioned theories, we can study the nature of intelligence and ponder as to which general and specific mental abilities are present in our client. But their evaluation can be done only through intelligence tests.

(h) *Information Processing Theory*: This theory is the most influential process-oriented approach to intelligence. This theory breaks down intelligence into various basic skills that people employ to take information, process it and then use it to reason and solve problems.

(i) *Sternberg Triarchic Theory of Intelligence*: Sternberg's theory of human intelligence (1977, 1985) includes Spearman's 'G' and underlying information processing components. This theory includes three sub-theories.

   (i) Analytical (Componential)
   (ii) Creative (Experimental)
   (iii) Practical (Contextual)

According to Sternberg, if intelligence is properly defined and measured, it will translate to real-life success.

(i) *Analytical Sub-theory*: This reflects how an individual relates to his internal world with the operations of meta components, performance components and knowledge acquisition components of intelligence.

(ii) *Creative Sub-theory*: This reflects the ability which allows people to adjust creatively and effectively to new situations. In these two abilities, novelty skills and automatization skills are associated with intelligence.

(iii) *Practical Sub-theory*: Practical intelligence means how the individual relates to the external world around him. People with this type of intelligence can shape their environment. The important asset of this theory is to avoid defining intelligence in terms of intelligence tests rather than performance in the everyday world.

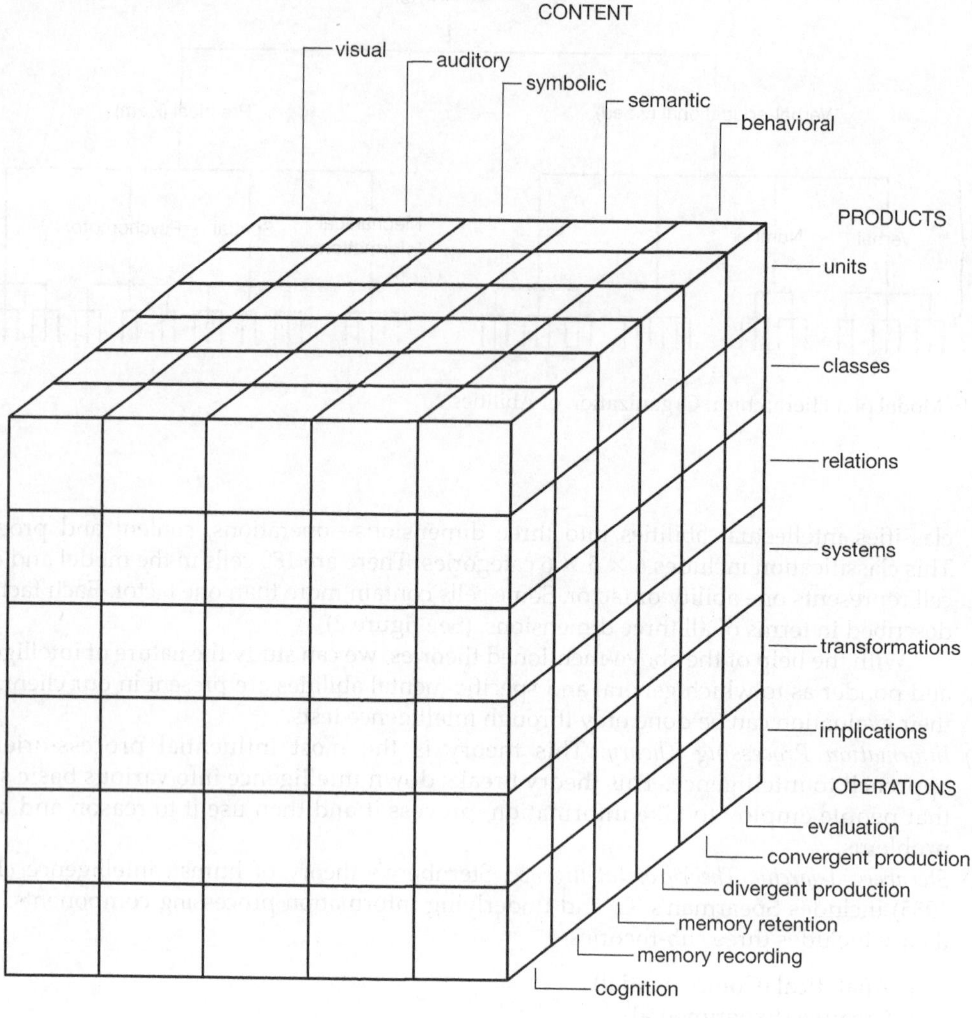

Figure 2: Three-Dimensional Model of the Structure of Intellect.

Measurement of Intelligence

The existence of individual differences was first accepted in 1875. After that a number of experiments were carried out. The foremost among them were on this subject conducted by Cattle and Gaulton. Experiments on intelligence tests were first conducted by Binet.

The basis of Binet's experiment was the observation that in a class some students learn very quickly and successfully while the others remain unsuccessful. Binet wanted to understand the mental ability responsible for this phenomenon. Binet, with the help of Simon, started devising such tests that would enable the mapping of this mental ability. It was in 1905 that Binet, with the help of Simon, devised the first intelligence test. It consisted of 30 questions arranged in the order of toughness level. This test was tried on 50 students.

In 1908 and 1911, modified versions of this test were brought out in which the term 'mental age' was used for the first time. After this, in 1916 Terman, with the help of his associates at

Stanford University, again brought modifications in the test and named it 'Stanford—Binet' test. It contained 90 questions. Its authentication was carried out on 1,000 students. Terman used the term 'intelligence quotient' for mapping intelligence.

Terman and Merrill further modified this test in 1960. This modified version contained more useful questions than its earlier version. The latest modification was carried out in 1973.

Intelligence Quotient

Intelligence tests are used to measure intelligence quotient. Intelligence quotient is the ratio of mental age (MA) and chronological age (CA). Chronological age is calculated from the date of birth whereas mental age is found out by tests. The formula for measuring it is:

$$IQ = \frac{MA}{CA} \times 100.$$

In order to avoid getting IQ in decimal, we multiply the proportion of mental age (MA) and chronological age (CA) with 100.

Mental age after a certain age does not increase with the increase in physical age. From IQ, we come to know of a person's intelligence level on the basis of which he may be given guidance for his future. To properly understand the concept of IQ, it is necessary to keep its limitations in view. Its limitations are as discussed below.

(a) IQ is the quantitative expression of an individual's intelligence.
(b) You do not obtain the same IQ in each test. Hence, IQ deduced from each test is different.
(c) Nobody is devoid of intelligence. Hence, there is nothing like 'zero IQ'.
(d) About constancy in IQ it has been said that even by testing through the same test again and again an individual's IQ can vary.
(e) Every youth's IQ does not remain constant. In some cases, significant variations can be observed.

IQ is a consequence of both heredity and environment. Hence, with the change in environment IQ can change.

It is on the basis of IQ only that the individuals are classified into different mental levels. If a youth's IQ is 100, we will treat him as being of average intelligence. If his IQ is more than 100, we will classify him as being of relatively sharper intelligence and if it is below 100, we will classify him as being relatively dull. Given below is a classification done on these lines:

Classifications	IQ's
1. Profound mental retardation	Below 20
2. Severe mental disability	20–35
3. Moderate mental disability	36–51
4. Mild mental disability	52–69
5. Borderline mental disability	70–79
6. Low-average mental disability	80–89
7. Average	90–109
8. High average	110–119
9. Superior	120–129
10. Very superior	130+

Other classifications like the above have also been made. The single truth that emerges from these is that the one with better IQ is proportionately more superior.

Many countries have adopted Binet's tests. Many other tests have been developed on their basis. Similarly, in India for the first time C. H. Rice developed an Indian Binet Performance Point Scale in 1922. Binet–Kamath version of the aforesaid test that has been developed in India is another.

Classification of Intelligence Tests

Tests occupy a very significant place in guidance. Hence, it is a must for guidance experts to have the comprehensive knowledge about the classification of intelligence tests.

(a) As per administrative practice, tests are of two types.

(i) *An Individual Test*: As the name suggests, this test can measure only a single person's intelligence at a time. All performance tests fall in the category of individual tests. While measuring intelligence it is necessary for the investigator to conduct tests only after establishing a cordial rapport with the subject. Only experienced and trained investigators should attempt such intelligence measuring tests.

Some of the important individual tests are (i) Binet–Stanford Test, (ii) Wechsler Intelligence Scale for Children (WISC), (iii) Wechsler Adult Intelligence Scale (WAIS), (iv) Burt's Reasoning Ability Test, (v) Minnesota Pre-School Test, (vi) Merill Palmer Mental Test, (vii) Gecil Development Index, (viii) Koh's Blocks Design Test, (ix) Bhatia Battery Test of Performance Intelligence and (x) Raven's Progressive Matrices.

(ii) *Group Test*: As is evident from the term, with the help of these tests more than one person's intelligence can be measured at a time. These tests were developed in the United States on the eve of World War I for testing soldiers' intelligence. During this period, Army Alpha and Army Beta tests were evolved. These tests are very useful for army, research, schools, industry, etc. Group tests are primarily verbal. In other words, these are based on the knowledge of language. These are easily manageable and do not require the service of skilled personnel.

However, these tests are not useful for problematic and young age children. Comprehensive study of intelligence is much wanting under group intelligence tests. Results of these group intelligence tests are not very reliable and acceptable as the interviewer is not able to establish adequate rapport with his subjects.

Some of the well-known group tests are (i) Army Alpha Tests, (ii) Army Beta Tests, (iii) Army General Classification Tests, (iv) Terman Group Test of Mental Maturity, (v) Dr. Sohan Lal Group Intelligence Test, (vi) Prayag Mehta's General Intelligence Test, (vii) Dr. S.S. Jalota's Group Test of Mental Ability and (viii) Raven's Progressive Matrices.

(b) On the basis of the subject matter and language, intelligence tests are of two types.

(i) *Verbal Test*: As it is clear from the title, intelligence tests which pre-dominantly use language in instruction, contents and responses are called verbal tests.

(ii) *Performance Test or Non-verbal Test*: In non-verbal and performance test, the problem is solved through constructive or passive actions. These actions include arrangement of pictures, picture completion, finding inaccuracies in pictures, picture puzzles, imitation, drawing a form, etc. The main utility of such tests is that through them intelligence level of the educated, uneducated, dull-minded, deaf–dumb children, foreigners or any person can be ascertained. Given below are the names of some practical tests: (i) Form Board Test, (ii) Proteus's Maze Test, (iii) Cube Construction Test, (iv) Alexander's Pass Along Test, (v) Pitner–Paterson Performance Scales and (vi) Bhatia's Battery of Performance Tests.

(c) On the basis of efficiency of performance intelligence, tests are of two types.

(i) *Power Test*: In power tests, an individual's skill in a particular area is tested. In these tests, questions are graded and no time limit is fixed.

(ii) *Speed Test*: In speed tests, all the questions are equally tough and are to be solved within a given time. The one who solves the maximum questions within the time given scores maximum marks. This gives us an idea about his mental speed.

Use of Intelligence Tests in Guidance

For successful and effective educational and vocational guidance, use of intelligence tests is essential to get a fair idea about the subject's mental ability. This information helps in giving educational and vocational guidance.

(a) Through intelligence tests, we can find which individual is dull, which one average and which one superior.
(b) Students classified on the basis of intelligence tests can be motivated through educational guidance to opt for right subjects and choose the right syllabus so that they do not encounter any difficulty in future.
(c) Individuals can be guided to choose a vocation or go in for vocational training according to the level of their intelligence. It is even possible to forecast the success of students.
(d) Intelligence tests play an important role in granting scholarships to students.
(e) Students should be divided into different sections in a class on the basis of their intelligence level. There should be separate classes for sharp and dull students. Choice of syllabus, the method of teaching and the teachers too should be decided on the basis of a child's IQ so that the child takes interest in his studies and discipline in the class is maintained.
(f) Through intelligence tests, a student's capacity to learn too can be gauged.

Emotional Quotient: Earlier, the function of intelligence known as IQ was given greater importance in all walks of lives. Recently, emotional intelligence (EI) also known as emotional quotient (EQ) has loomed large on the psychological horizon and claims greater attention than intelligence in general.

Steves has defined emotional intelligence as 'The mental ability we are born with which gives us our emotional sensitivity and our potential for learning emotional management skills that help us maximize our health, happiness and survival'.

Goleman stated that only about 20 per cent of the person's success in life is a result of IQ. It is rarely EI or EQ that contributes the rest 80 per cent.

(a) EQ is understood to be a matter of degree with no relation to intelligence quotient.
(b) Feeling of anger, unhappiness, failure, disappointment, frustration, obligation, guilt, bitterness, dependence, depression, loneliness, instability, despondence and lethargy are the main consequence of low emotional quotient.
(c) High EQ results in feeling of happiness, motivation, appreciation, friendship, self-control, satisfaction, freedom, peace, desire, awareness, balance.
(d) There is no genetic fixation as far as emotional intelligence is concerned.
(e) EQ continues to develop lifelong with age.

Aptitude Tests

One of the main reasons for individual differences is the difference in aptitudes. It is on this basis that one is able to become a doctor while the other one is fit to become an engineer and the third one would succeed as a musician. It is important to understand as to what is an aptitude. An aptitude is a person's special ability, or in other words, his inherent skill. There is, however, no unanimity among scholars on the subject of aptitude.

According to Traxler (1966), 'An aptitude is a present condition which is indicative of an individual's potentialities for the future'.

According to Warren, 'An aptitude is a condition or a set of characteristics indicative of an individual's ability to acquire with some specific knowledge, skill or set of responses such as the ability to speak a language, to become a musician, to do mechanical work, etc'.

Jones (1971) says, 'An aptitude is not an ability, but it helps to predict the probable development of certain abilities. A test of an aptitude may reveal abilities as well as skills, but the significance of the test is in revealing potential abilities and skills'.

Jones has clarified the difference between achievement, ability and aptitude.

- *Achievement*: It describes the past. It indicates what has been done.
- *Ability*: It is related to the present. It is an indicator of skills, habits and abilities present in the individual that make him capable of doing something.
- *Aptitude*: It indicates towards the future. It forecasts as to what success an individual would achieve in his profession after training on the basis of his present habits, skills and abilities.

According to Bingham (1937), 'An aptitude is a characteristic or a set of conditions that are symptomatic to the individual'.

He describes the following characteristics of aptitude.

(a) An individual's aptitude is the sum total of his present conditions or abilities that are indicative of his capabilities. This capability is dependent on the final outcome of both inherent and environmental circumstances.
(b) An aptitude is not something concrete. It is an abstract term. It indicates a person's abilities. It is ingrained in his personality.
(c) An aptitude gives an indication of future only in the real state of affairs. It is a collective representation of abilities, pointing towards the capabilities. These tests are no measure of future success. The figures of these tests are just a means of estimating these capabilities.
(d) The readiness to acquire competence in some vocation or profession does not necessarily indicate aptitude. Apart from an aptitude the individual should also have interest in that vocation.

According to Super (1962), there are four characteristics of an aptitude. (i) Specificity, (ii) unitary composition, (iii) facilitation of learning and (iv) constancy.

Skinner has described an aptitude as 'special skill', 'knowledge' and 'interests'.

Nature of Aptitude

To understand the nature of aptitude, it is necessary to ponder over the following facts.

(a) *Is Aptitude Inherent or Acquired?* Till the beginning of the twentieth century, psychologists believed that aptitudes are inherited. But research has led them to believe that apart from the inheritance environment, and circumstances too play a role in the development of aptitudes. Research has now confirmed that both heredity and environment influence intelligence, aptitude, interests and abilities.
(b) *Is Aptitude Fixed or Subject to Change?* It is a contentious issue that requires research-based evidence. Psychologists are now open to the suggestion that aptitudes can be altered to some extent through education, training and circumstances. At the same time, it is true that it is impossible to alter aptitude instantly.

(c) *Is Aptitude Unitary or Multi-Elemental?* Earlier it was believed that aptitude is unitary in nature. But modern research has revealed that aptitude is multi-elemental. These do not result from a simple symptom. Kelly has described seven elements. These are numerical, motor ability, mechanical, social, verbal, musical and artistic. Subsequently, after Kelly, psychologists have put their number at more than 30.

Aptitude and Other Terms

(a) *Aptitude and Ability*: The main difference between ability and aptitude is that ability is related to the present, however, aptitude gives an indication of the future.

(b) *Aptitude and Achievement*: Achievement is related to the past or what has already been done. Aptitude has to do with an individual's ability to achieve something in the future or the extent to which an individual can go.

By measuring an individual's aptitude, we can have a measure of the success he is going to achieve in different spheres. Aptitude measures an individual's present potential. Only on the basis of these results a forecast can be made about a person's future achievements.

(c) *Aptitude and Intelligence*: Intelligence is concerned with general mental ability. On the other hand, aptitude connotes specific aspects of intelligence like mechanical, artistic, professional, sensory, perceptual and motor abilities.

(d) *Aptitude and Interest*: According to psychologists, interest and aptitude go side by side and act in unison. Both influence an action either in terms of success or failure. For example, an individual has got aptitude for something, but does not take interest in it. Similarly, an individual may have interest in something, but may not have an aptitude for it.

In the field of guidance, the knowledge of aptitude helps a counsellor in counselling an individual as to in which course or vocation he would have better chances of success.

Aptitude Tests

Scholars have developed different aptitude tests for measuring aptitude. These aptitude tests are used to select personnel for different professions and for the selection of subjects in schools. In order to carry out guidance, along with the testing of other abilities, testing of aptitude is also necessary. The aptitude tests are to some extent like intelligence tests. The different types of aptitude tests are described below.

(a) *Clerical Aptitude Tests*: For carrying out office work properly, skilled clerical staff is required. These tests have many characteristics. According to Bill, 'Clerical duties include the gathering, classification and presentation of data of all sorts, and the analysis and use of these data in planning, executing and determining the results of operation'.

Super mentions two main characteristics of a clerk are (i) speed and (ii) accuracy.

In an office, a person who can work with numerical and verbal symbols with speed and accuracy has got the ability to work as a clerk.

According to Bingham, 'The aptitude for clerical work is evident from four types of abilities':

(i) *Perceptual Ability*: The ability of grasping figures and words written on a paper with speed and accuracy.

(ii) *Intellectual Ability*: The ability to comprehend the meanings of words and symbols.

(iii) *Mental Skill*: The skill to speedily and accurately add and multiply figures.

(iv) *Motor Ability*: The ability to use fingers and hands for working with paper, pencil, typewriter and computer.

Numerous tests have been devised for measuring the aptitude for clerical work. A few among them are described below.

(i) *Minnesota Vocational Test for Clerical Workers*: This test is used both for individual and group testing. The test duration is 35–40 minutes. It is used in the field of education also. With the help of this test, the aptitude for typewriting, filing work, book-keeping, sorting of mail, etc. is tested.
(ii) *Clerical Test*: This test was developed by British National Institute of Industrial Psychology. This test has been divided into seven parts by which seven types of abilities related to clearical job are evaluated.
(iii) *Thurston's Examination in clerical work.*
(iv) *Detroit clerical aptitude examination*.

(b) *Mechanical Aptitude Tests*: There are mainly three characteristics of mechanical aptitude.
(i) Location-related sense and perception.
(ii) Manual skill with perfect synchronization among all organs.
(iii) Mechanical abilities of energy, speed, patience, etc.

For all mechanical occupations, the above three abilities are essential but these need to be necessarily present in equal measure. The guidance expert simply measures the amount of these abilities and counsels about joining a suitable occupation. By keeping these factors in view, various mechanical aptitude tests have been developed. Some of the tests described are as follows.

(i) *Minnesota Mechanical Aptitude Test*: This test was first developed for junior high school students. In this test, 33 mechanical parts have been included. These parts keep lying in three boxes. In the first box, there are nine parts, in the second box eight and in the third one 16. In the test, the students are asked to put together the parts in each box and complete an item. A fixed time is given for each box. For the first box it is 18 minutes, for the second 21 minutes 5 seconds and for the third 16 minutes.
(ii) *O'Rourke Mechanical Aptitude Test*: This test is in two parts. In the first part, there are pictures and in the second part there are verbal questions. This test is based on the premise that individuals with mechanical aptitude can acquire knowledge about machines in a shorter period than those without this aptitude.
(iii) *Johnson's O'Connor's Wiggly Test*: This test is generally used for selecting people for training in engineering, draughtsman ship and other highly technical professions to measure the ability to visualize three-dimensional structures. O'Connor also uses a finger dexterity test and a tweezers dexterity test to discover aptitude for certain types of small assembly work.
(iv) *Stenquist Test for Mechanical Aptitude*: This test was developed by Stenquist. In this test too students are asked to assemble certain parts within a fixed time by using given mechanical methods. The candidate's suitability for that occupation is determined by the speed of assembling. In this test, there are also pictures of certain machines which the candidate is asked to identify.

(c) *Teaching Aptitude Tests: Pandey's Teaching Aptitude Test*: This test was developed by K. P. Pandey of Jiyaji University in 1968. This test is extremely useful for selecting teachers for primary schools in Uttar Pradesh and in other Hindi-speaking regions. Under this test, there are eight sub-tests as (i) vocational knowledge, (ii) verbal knowledge, (iii) basis of results, (iv) sequence, (v) marking, (vi) logical selection, (vii) general information and (viii) comprehension of lessons.

Aptitude Test for Elementary School Teachers: This aptitude test was developed by S. N. Sharma in 1969. This test is scripted in Hindi. It has five sub-tests as (i) mental ability, (ii) behaviour towards children, (iii) adjustment, (iv) vocational information and (v) interest in the vocation.

Pandey's Professional Test for Teachers: In 1972, B. G. Pandey developed a vocational test for teachers. By this test, abilities that are essential for a teacher are measured.

(d) *Musical Aptitude*: Knowledge of musical aptitude is measured on the basis of following abilities.

(i) *Motor Aspect*: Before using any musical instrument it is necessary to know all its functions.
(ii) *Perspective Aspect*: Differentiating sensory perceptions.
(iii) *Interpretative Aspect*: Perceptual evaluation of rhythmic finesse.

To find out an aptitude for music, a number of tests have been developed. These are as follows.

Seashore Musical Test: In 1916, Seashore developed a test for testing musical capacity. In 1920, Seashore presented the following list of factors of the musical mind:

Musical sensitivity:

(i) *Simple form of impression*:

- Sense of pitch
- Sense of intensity
- Sense of time
- Sense of extensity

(ii) *Complex forms of appreciation*:

- Sense of rhythm
- Sense of timbre
- Sense of consonance
- Sense of volume

(iii) *Musical action: Natural capacity for skill in accurate and musically expressive production of tones (vocal, instrumental or both)*

- Control of pitch
- Control of intensity
- Control of time
- Control of rhythm
- Control of timbre
- Volume

(iv) *Musical memory*

- Auditory imagery
- Motor imagery
- Creative imagination
- Memory span
- Learning power

(v) *Musical intellect*

- Musical free association
- Musical power of reflexion
- General intelligence

(vi) *Musical feeling*

- Musical taste
- Emotional reaction to music
- Emotional self-expression in feeling

(e) *Differential Aptitude Tests*

(i) *Rao's Differential Aptitude Testing Project*: This project was initiated by N.C.S. Rao in 1962 to measure the aptitude of class eight students and to have an idea about their future achievements.

(ii) *Mukherjee's Differential Aptitude Test Battery*: In 1966, M. Mukherjee of Calcutta University developed differential aptitude test. There are seven sub-tests within it:

- Use of English
- Clerical aptitude
- Knowledge of maths and aptitude
- Knowledge of science and aptitude
- Technical comprehension
- Verbal reasoning
- Abstract reasoning

This test is used to measure the dominant abilities of students studying subjects like science, commerce, home science, humanities, agriculture, technical subjects, fine arts.

(f) *Artistic Aptitude*: For testing the aptitude for arts mainly two methods are employed:

(i) First, children are asked to draw basic pictures.

(ii) Secondly, they are asked to critically examine the pictures already drawn and describe their good and bad points.

A child's art capability can be judged best by examining his artworks. Some of the well-known aptitude tests are as follows.

- Horn's art aptitude index
- Nauber's art ability test
- Mcadory's art test
- Mayer art appreciation test

(g) *Scientific Aptitude Tests*

(i) *Venkatraman's Aptitude Test in Science*: In 1970, C. Venkatraman developed this test in order to gauge secondary students' aptitude for science. In this seven sub-types of aptitude are tested:

- Numerical
- Locational
- Logical
- Differential

- Mechanical
- Relation between cause and effect, vii) Ability to draw conclusion from experimental data

(ii) *Dave's Scientific Aptitude Test*: This test was developed by B. M. Dave in 1964. This test is used to study high-school students' aptitude for science. It helps to select able students for science stream at the University level. Science aptitude tests are conducted on the basis of the following criteria:

- Scientific comprehension
- Mechanical reasoning
- Counting ability
- Place relationship
- Scientific information

Importance of Aptitude Tests

Aptitude tests help in understanding an individual's capability and ability. Only on the basis of these capabilities, a counsellor is able to offer educational or vocational guidance to the youth.

Aptitude test enables a counseller to help a student to choose his subject after he has passed out of high school. Special aptitude tests help in selecting candidates for special occupations. Aptitude tests also help in predicting future success.

Discovering individuals' skills and abilities through aptitude tests can help in planning the course of their development in consonance with their abilities. Only through these tests suitable people can be selected for various posts.

In our country, a person chooses his occupation without any consideration to his abilities. The unfortunate result is that most people keep changing jobs in different occupations, and seldom taste success. This results in loss of money, energy as well as time. To obviate this wastage it is important to popularize aptitude tests. The need is to develop aptitude tests indigenously, tailored to our conditions and answering our needs.

Achievement Tests

Due to individual differences, even after studying in the same class and receiving education from the same teacher, the level of learning is found to be different in different students. In order to understand this difference, achievement tests were devised.

Achievement test is conducted in a school after a student has been imparted knowledge in different subjects. In this test, a teacher can find out about the progress made by a student in the class. Achievement test has been variously defined by scholars. Some of them are given below.

According to Bingham, 'Measurement of past accomplishments, both in and out of the school, when judged in relation to length and character of the training or experience, is called achievement test'.

In the words of Super, 'An achievement or proficiency test is used to ascertain what and how much has been learned or how well a task can be performed. The focus is on the evaluation of the past without reference to the future except for the implicit assumption that acquired skill and knowledge will be useful in their own right in the future'.

In such a test, consideration is given not only to the absolute achievement but also to the related success or relative achievement. For success in an achievement test, much importance is not given to any prescribed level. For example, a youth has got 90% marks. Here, 90% is not as important as the fact that he stands above so many students. Again, one student gets 60% marks and the second gets 80% marks. Here, 60% marks is not as important as the fact that the second student has got

20% more than the first one. This type of comparative evaluation is considered to be the basis of relative achievement. In terms of absolute achievement it is necessary to get minimum 60% marks for being placed in the first division, 48% minimum marks for being placed in the second division and 36% minimum marks for being placed in the third division.

Types of Achievement Tests

There are two types of achievement tests: standardized tests and teacher made tests.

Standardized Tests

Standardized tests are those whose reliability and legitimacy are ensured. The other characteristics of standardized tests are as follows.

(a) Standardized tests are designed by experts.
(b) Standardized test are designed for different subjects and different classes.
(c) While designing standardized tests, the number of questions is very large.
(d) These are designed according to set principles and rules.
(e) The questions given in these tests are to be solved within the given time frame and according to the directions given therein.
(f) These tests have definite directions for evaluation and marking.

Standardized tests are of two types: (a) general standardized achievement batteries and (b) specific standardized achievement batteries.

(a) *General Standardized Achievement Batteries*: (i) California Achievement Test, (ii) Metropolitan Achievement Test, (iii) Stanford Achievement Test, (iv) SRA Achievement Test, (v) Sequential Test of Educational Progress, (vi) Iowa Test of Basic Skills, (vii) Cooperative General Achievement Test.
(b) *Specific Standardized Achievement Batteries*: (i) Mathematics Readiness Test, (ii) Reading Readiness Test, (iii) Vocational Achievement Test.

These tests are designed to measure vocational competence of the subject. They are also known as trade tests. They are used to see competence level of a person, post-vocational training, vocational experience in a particular trade and his contribution to the trade.

SRA Series:

- SRA test of educational ability for elementary stage
- SRA test of educational ability for high school

Achievement tests have been designed in India too. Allahabad's Dr A. E. Harper has designed the English language achievement tests. In Baroda University, achievement tests have been designed for geometry, algebra and arithmetic, general science, physics, chemistry and history. In Jamia Milia, Delhi, achievement tests for social sciences and hindi have been designed.

Teacher Made Tests: An achievement can also be measured with the help of tests designed by a teacher to ascertain the progress made by the students in different subjects. The success of these tests depends on the teacher's proficiency in designing them. But these tests are more often than not subjective and lack reliability.

Designing an Achievement Test

While designing an achievement test, the objective of the test must be clearly understood. Then the level for which the test is being designed has to be understood. Thereafter, questions should be framed in such a way that no part of the syllabus remains uncovered. Questions, however, can be framed in different ways. Matching type, True-False type, Completion type, Multiple-choice type test, Classification type test, Best-answer type test, Simple recall test.

Matching Type Test: Questions are divided into two parts. One part is kept as it is while the other part is disarranged. Students are asked to rearrange the second part like the first part. It is very useful to test a student's knowledge about an important current news where there is no chance of total recall. By this test, the ability to relate and classify them can be ascertained. The questions under these tests are simple. However, the following points should be kept in mind:

(a) In both the parts, there should be equal and similar questions.
(b) In both the parts, the number of facts should be maximum seven.
(c) The first part should be kept in order. For example, written below in the first part are the names of some historical buildings. These are to be conjoined with the disarranged names of the cities in the second part.

Part 1	Part 2
Taj Mahal	Jaipur
Red Fort	Agra
Hawa Mahal	Delhi

True-False Type Tests: These tests are frequently used. In these questions, some sentences with true statements and other sentences with false statements are given. The student is supposed to write 'True' or 'Yes' against the correct statement and 'No' or 'False' against the wrong statement. Technically also this type of questions are believed to be the best because their construction as well as marking process both are very simple.

For Example: Given below are some false and true statements. Written against each are the words 'True/False'. In the case of true statement the word 'True' is to be ticked (√), while in the case of wrong one the word 'False' is to be ticked (√).

Completion Type Tests: They are also called Sentence Completion Tests. These questions test a student's knowledge about an important event or fact. In these sentences, an important word or part of sentence is left out and the student is asked to complete it. *For example, given below are some blank spaces which have to be completed.*

(a) Pakistan's capital is ________________.
(b) Ganges river is in ________________.
(c) Kumbh Fair is held in ________________.

Multiple-Choice Type Tests: Given in these tests are three or four possible answers to each question. The student is required to mark (√) on the correct answer. *For example*:

(a) In India where maximum tea is grown:
    Uttar Pradesh, Maharashtra, Assam
(b) Bikaner is in which state:
    Madhya Pradesh, Rajasthan, Uttar Pradesh

Classification Tests: In these tests, some such words are given of which all but one are mutually related. Students are asked to underline the word which is not related to the rest. *For example*:

(a) Pen, Pencil, Crayon, Ink, Table
(b) India, China, Pakistan, America, Ganges

Best Answer Type Test: In these tests, some questions are given together with their possible answers. Among all the answers one answer is the most suitable. The students are asked to mark (√) against the most suitable answer. While framing these questions special attention should be paid to the answers. Answers should be clear, simple and relevant to the question. *Some examples are given below*:

The President is the main ruler of the country because

(a) He is the most powerful.
(b) People accept him as the main ruler.
(c) He is the most capable.

Simple Recall Test: In these tests, a student is asked to write the answer in the space provided against the question. *For example*:

(a) In which city of India is the Howrah Bridge situated? ( )
(b) In which state of India is Agra? ( )

Oral Tests

Achievement tests are sometimes conducted orally as well. At the primary school stage when a child is unable to write properly his achievement test is done orally. Even in higher classes, after practical examinations viva voce is held which is a form of oral test. The main advantage of this test is only this that it leads to a quick evaluation of a student's achievement. But the main drawback with this test is that sometimes even an otherwise intelligent student cannot answer the questions properly due to lack of confidence. This adversely affects his achievement level. Another drawback is that at times the teacher, influenced by a student's personality level, commits injustice by awarding him either more or less marks. These tests lack objectivity.

For successful guidance, it is important to know a student's capacity to learn and gain experience. This knowledge can be gained only through the achievement tests. There are numerous students in each class. They have different abilities. Some students are intellectually sharp, others are dull. If the teacher adopts the same method for teaching both types of students, it would be improper for both of them. Hence, it is important to form different sections on the basis of achievement tests and provide students educational or vocational guidance according to their mental level and learning ability.

Achievement tests are very useful in guidance and counselling.

(a) *Finding Out Students' Talents and Developing Them in the Right Direction*: The main aim of education is to achieve a student's all-round development. An individual's development is not possible without knowing his talents. A guidance expert can find out with the help of achievement tests as to which student has got talent for and interest in which subject. On the basis of this knowledge, a guidance expert can help a student in the choice of subjects.
(b) *Students' Success can be Ascertained from Time to Time*: After ascertaining a student's success status, a guidance expert can also find out the pace of his progress in different subjects.
(c) *Counselling the Guardians*: On the basis of the results of achievement tests, even students' guardians can be given suitable counselling so that they may encourage their wards in the selection of suitable subjects. The proper subject choice helps a student in proper vocational choice because subject choice is directly related to the vocation.
(d) *Counselling the Teachers*: The result of achievement tests can help a teacher in reassessing his teaching style because success in achievement tests depends not only on students' ability but also on the teacher's performance and the teaching methods adopted.

If majority of the students' achievement results are not satisfactory, then the teacher should take it to be his failure and try to reform his teaching style. For the teacher this is self-guidance. This reform will ensure not only children's progress but also that of the community.

(e) *Help in Preparing Cumulative Record*: The achievement tests help in preparing the cumulative record. In which subject a student has made how much progress becomes clear from this record.

(f) *Help in Vocation Selection*: The achievement reports are very useful for selecting of vocations. People in business organizations can be classified on the basis of these reports. The results of these reports can also be helpful in deciding about promotions.

It is evident now that achievement reports can help in educational, vocational and personal guidance.

Interest Inventories

In every individual's, life interests play an important role. What an individual will do is determined mostly on the basis of his interests. Interests are acquired motivations. When an individual is free to do some work or perform a function, he chooses only those works in which he is interested. An individual's interests determine this association. Hence, for the purpose of guidance, be it educational or vocational, an individual's interests must be ascertained.

Generally, people believe that an individual's interests can be ascertained by asking him about them. But in this age of science such ad hoc approach does not hold any water. Psychologists have, therefore, developed a number of tests to measure the depth of interest.

We can describe interest as a feeling of association. In popular parlance, anything with which we get associated or which gets associated with us is called an interest. For example, I am interested in art. In other words, art is associated with me. This association can be present or may be rooted in the past. From the point of view of psychologists, things or acts that give us mental satisfaction or the ones we can perform successfully and deftly are called our interests. We can also call our interests 'our likes'. But it certainly does not mean that since I am interested in art I cannot do anything else.

Interest does not have any adverse impact on other activities because it is just a mental fixation. Our interests play very significant role in our lives because these are the source of strong motivation for attainment.

Different psychologists have defined interests as.

According to Guilford (1964), 'Interest is a tendency to give attention, to be attracted by, to like and find satisfaction in an activity, object or person'.

In Bingham's words, 'An interest is a tendency to become absorbed in an experience and to continue it'.

In Drever's view, 'Interest is disposition in its dynamic aspect'.

As per Eysenck, 'Interest is a tendency to behaviours oriented towards certain objects, activities or experiences, which tendency varies in intensity (and general ability) from individual to individual'.

According to Murphy, 'Interests are conditional stimuli related to goal objects and expressed as likes or dislikes of activities, objects or characteristics of people in an environment'.

Development of Interests

How, why and in what order do interests germinate and develop in an individual? According to psychologists, interests are acquired tendencies. Their origin lies in psychosomatic factors, and their growth is influenced by heredity and environment. Hence, these are both inherited and acquired. In Super's view, the development of interests though influenced by inherited aptitudes and endocrine glands, opportunities, facilities and social appreciation also plays a significant role.

As opposed to Super's views, modern thinkers believe that interests rather than being inherited are primarily acquired.

Types of Interests

Interests are primarily of four types. These are as follows.

(a) *Manifest Interests*: Those interests which a person, instead of expressing through words, expresses through his behaviour are called manifest interests. For instance, some people are fond of watching movies, television or cricket while others go out to listen to discourses. Interest exhibited through these acts is more real.

(b) *Expressed Interests*: These are those interests which a person expresses through words. These interests can be known by asking a person about it. For instance, we can ask a student as to in which subject he is more interested. Usually, it has been observed that interests expressed verbally are not all that reliable.

(c) *Inventoried Interests*: These are those interests which we come to know through verified written records or tests.

(d) *Tested Interests*: Tested interests are those which we come to know from the significant similarity between a person's knowledge of some subject and the marks obtained by him in that subject. In other words, if a person's knowledge of some subject and the marks obtained by him in that subject are matching then we can say that he is interested in acquiring knowledge about that subject. The knowledge about these interests can be ascertained through different tests developed for the purpose.

From a study of different definitions and types of interests, we find that interests have certain characteristics.

Characteristics of Interests

(a) Interests are a part of our personality.
(b) Interests are inborn but can be influenced by environment, that is, these can also be acquired.
(c) Interests are not permanent. Interests develop and undergo change with age and time.
(d) Interests are also closely inter-related with the abilities. If an individual has got an interest along with an ability there is a possibility of his progress.
(e) Interests vary individually. That is why one individual wants to become a doctor while another an engineer.
(f) Interests are assimilated motivations for attainment.
(g) Interests are related to those feelings which give an individual pleasure or satisfaction.
(h) Interests are either manifest, expressed, inventoried or tested.
(i) Professional and non-professional interests go side by side.
(j) Interests are just a fragment of an individual's behaviour.

On the basis of characteristics of interests stated above, we can very well understand the nature of interests. These characteristics of interest are helpful in giving guidance or counselling to an individual.

Measurement of Interests

By measuring interests, we come to know whether an individual is interested in a particular vocation or not. Among general lists of this type mention must be made of Margaret E. Hoppock's checklist of occupations.

Apart from these general inventories, some other inventories too have been compiled in which along with the vocation, a chance is also given for expressing different aspects of personality. This interest inventory was first compiled in 1919 to 1920 by Carnegie Institute of Technology.

In 1921, Moore compiled an inventory of interests to find out the mechanical and social interests of engineers. In 1924 to 1925, Crage compiled different types of interest inventories to measure interests. In 1927, Korn Hausser compiled a general interest inventory. In 1938, Kuder compiled Kuder Preference Record. It was revised in 1951. It has served as a useful interest inventory since then. Guilford and his associates (1948) also prepared pro forma for the survey of interests. This interest preference reckoner is based on cause analysis and is quite prevalent. Another cause analysis-based preference reckoner was compiled by Thurston in 1953.

In India probably it was the Allahabad Bureau that prepared a vocational interest preference reckoner in 1956 on the lines of Kuder's Preference Record. In the same years, Educational & Vocational Bureau in Bihar compiled an interest preference reckoner again on the lines of Kuder Preference Record.

In 1962, Dr. Pandey designed an interest test for measuring the interests of adolescents. In 1967, Dr R. P. Singh's interest preference test was accorded the status of a standard test by Allahabad Bureau. In 1970, S. P. Kulshreshtha's vocational interest test was prepared. In 1973, Dr Mahesh Bhargava compiled a vocational preference measurement inventory.

Strong's Vocational Interest Blank: E. K. Strong (1938) of Stanford University compiled a vocational interest blank and got it standardized. This questionnaire is quite old. Strong compiled it for men only. He revised this questionnaire in 1966, and compiled one for women too. With the help of this questionnaire, an individual's like or dislike for any vocation can be found. In this questionnaire, there are 420 test items related to different vocations, entertainment activities, school subjects and individual characteristics.

This interest preference questionnaire by Strong was completed by numerous lawyers, doctors, teachers, traders, insurance workers, salesmen, farmers, dentists, etc., and through this the knowledge of their likes and dislikes was collated. This way Strong found that interests of people working in a particular profession are different from those of others.

For mapping interests, the individuals are asked to complete these questionnaire. On the basis of the marks obtained therein, their interests are compared with those who are successfully working in these professions. As such these questionnaires do not map an individual's ability but are only a comparative study.

This questionnaire has five versions as under.

(a) For those men who have completed their education.
(b) For those women who have completed their education.
(c) For those males who are still pursuing their studies.
(d) For those women who are still pursuing their studies.
(e) For males whether they are studying or not.

(i) This questionnaire is ideal for 17-year-old boys.
(ii) 15- to 16-year-old males and females can also use it.
(iii) Boys below 15 years are not eligible for this test as their interests are not stabilized as yet.

Responses given in the questionnaire are evaluated according to specially designed parameters called keys—which stood for different professions like mathematician, lawyer, physicist, psychologist, architect, journalist, chemist, dentist, teacher, physician, superintendent, secretary, artist, etc.

Special directions for completing this questionnaire are printed on the questionnaire itself. Students are explained the importance of these directions so that they answer all the questions truthfully. Supervision is not very necessary while the questionnaire is being completed because there is no right or wrong answer. Completing the questionnaire should ideally take 30 minutes. But 90 per cent students take around 50 minutes to complete the questionnaire.

This questionnaire where each key stands for different vocation is based on the practical aspect. As such it is more reliable and acceptable. Evaluating 420 test items takes lot of time. With the use of evaluation stencils the whole process can be completed within 15–20 minutes.

While analyzing the marks, it must be borne in mind that these are not a measure of abilities.

Kuder's Preference Record: There are a number of versions of Kuder's preference records, like Industrial Preference Record, Vocational Preference Record, Individual Preference Record, etc. In the Vocational Preference Record, there are 168 test items, each item having three options. A student has to mark these items in the order of his preference. In the entire record, there are 10 interest area of measures namely, outdoor, mechanical, computational, scientific, persuasive, artistic, literately, musical, social service and clerical.

With the help of this preference record, the interests of high-school students and adults can be measured.

Cleeton's Vocational Interest Inventory: McKnight & McKnight Company first published this inventory. This inventory has been found to be useful for school students and adults. There are separate versions for men and women. This inventory too is based on the same principles as the ones in the above described inventories. But this inventory does not give importance to those test items towards which the student is careless.

In the mens' version, there are 630 test items and 40 questions that are to be answered either in 'yes' or 'no'. For women also the same system is followed and test items are divided into nine categories.

Scoring more marks in a group indicates interest in that vocation. Among the inventories for men are those for engineer, priest, teacher, social worker, life insurance worker, sales man, biologist, scientist, etc., each one of which is separately categorized.

Stewart and Brainard's Specific Interest Inventory: It is available in four different versions—for men, boys, women and girls. Inventories for girls and boys are meant for those between 10 and 16 years of age. In each version, there are 20 groups of five questions each. Questions can either be answered or just tested. This work can be done in five ways because in each group there are five different questions. As such there can be only five types of responses from each respondent from like to dislike.

These 20 groups are related to 20 different types of interests which are as follows: artistic, commercial, creative, imagination, emotion expression, esthetic, experimental, leadership, mechanical, musical, observation, order, outdoor, physical, scientific, social study and local expression and each interest has been divided into five parts. For example, mechanical interest group has been divided into five parts, viz

(a) Construction
(b) Installation
(c) Repair
(d) Designing
(e) Operation

There are other interest inventories as well:

(a) Hepner's Vocational Interest Quotient
(b) Thurston's Interest Schedule
(c) Manson's Vocational Interest Inventory
(d) Lee Thorpe's Questionnaires
(e) Guilford, Schneidmann, Zimmermann Interest Survey

Personality Tests

Personality is the most important aspect of an individual because while studying personality we study an individual in totality. It encompasses an individual's complete external and internal characteristics on the basis of which we can distinguish one person from the other. Personality involves all those mental activities which influence an active individual's personality, and is related to the environment. It is an individual's way of adaptation to his surroundings. An individual behaves to adapt himself to his surroundings. There is a sort of selectivity in this behaviour.

This selectivity is found in different measures in different individuals. This specific selectivity or characteristic aspect of selectivity symbolizes personality. This distinguishes one individual from the other. But personality is not static or fixed. It is a complex of attributes, constantly changing with changing circumstances.

A study of personality is extremely significant in the process of guidance and counselling. An individual's personality is the sum total of intelligence aptitude, capability, interest, etc. Guidance is given to the individual and not to his aspects. The study of an individual is the study of his personality.

Before defining 'personality', we must know the origin of the term 'personality'.

From the historical point of view, the term personality has come from the Latin word *'persona'* meaning dress, veil or mask. In the classical age, while staging plays, actors used to put on masks and fanciful dresses. The difference in dress and facial appearance signified the difference of character. In the psychological context, this meaning of personality is extremely narrow. This is because a mask can bring about a change only in the external appearance. But external appearance does not give us much idea about his personality. It is essential to know his internal characteristics without which it is impossible to describe his personality.

Some people believe that personality is what influences others. Hence, we can describe it as a social stimulus value. But by doing so we overlook the internal characteristics of the individual. According to this view, man is nothing more than a structure of bones and flesh.

Allport and Woodworth have defined personality from the psychological point of view. Allport's definition is believed to be very extensive. Personality has been described as the sum total of man's physical, mental, emotional, social and behavioural systems. It is the essence of an individual's tendencies, feelings, emotions, intelligence, experiences, habits, appearance, memory, perception and behaviour patterns. An individual's dress, reservedness, style of living, emotional reactions represent his personality.

According to Allport, 'Personality is the dynamic organization within the individual of those psycho-physical systems that determine his unique adjustment to the environment'.

Allport has, however, ignored the social influence on an individual's personality. The Indian thinkers have pondered over personality through ages. In *Sankhya Darshan*, Kapil Muni ascribes three characteristics of personality—*Satto Guna* (preponderance of truth, equanimity and peace), *Rajo Guna* (preponderance of passion, emotion, provocation and action) and *Tamso Guna* (preponderance of inertness, indolence, anger and malice). An individual's personality is determined by the extent to which each of these *gunas* (quality) is inherent in him.

Burgess presents a sociological viewpoint of personality, 'Personality is the integration of all traits which determine the role and status of a person in society. Personality might be, therefore, as social effectiveness'.

In the words of Woodworth (1958), 'Personality is the quality of individual's total behaviour'. An individual can never develop himself living outside society. Just like the cells that grow within the body, an individual grows in society.

According to Valentine, 'It is the sum total of innate and acquired dispositions'.

Eysenck (1959) too, while defining personality, talks about its different aspects, 'Personality is the more or less stable and enduring organization of a person's character, temperament, intellect and physique which determine his unique adjustment to the environment'.

Development of Personality

An individual's personality can be determined only through tests. But in order to understand an individual's personality it is necessary to understand the factors that influence his personality. Broadly, there are three factors that influence an individual's personality:

Hereditary factors: We can describe the hereditary factor as an individual factor or living factor. Under this the following factors influence the personality:

(a) Constitution structure
(b) Health
(c) Intelligence
(d) Sex differences
(e) Nervous system
(f) Endocrine glands
  (i) Thyroid glands
  (ii) Parathyroid glands
  (iii) Adrenal glands
  (iv) Pituitary glands
  (v) Sex glands

Environmental factors

(a) Family environment
(b) Education
(c) Neighbourhood environment
(d) Financial condition
(e) School environment
(f) Physical or geographical environment
(g) Social environment
(h) Cultural environment

Psychological factors

Psychological factors like motivation, character, intellectual capabilities, attitudes and interests, etc. play main role in the development of personality.

Thus, an individual's personality is not influenced by a single factor but by multiple factors. Hence, in order to develop a child's personality, teachers and parents should regulate these factors.

Assessment of Personality

Psychologists have used various techniques to evaluate one's personality.

Personality Evaluation Techniques are as follows.

Subjective Methods

(a) *An Autobiography*: In an autobiography, an individual writes his life story and the readers evaluate his personality by going through it. The writer describes the subjective version of his experiences, interests, wishes, etc. This method is not very reliable because of the following:

(i) In an autobiography, a writer also writes certain fictitious things.
(ii) An individual describes his qualities and achievements in hyperbolic terms.

(b) *Interview Method*: Interview is the commonly used method for testing one's personality. This is the most commonly used method for selecting candidates for private and government jobs. In this test, the examiner and the examinee sit facing each other and the examinee answers the questions put forth by the examiner. From the answers given by the examinee, an assessment of his interests, wishes and expectations can be made. His demeanour, approach, manners and the way he answers questions also help in assessing his personality. The main flows of this method are:

(i) It is more time consuming.
(ii) A competent examiner is required.
(iii) Sometimes a person cannot answer questions properly.

But if the interviewer is trained and gathers facts in a controlled manner, the results obtained can be reliable and valid.

(c) *Questionnaire Method*: For evaluating social aspects of one's personality like sociability, self-exposition, etc., questionnaire is widely used in psychology. There is a series of selected questions, the answers to which give an insight into an individual's personality. These questions have two or three alternatives like 'yes', 'no' and '?'. The examinee marks (√) on the correct word and (×) on the wrong word. From the questionnaire, different attributes of personality like self-confidence, sociability, introversion, extroversion, dominance, subservience, etc. become apparent.

Four important types of questionnaires are as follows.

(i) *Closed Questionnaire*: In this questionnaire, the questions are answered in 'yes' or 'no'. Here are some sample questions:

- Do you like gossiping? *yes/no*
- Do you feel happy when guests come? *yes/no*

(ii) *Open Questionnaire*: In this questionnaire, as is apparent from its name, instead of answering the questions with 'yes' or 'no' full answer is to be written, for example

- What are your views on changing social values?
- What are your views about Kargil War?

(iii) *Pictorial Questionnaire*: Questions are answered by marking the pictures.
(iv) *Mixed Questionnaire*: In this questionnaire, there is a combination of all the above three types of questionnaire.

The main drawbacks of this method are:

(i) People feel hesitant to answer the questions clearly and honestly. Hence, it is very difficult to get correct answers for all the questions.
(ii) Sometimes questions are ambiguous—the examiner means one thing while the examinee derives a different meaning. As a result, the examinee gives a wrong answer by understanding the question wrongly.

Despite the above drawbacks questionnaire method is widely used. A questionnaire can be given to a single person at a time or even distributed among a group as required.

(d) *Case Study Method*: To study an individual's vices, virtues and peculiarities, biographic or case study method is used. In this method, information about the individual, under study, is collected from different sources. This information is extracted from his diaries, documents, family, school, office, relatives and friends and analyzed to arrive at conclusions about the subject's personality. This, in a way, provides a window view of an individual's complete personality. By this method, most of the adjustment capabilities of an individual can be studied.

The main requirements are:

(i) Patience, labour and time involved in collecting and recording information about any individual under study.
(ii) Special training for the personnel associated with the study.
(iii) Frankness and honesty in collecting, compiling and analyzing data.

Objective Methods

These methods take into account an individual's external behaviour. Hence, these methods are more scientific and reliable.

(a) *Observation Method*: An individual's personality can also be evaluated through observation but this is an ongoing process. Observation is of two types:

(i) *Controlled Observation*: In controlled observation, the individual is aware of his behaviour being observed. Quite often then not he adopts artificial behaviour.
(ii) *Uncontrolled Observation*: In uncontrolled observation, the individual is watched without his knowledge. Care is taken to ensure that he is not aware of his being observed. Through this type of observation, an individual's personality unfolds itself clearly. This method can be used for children very successfully.

(b) *Sociometric Method*: Through this method, the social aspect of an individual's personality is evaluated. This method was designed by Moreno. In this method, an individual is asked about his likes and on the basis of facts provided, a sociograph is drawn. This sociograph is analyzed to study an individual's personality.

(c) *Rating Scale Method*: Another way of evaluating personality is the rating scale method. Basically, this method is used in two ways—the subject is asked to answer some questions related only to a few aspects of his personality. The way the subject replies, or chooses answers from the given ones tells about his personality. In the other method, the subject is placed in real situations and his behaviour and reactions studied. For instance, to test someone's qualities of honesty and hard work, he may be assigned some tasks.

In this evaluation method, there are mainly two types of rating scales:

(i) *Relative Rating Scale*

In this method, a number of people are placed in the order of their relative seniority. For instance, if the relative sociability of 10 people is to be evaluated then the most sociable among them will come on the top and the least sociable at the bottom of the scale. The rest would be placed between them at their relative places.

(ii) *Absolute Rating Scale*

As is clear from its title, here people are not compared. They are rather placed in the impartial categories as per predetermined characteristics. For instance, if some individuals are to be evaluated for humility, questions are split into 5 to 7 sections.

Five-Category Rating Scale

1	2	3	4	5
Disagree	Somewhat Disagree	Uncertain	Somewhat Agree	Agree

In whatever category a person scores the maximum points, he will possess the quality of that category.

At first sight, this method of evaluation appears to be very simple. But a very competent evaluator is needed to use it. The biggest drawback of this method is that while answering questions the person risks the chance of being partial because most people do not see faults in their dear ones.

Another difficulty with this method is that on seeing a single good or bad quality in a person, we start viewing the rest of his character in that very light.

Despite the above shortcomings, this method of evaluation is quite popular in both the social and the industrial spheres.

(d) *Situational Tests*: As is clear from the term, the negative and the positive points of an individual's personality are evaluated by placing him in a special situation. This method is like performance method. The only difference is that in the performance method the individual is given certain tasks to perform.

(e) *Performance Method*: Performance method was designed by May and Hartshorne. In this method, the characteristics of an individual's personality are evaluated by giving him a specific task for performance. For instance, in order to test childrens' honesty, 8–10 weight measures with minor differences were placed together. These were to be arranged in the order of their respective weights. Each measure's weight was written at its bottom. The honest children found problem and took time in placing them in the order of their weight. But the dishonest among them read the weights at the bottom and quickly placed them in order.

(f) *Personality Inventories*: For personality evaluation, the different types of personality inventories are commonly used. In the personality inventories, there are questions regarding a particular aspect of personality. There are two or three alternatives against each question. After reading these the candidate has to give his reaction by marking tick (√) against 'Yes', 'No' or '?' These inventories can be used both for an individual as well as for the group tests. This saves a lot of time and expense. But there are some shortcomings:

(i) Through this method, the unconscious part of one's personality cannot be studied.
(ii) The candidate may aver wrong meaning from the question and answer accordingly.
(iii) In group tests, there is a chance of copying.

Some important inventories are as below.

- Minnesota Multiphasic Personality Inventory
- Bernreuter Personality Inventory
- Bell's Adjustment Inventory
- Freud Heidbreder's Introversion-Extroversion Test
- Cattell Sixteen Personality Questionnaire
- Maudsley Personality Inventory
- California Psychological Inventory
- Woodworth's Personal Data Sheet

Inventories used by Manovigyan Shala, Allahabad (UP), are in four sections.

(i) Your Home and Family
(ii) Your School
(iii) You and Other People
(iv) Your Health and Other Problems

There are 30, 40, 45 and 40 problems in the four sections, respectively. In all there are 155 problems. In the inventory, questions are in the form of problems. The candidate after carefully reading the questions (√) marks the problems relating to him.

For example:

(a) Your Home and Family

(i) My parents keep me under strict control.
(ii) I do not like staying away from my parents at all.

(b) Your School

(i) I do not enjoy playing unless I am made the captain of the team.
(ii) I feel depressed when I see other boys in problem.

(c) You and Other People

(i) I get angry very soon.
(ii) I can't make friends easily.

(d) Your Health and Other Problems

(i) I wish my body were sound and beautiful.
(ii) I get tired very soon.

This inventory helps in getting information on an individual's problems and his psychological needs in different spheres of life. This method is similar to the questionnaire method. In this method, questions concern the subject person alone. But in the questionnaire method, the information on other things, apart from the subject person, is also collated.

Projective Techniques: The most popular and prevalent method of personality evaluation is the projection technique. This method, as is evident from the term, is based on the principle of attribution or projection. It was L. Frank who first used the word 'projection'. It means to act or see an object in the light of own personality. Through this technique, we can study the unconscious behaviour while other techniques enable us to study the conscious behavior only.

Projection technique has the following characteristics:

(a) The material used in this technique is vague or formless.
(b) It is used to study an unconscious behaviour.

(c) In this technique, an individual is completely free to express his views, feelings, emotions and experiences.
(d) An individual can make use of any means to record his response like social, intellectual, verbal, physical, etc.
(e) It is a holistic technique. It helps to evaluate on individuals personality.
(f) The purpose of the test is disguised. The individual is not informed about the purpose of the survey to ensure veracity of responses. Otherwise his responses would lack reliability.
(g) These techniques can be used to study the personality of both normal and mentally disturbed individuals.
(h) The results obtained and conclusions drawn through these techniques are more reliable and valid than ones obtained through other techniques.

Merits of Projective Techniques

(a) The field of projective methods is very extensive. Many aspects of an individual's personality can be evaluated.
(b) Through this method subconscious as well as unconscious behaviour of an individual can be studied.
(c) The results and conclusions derived from the techniques are more reliable and valid than those obtained from other techniques.
(d) These techniques can be used on both the normal and mentally disturbed individuals.

Demerits of Projective Techniques

(a) The development and standardization of these techniques is a cumbersome task.
(b) The management, compilation and interpretation of data in these techniques require the services of trained personnel.
(c) Till adequate rapport has been established between the instructor and the respondent, there is little possibility of obtaining meaningful data.
(d) The materials used in these tests are very expensive and time consumed is much more.
(e) In these techniques, there is better respondent involvement.
(f) There is also the fear of arriving at wrong conclusions.

Rorschach Inkblot Test

(a) *Material*: This test technique was invented by Swiss psychiatrist, Hermann Rorschach, 1921: This is the most successful test. For this test, Rorschach took 10 cards on which ambiguous inkblot-like caricatures are printed. On the five cards, there are completely black caricatures, on two cards there are black and red caricatures, and on the rest three there are multi-coloured caricatures. Hardly any meaning can be discerned from the 10 caricatures so made.
(b) *Procedure*: The individual whose personality is to be evaluated is given those 10 cards, one by one at a time. He is asked to describe the caricature on the card. These blots give an impression of different objects, such as man, bosom, girls with bugle, sparrows, animals, phantoms, etc.

There is no time limit for this test, but the amount of time taken by the subject to visualize those caricatures as distinct images is noted down. Besides time, the candidate's reactions on watching the caricatures, his way of holding the cards and his facial expressions are also recorded.

(c) *Analysis*: Thereafter, responses are marked for analysis. For marking the responses the following points are observed.

(i) *Location*: Which part of the caricature the respondent reacts to is taken into account? Does he react to the whole of the caricature or a particular portion? If he reacts the caricature whole, then it is marked as (w). If he describes it in very loud terms, it is marked as (D). If he looks at small details deeply, it is marked as (d). In case he gives his reaction about blank spaces, it is marked as (s).

(ii) *Contents*: The respondent's perceptions noted down. Imaging a human figure is marked (H), an animal figure (A), a natural scene (N) and other objects like a vessel or an umbrella (O).

(iii) *Determining Elements*: What made the respondents react—the shape of the inkblot, its colour or its speed is recorded. The shape would be depicted by (F), colour by (C), speed by (M) and the loudness of colours by (K).

(iv) *Interpretation*: Observation recorded and evaluated is then interpreted. From this, we get full information about the respondent's nature, his observation power, emotional maturity, range of imagination, state of mind and intelligence level. But while interpreting, the respondent's social and financial conditions should also be borne in mind.

This technique is used in the individual cases. Hence, it involves a lot of time and cost. It can be conducted by qualified persons only.

This technique is used for detecting mental illness. It is equally useful in the field of guidance as it enables us to learn about an individual's various abilities, normal tendencies, and on their basis, his capabilities and potential.

Thematic Apperception Test (TAT)

This test was designed by Morgan and Murray in 1943. In this test, there are 30 cards with meaningful pictures, related to day-to-day life. Ten pictures are for men, 10 for women and 10 for both. Each person is shown 10 specifically selected pictures. In this test, the respondent is shown these cards one by one. The respondent, after observing each card, uses his imagination to write a story within a given time. The respondent has to keep in mind certain aspects like what must have happened before, what is depicted in the picture and what is happening now?, who are the people in the picture?, what are they thinking? and what would be the outcome?, etc.

Through transplantation, the individual unknowingly relates certain aspects of his personality to the story. The individual uses the story as a return to express his natural wishes, emotions, sentiments, tendencies and desires.

After a certain gap time, the respondent is again asked to clarify the story's details. This way, the first and second narrations are compared and analyzed. While analyzing the narratives, time taken by the respondent, his behaviour, demeanour, disposition, doubtfulness, etc. are documented in detail. From this the respondent's power of imagination too can be evaluated.

There are a number of ways of analyzing it. Anyway, the analysis is structured but qualitative. An experienced and competent psychologist can certainly discover many characteristics of an individual's personality from this test.

However, it is more reliable than Rorschach's Test. When an individual is shown the same picture repeatedly his reaction would be almost the same. He may tell one story earlier and another later, but the underlying theme would be the same. Since this test does not accord marks to the respondent's reaction, it has failed to gain the status of a fully objective test. Despite this limitation it is a comprehensive personality test—widely used in personality-related research, guidance and clinical sphere. This test was adapted to Indian needs by Uma Chowdhary in Calcutta. But she has indianized 14 pictures only.

Word Association Method

This method was first used by Galton in 1879 in his psychology laboratory. He designed an inventory of 75 words and experimented it on himself. He discovered that by remembering associated words some mental pictures and symbols get registered in the brain. The number of these pictures and symbols, and their clarity depends upon the power of association. After Galton, Jung too adopted this method and prepared an inventory of 100 words. Jung's objective was to find out the glands responsible for emotional behaviour. In this technique, the investigator tells the subject—I will speak before you certain words one by one. You listen to them carefully and after hearing them whatever first word occurs to you please tell me. The word spoken by the investigator is called the 'stimulus word' and the word uttered by the respondent is called the 'response word'. The time gap between these two words is called 'reaction time'. The analysis of this method is done on the basis of both the response word and the reaction time. Jung divided the response word in the following categories:

(a) Egocentric
(b) Super Ordinates
(c) Opposite Words
(d) Speech Habit

Sentence Completion Test

This technique was first used by Pyne and Tandler in 1930. It had 20 sentences like 'I feel good because ____________________'. The respondent has to complete these sentences quickly. In this technique, the respondent uses only those words that express his fear, anxieties, wishes, etc. This technique senses the characteristics of personality and is reliable. It has enough distinguishing quality, and hence is very important for guidance.

Play and Drama Method

This personality evaluation technique, in which the respondent freely expresses his emotions was designed by Moreno 1953. Its clinical efficacy depends on the competence of the investigator or the surveyor and the analysis of the respondent's emotive exposition. Even utterances spoken by the respondent while playing are noted down.

Guidance and Personality Tests

Personality tests carry a lot of significance in guidance and counselling. Through guidance and counselling, we do not guide a single aspect of personality like intelligence, interests, capability, etc. We rather provide guidance for the total personality. Intelligence, aptitude, capability have no independent existence as such. For the study of personality these are interdependent. Hence, while evaluating human personality with the help of various personality evaluation techniques, the purpose of guidance is not served unless intelligence capability and aptitude tests too are used as complementary tools.

Summary

To understand a person it is essential to collect and analyze information on different facets of his life. It is on the basis of this information that a guide or a counsellor can decide the type of guidance that might be given to a person.

A person's family and social environment influence his personality. Hence, for studying a person collecting data about his family and social environment is essential. It is also essential to have knowledge of his mental abilities, interests, aptitudes and personality. After knowing all these abilities, a counsellor can impart educational and vocational guidance.

Which individual can perform which work better depends on, apart from his intelligence and competence, to a large extent on his interests. In every individual's life, interests play an important role because what an individual will do and how is determined mostly on the basis of his interests.

One of the main reasons for individual differences is the difference in aptitudes. It is on the basis of aptitudinal differences that one individual is able to become a doctor while the other an engineer and a third one a musician. In the field of guidance, knowledge of aptitude helps a counsellor in counselling an individual as to in which profession or vocation he would have better chances of success.

To understand an individual's personality, we must study the coordination of his inherent physical and psychological traits. Personality is that total which encompasses an individual's complete external and internal characteristics on the basis of which we can distinguish one person from the other. From these traits, we come to know about an individual's adjustment with his environment.

For giving educational guidance to a student, it is very important to know his adjustment level, his relations with his friends, parents, teachers and peers; his reaction in different situations, etc.

3

Understanding the Individual: Non-testing Techniques

Effective guidance is dependent upon accurate and comprehensive information about the individual.

Psychological tests are considered useful devices for providing objective psychological information about the individuals characteristics such as intelligence, aptitude, interest and personality etc.

Therefore, a Psychological test is essentially an objective and standardized measure of a sample of behaviour.

From Psychological tests we observed more than once that they are not infallible. They are not goals in themselves until they supplement other information that is available concerning the client; it is then we used non-testing techniques.

Non-testing techniques have been found to give useful and detailed information, but they suffer from subjective errors.

Clinical and counselling Psychologists used a wide variety of tests but the use of tests by samples of clinical and counselling Psychologists differ in their theoretical orientations and work setting.

Psychological tests are used for diagnosis and interpretation purpose. It can also be used in selection of subjects in schools and colleges, promotion in school, entrance to college, to enter in part-time or full-time job and counselling for several purpose.

Hence to understand an individual's behaviour, it is important to understand the difference between testing and non-testing techniques.

Difference Between Testing and Non-testing Techniques

(a) Testing techniques are impartial and objective whereas non-testing techniques are subjective.

(b) Through testing techniques, information is gathered in a form that can be used by guidance expert to derive the same meaning. The information derived through non-testing techniques may not convey the same meaning to every guidance expert.

(c) Gathering information through testing techniques takes less time than through non-testing techniques.
(d) Facts about personality or behaviour can be directly ascertained through testing techniques while it is not directly ascertained through non-testing techniques because it provides detailed information.
(e) Evaluation is difficult through non-testing techniques.
(f) Testing techniques also help in identifying students needing special help.

Though testing techniques are much more useful, these have some inherent drawbacks also.

Drawbacks of Testing Techniques

(a) Testing techniques do not provide comprehensive evaluation.
(b) At times, these tests are used for purposes other than for which they have been designed.
(c) Testing techniques help to gauge a student's capability of doing but these cannot goals in themselves.
(d) Testing techniques are a component of guidance programme but these techniques do not constitute its whole.
(e) Testing techniques do tell us what a student might achieve in case of a test but cannot tell us what he might do in other situations.

Informal information can also help the counsellor to know more about an individual. In the process of guidance, any incomplete information can create one or the other problem for the individual. As such, information from people with whom the individual remains more in contact should be collated. It is believed that an individual chooses and befriends persons of his own kind.

To get information about a student, contact should be established with his teachers, classmates, playmates and peer group. In order to provide guidance, one should employ the knowledge of non-standardized techniques, apart from the standardized test techniques.

Some non-standard techniques are as follows.

(a) Anecdotal record
(b) Autobiography
(c) Observation
(d) Rating scales
(e) Questionnaire
(f) Interview
(g) Cumulative record information so culled from all above techniques, helps in understanding the individual.

Anecdotal Record

Anecdotal method is frequently used in schools. In this method, a student's work, behaviour or an important event of his life is mentioned. This method is more useful for teachers because being overworked they forget about a student's special behaviour. Hence, whenever a teacher finds an event or behaviour of a student to be of special significance, he must note it down in the anecdotal record.

Different psychologists have defined anecdotal record in the following terms.

According to Jones, 'It may be defined as "on the spot" description of some incident, episode or occurrence that is observed and recorded as being of possible significance. When these reports are collated they are known as anecdotal record'. Strang has defined it as follows. 'Anecdotal record is a specialized form of incidental observation. It is a description of the child's conduct and personality in terms of frequent, brief, concrete observation of the pupil made and recorded by the teacher'.

According to Brown and Martin's (1938), 'Anecdotes are descriptive accounts of episodes or occurrences in the daily life of students'. According to Rath: 'An anecdotal record is a report of a significant episode in the life of a student'.

Types of Anecdotal Records

Anecdotal records are used for guiding a student. The most important types of anecdotal records among different types of records are as follows.

(a) The first type of record contains only the objective account of a student's behaviour. In this type of record, there are no comments.
(b) In the second type of record, brief comments along with the subject's behaviour account are noted down.
(c) In the third type of record, problems related to his/her behaviour are noted down.
(d) In the fourth type of record, student's behaviour along with his good and bad qualities, and suggestions for improvement are mentioned.

Steps in Anecdotal Record

The main steps in the anecdotal record are as follows.

(a) *Getting Cooperation*: Cooperation is the first step that is sought. It is needed to collate information about the student whose anecdotal record is being compiled, so that the teacher can document his behaviour judiciously.
(b) *Length of Detail*: In the second step, care is taken to see that the teacher records only the relevant information of a student which is necessary. This means the teacher would concentrate only on the limited points, and hence the account would be clear and useful.
(c) *Preparing the Circular*: The third step involves preparation of a form by the teacher to enter details of the anecdotal record. There are four columns in this form. In the first column, the teacher enters the date, in the second column: the place, in the third one: the event and in the last column: the comments. On the top of the form, the name and the class of the student are mentioned. At the end of the columns, space is provided for the examiner or the teacher to sign.

Anecdotal record has the following format:

ANECDOTAL RECORD

Student's name ________________
Class ________________

Date	*Place*	*Event*	*Comments*

Examiner ____________

(d) *Procuring the Main Narrative*: Quite a few things happen in the course of study in the classroom which form the material suitable for writing an anecdote. The teacher, however, cannot disturb teaching to record those events. If the teacher does so, continuity would be disturbed and the students' attention distracted. In such a situation, the teacher should make use of certain symbols so that after the class is over, on seeing the symbol the event is recalled and recorded in the form.

(e) *Main File*: It is essential to file each student's anecdotal narratives so that whenever required they can be easily retrieved and referred to. These narratives should be kept in the counsellor's office.

(f) *Summary*: Once a month, each student's narratives should be summarized. The annual summary should be prepared by the counselor only.

Advantages of Good Anecdotal Records

Educational significance of an anecdotal record is evident from its benefits:

(a) Anecdotal record generates a teacher's interest in a student, leading to a healthy rapport between the teacher and the taught.

(b) On the basis of anecdotal record, a teacher can form an accurate opinion about a student's personality and also find out how the student is forming up.

(c) New teachers can get full knowledge about each student by going through these records.

(d) With the help of anecdotal records, a teacher can, keeping in view the interests and needs of students, suitably modify and change the syllabus.

(e) With the help of anecdotal records, a counsellor can have advance knowledge of a student's problems, and when a student comes for the interview, the counsellor finds it easier to do his job because of the advance knowledge.

(f) These narratives help in rationalizing various actions of a student in different situations. This helps the counsellor in providing guidance.

(g) After studying these anecdotal records, a teacher is tempted to take more interest in a student's development rather than providing mere bookish knowledge to them.

(h) These narratives are helpful in problem solving.

(i) While standardized tests evaluate personality, anecdotal records play a corroborative role in evaluation.

Limitations of Anecdotal Records

However, anecdotal records suffer from certain limitations. These limitations are as follows.

(a) *Subjectivity*: Anecdotal records are subjective type. It is totally dependent on the teacher's version. Thus, chances of the narrative being tax are higher. While writing the anecdotal record, the event must be watched very carefully so that the description is vivid, objective, impartial and brief.

(b) Writing these records is a difficult task because of the spiralling number of students in schools. Even if narratives are prepared for all the students, then preserving them becomes a difficult task.

(c) The main account should be kept secret as they are confidential. Only the counsellor should have access to it. There is no need to keep the summary secret because it does not have an account of any particular event. The main account of a student's behaviour should be accessed only by the counsellor. The summary, however, is open to all as there is no direct reference to any incident.

(d) These accounts are available for either brilliant students or those who are at the lower end of the ladder. Teachers hardly pay any attention to the average level students.

(e) These narratives by mentioning either good or bad deeds do not give a balanced account of student's activities.

Autobiography

Biography is a popular method. An autobiography means somebody's account of life written by himself. It is a subjective method. In an autobiography, an individual writes his experiences of different moments and events in his life, starting from his past, that is, from his childhood to the present. In an autobiography, an individual mentions his interests, objectives, achievements, wishes, events, reactions, etc.

Types of Autobiography

An autobiography is generally of three types.

(a) *Directed Autobiography*: In this type of autobiography, an individual is not fully free. A student is given clear directions as to in what context he has to write and what type of information he has to give. He is given an outline or a questionnaire, and he writes his autobiography accordingly. A directed autobiography is somewhat like this:

(i) Family
- Family's financial condition and intra-family relations
- Religion
- Social environment

(ii) Places where you have lived earlier
(iii) Place where you are living at present
(iv) School experiences
- Early days in the school
- Experiences of primary school
- Different schools in which a student has studied
- Friend circle in the school
- Co-curricular activities in the school and hobbies
- Teachers
- Subjects of interest

(v) Personal views, interests and aptitudes
(vi) Involvement in national problems

(b) *Non-directed Autobiography*: In non-directed autobiography, there is no restriction of any type on the individual. An individual can write freely anything in any way according to his own wishes. But this method is not organized as no directions are given to the individual on what to write and how to write non-directed autobiography.

(c) *Mixed Autobiography*: It is a mix of both the directed and the non-directed autobiographies. Directions are given to obtain specific information. Beyond that the student is free to write his experiences the way he likes to write.

Advantages of Autobiography

Information gathered from the student in the autobiography method helps the counsellor in providing guidance to the student. He writes down many useful things in his autobiography that he might not tell the counsellor when asked by the counsellor.

The following things about the usefulness of autobiography deserve mention as follows.

(a) An autobiography allows a fair peep into an individual's life, thoughts and views.
(b) The method of autobiography bolsters his power of expression.
(c) An individual can give free expression to his suppressed emotions by writing an autobiography. It helps him to relieve from his tensions.
(d) This method saves both money and time because students can be made to write their autobiography sitting in a group.
(e) The teacher gets to know about a student's creative abilities, vocabulary, spellings and the style of writing.

For making the method of autobiography more useful, students should be encouraged to read the autobiographies of great men. This would help them understand the significance of writing an autobiography.

According to Wright Stone, Justman and Ravins, 'The value of autobiography also depends on the conditions under which it has been written'.

An autobiography has relevance only when a student is himself prepared to write and knows its results. The gentleman who commissions the writing of autobiography should enjoy the confidence of the student, and the student should be assured that the information given by him would be kept confidential.

Limitations of an Autobiography

(a) Many a time a student exaggerates his qualities.
(b) He sometimes writes unnecessary details.
(c) Sometimes he cannot put forward his point of view properly for want of expression.

Observation

It is a very important tool for collecting information about an individual. The method of observation is an age-old technique. Even when psychology had not developed as a subject, an individual's behaviour was studied through observation. It is a very exhaustive method because it is used extensively in every sphere of activity, be it medicare, education, astrology or even guidance.

The cornerstone of studying human behaviour is observation. Through this method, data on different types of human behaviour and activities are gathered. Observation is also basically a subjective method but to be useful it has to be made objective and reliable.

Carter V. Good and Skates have written about the technique of observation. It is as follows.

(a) 'Observation is specific—It is not haphazard looking around for general impressions'.
(b) 'Scientific observation of behaviour is systematic—It is not chance dropping in on a situation apportunistically'.
(c) 'Observation is quantitative—By recording the number of instances, certain types of behaviour are noted'.
(d) 'Observation is recorded immediately—Notes are made promptly rather than drawing from memory'.
(e) 'Observation is an expert job—Being done by someone trained to do such job'.
(f) 'Observational results can be checked and substantiated to ascertain reliability and validity'.

Good has defined observation as 'Observation deals with the overt behaviour of persons in appropriate situations'.

Types of Observation

Observation is done according to the situations. Hence, the person providing guidance will have to assess the situation define deciding upon the type of observation needed. Observation can be categorized as controlled and uncontrolled observations. Standardized and natural observations are also described below.

Controlled observation: Controlled observation is done in some specific conditions. In this type of observation, time, place, conditions and observation units are pre-determined.

Uncontrolled observation: In uncontrolled observation, the observer is given freedom. He himself decides upon the circumstances and the type of behaviour is to be observed.

Standardized observation: Under standardized observation, an individual's behaviour is observed when he is examined. This examination technique also helps to throw light on a number of his attributes.

Natural observation: In natural observation, an individual is generally watched in a real situation.

Steps of Observation

(a) *Selection of Various Aspects of Behaviour for Observation*: The biggest problem in observation method is deciding upon the aspects of behaviour that should be observed. While observing activities of an individual in a particular situation some activities may get left out. Sometimes even significant things get omitted. Therefore, for the purpose of observation some selected aspects of an individual's behaviour should be pre-determined so that the observer concentrates on those aspects only.

(b) *Making Clear the Meaning of Selected Behaviour*: The meaning of determined behaviour should be made clear so that if two different observers are watching an individual's behaviour there is consistency and reliability in their conclusions.

(c) *Training of Observers*: It is important to train observers. If the observers are not trained the marks awarded by them shall not reflect the real position. To minimize the margin of error in their conclusions they are made to undergo practice.

(d) *Quantifying Observation*: It is necessary to substantiate the observed behaviour. This substantiation is in terms of numbers. Keeping count of the number of times a student repeats the same behaviour is substantiating the observation.

(e) *Report Writing or Data Recording*: It is necessary to immediately record an observed fact. It is ideal to use code words for different types of behaviour. Apart from this, tape-recording, recording on CD or floppy and photography are appropriate recording techniques. But the person under observation should not know this fact, otherwise he will not behave naturally.

Principles to be Followed in Observation

(a) *Observe the Whole Situation*: While observing, the teacher should not only limit his attention to the behaviour of the student but should also limit the conditions under which he is working.

(b) *Observe Students in their Routine Activities*: Students should be observed through their daily activities, for instance, how does a student behave while studying in the classroom, in the playfield or while moving from one classroom to the other classrooms.

(c) *Observation Over a Long Period*: Students' behaviour should be observed over a long period. This helps the observer to arrive at any definite conclusion.

Benefits of Observation

(a) Observation is useful both in individual and group situations.
(b) Observation reveals an individual's original behaviour. Hence, it is more reliable and objective.
(c) Everybody can use observation method.
(d) Observation is more useful for studying young children because their vocabulary is limited at this age. Therefore, study of their behaviour is possible only through their emotional reactions and other activities.
(e) Observation can be done not only in special situations but should also be done in normal situations.
(f) This method is also economical because this method is independent of a lab or any tools. Information gathered through this method is more reliable.

Limitations of Observation

(a) Many a time observation is not impartial because students can influence the teachers through their conduct and personality. Hence, while observing the students, the teacher looks at their good points only and overlooks the seamy side. Teacher's conclusions are therefore clouded—this has been described by the Psychologists as the 'halo effect'.
(b) Observation varies from individual to individual. Therefore, accounts given by different observers do not tally with each other.
(c) Observation fails to study the unconscious behaviour and the inner working of an individual's mind. Only the external behaviour can be studied through it.
(d) The physical and mental state of the observer's influences the observation.
(e) Sometimes an individual adopts artificial behaviour, leading to faulted observation.

Rating Scales

Rating scale has been devised to measure the personality of an individual. It is also helpless of procuring objective information through classification. In the field of education, a teacher can improve his teaching through classification. He can affect modification in the syllabus according to the requirement of the students and also bring about necessary administrative improvements at the school level. In industrial organizations, this method is used while giving promotions and increments to their employees. Through this method, we can also systematize expression of opinion on a specific objective.

According to Wright Stone, 'Rating scale is a selected list of words, phrases, sentences or paragraphs following which an observer records a value or rating based upon some objective scale of values'. In the words of A.S. Barr and his colleagues: 'Rating is a term applied or judgement regarding some situation, object or character. Opinions are usually expressed on a scale of values. Rating techniques are devices by which such judgements may be quantified'.

As per Ruth Strang, 'Rating is, in essence, directed observation'.

Rating scale is nothing but quantifying the essence of facts evaluated through classification.

Types of Rating Scales

Rating scales are of different types. The main ones are as follows.

(a) *Graphic Scale*: This method is widely used. A straight line is drawn and divided into many parts. In each part, a number of adjectives are written. The evaluator has to mark any one of these. Graphic scale is also known as Behavioural Statement Scale. Millford has evolved the following principles for making a graphic scale mentioned as follows.

(i) Length of the line should be about 5 inches.
(ii) The line should not be cut into pieces.
(iii) Three to five adjectives should be used: Two superior one neutral and two inferior.
(iv) Average or neutral words should be in the middle.
(v) Divisions on the line should be equidistant.

The use of graphic scale is as follows.

(i) Being simple it can be easily understood.
(ii) It can be filled in quickly.
(iii) The judge gets the chance to ask for minute distinctions.
(iv) In this method, there is the choice of making a comparative judgment.

(b) *Numerical Scale*: In this method, marks are associated with certain indicators. Students get marks on the basis of abilities, for example, three-point scale, five-point scale, seven-point scale. If it is a three-point scale then in this scale each statement will have three answers. The student ticks (√) one out of these three answers with which he agrees.
(c) *Rank Order Scale*: It is a statistical technique. In this method, ranks are mentioned in the descending order. Students are ranked by the evaluator according to their ability or performance. Different teachers who teach a student help in this work. Rank steps given by different teachers to each student are totalled. The average of all the steps is the final rank.
(d) *Paired-Comparison Scale*: In this method, each person is compared with others in the group. Thereafter, the findings are statistically analyzed and the individuals arranged on the scale according to their comparative qualitative standing.
(e) *Forced Choice Scale*: It has been observed that in the descriptive and illustrated comparative order determination the evaluator cannot vouch for his finding with any degree of certainty. To overcome this shortcoming, forced choice scale is used. In this method, the evaluator has to select one pair among pairs of two alternatives each. This method helps in knowing a person's view with certainty.

Suggestions for the Construction of Rating Scales

(a) The first task is fixing the number of gradations for a scale. If the gradations are few, the evaluator does not get the chance to make fine distinctions. But if the number of gradations is increased then probably the evaluator will not be able to use all of them. According to Symonds, the number of gradations should be seven.
(b) The statements used should be objectively defined. The evaluator should get the chance to observe the qualities of the individual in different situations.
(c) Instructions for the use of rating scales should be clear.
(d) The evaluator should be trained and intelligent.

Demerits of Rating Scales

There are certain drawbacks of rating scales. They are as follows.

(a) *The Error of Leniency*: If the evaluator is acquainted with the individuals being evaluated there can be leniency in judgment.

(b) *Halo Effect*: According to this effect, once a person gets influenced by someone then that impression persists.
(c) *Logical Error*: When an evaluator finds similarity between the performance of two youngsters, he gives them the same grading. This type of evaluation cannot be impartial.
(d) *Difference Between the Quality of Judgment of Two Different Evaluators*: It is natural that there would be difference between the evaluations done by two different evaluators. Because they being two different individuals their evaluation capabilities are bound to be different from each other.
(e) These ratings are subjective, hence are not fully reliable.

Advantages of Rating Scales

(a) This method acquaints the teacher with a student's working.
(b) By compiling a student's progress report, it helps parents to know about their child's abilities. Further on its bases, a student's rank in the class can be mentioned.
(c) On the basis of the conclusions drawn by this method, a student becomes aware of his shortcomings and is inspired to overcome from them.
(d) Conclusions based on this method help administration in taking appropriate decisions in matter of appointments, transfers, promotions, etc.
(e) This method also helps selecting children for admission.

Questionnaire

In psychology, questionnaire is widely used for gathering information concerning an individual. A questionnaire is an inventory of some selected questions compiled for collating information about an individual's personality.

Goode and Hatt have defined questionnaire as follows: 'The word questionnaire refers to a device for securing answers to questions by using a form which the respondent fills in himself'.

According to Barr, Davis and Johnson, 'Questionnaire is a systematic compilation of questions that are submitted to a sampling of population from which information is desired'.

Types of Questionnaire

Questionnaire is of many types, but among them two are most important mentioned as follows.

Closed Questionnaire: In this, answers to the questions are given in 'yes' or 'no', or by ticking (√) a choice among a number of given responses. Some illustrative questions are given below:

(a) Do you like gossiping? *Yes/No*
(b) Do you want to have more friends? *Yes/No*

In this questionnaire, an examinee writes nothing on his own. The benefits of this method are as follows.

(a) Giving answers is simple.
(b) Takes less time.
(c) It is objective.
(d) Listing and explanation is easy.

The Open Ended or Unrestricted Questionnaire: In this technique, the examinee instead of answering in 'Yes or No' writes the full answer. For instance,

(a) What are your views on Indo-Pak relations?

(b) The impact of earthquake in Gujarat and how has it affected the people psychologically. What are your views in this regard?

The person giving the answers is free to express his views. But this method is time consuming.

Characteristics of a Good Questionnaire

(a) Questions included in the questionnaire should be clear, appropriate and in keeping with its objectives.
(b) The order of the questions should be appropriate—starting with general and simple, and leading to specific and tough.
(c) Directions in the questionnaire should be clear and comprehensive.
(d) Each question should represent only one view at a time.
(e) The language should be simple and unambiguous, so that answers can be written without any confusion.
(f) Questions should be objectives and the number of questions as far as possible should be limited.
(g) Marking explanation should be simple and intelligible.
(h) Questionnaire should be attractive enough in its format and design.

Interview

Interview is an important and widely prevalent technique of gathering information in the field of guidance and counselling. It is a necessary component of guidance and lies at the heart of any counselling programme. In every sphere, an individual comes across various problems. For understanding these problems and helping the individual in their resolution, interview comes in as a handy tool. It is a subjective technique.

Meaning of Interview

The technique of interview is used in different fields. Interview has been described as a conversation with a definite purpose. In the words of Goode and Hatt, 'The interview is in a sense the foundation upon which all other elements rest, for it is the data gathering phase'.

In this technique, the interviewer and the interviewee converse in a friendly atmosphere sitting before each other and the necessary information is gathered. Interview is also believed to be the pivotal point of counselling. Pauline Young has defined interview as 'a systematic method by which a person enters more or less imaginatively into the life of a comparative stranger'. In the opinion of John G. Darley, 'Interview is a situation in which the client can gain better understanding of himself'.

From the study and the analysis of the above definitions of interview the following facts emerge:

(a) In an interview, two different persons interact facing each other.
(b) Interview is also a means of establishing contact with each other.
(c) The interviewer has a prior knowledge of the objectives of interview.
(d) During the brief span of interview, apart from gathering information about an individual, the interviewer gets a peep into the interviewee's personality from his demeanour and behaviour which is not the case with other techniques.
(e) Interview is the most widely used technique. It can be used for people coming from diverse backgrounds and under all conditions.

(f) Professional people are needed to conduct an interview, who can skim out desirable information from the candidate by putting relevant questions without causing any embarrassment.

(g) The process of interview is as much dependent on the interviewee as on the interviewer.

Types of Interview

Interviews are of many types, some of which are described below.

(a) *Employment Interview*: For a new appointment in any office, suitable candidates have to be selected. The purpose of this interview is to determine the suitability of a candidate for the post in question. Job-related questions are asked from the candidate.

(b) *Informative Interview*: In this type of interview, a candidate's achievements and explanations about marks obtained by him in different exams are asked. Providing information to youngsters on various vocations, professional opportunities, educational and training institutes, etc. is also described as an informative interview.

(c) *Counselling Interview*: Interview is supposed to be the mainstay of the process of counselling. The objective is to develop in the youngster the ability to solve his problems and realize his potential.

(d) *Research Interview*: In this interview, questions regarding research are asked from a number of people. Therefore, facts are gathered.

(e) *Diagnostic Interview*: Diagnostic interview is one where questions are asked to ascertain the causes for a person's problems. Gathering facts is an important part of diagnosis.

(f) *Group Interview*: In this type of interview, 10–12 persons with similar problems are made to sit in a group. In this interview, everybody's equal participation should be ensured so that each one of them comes to realize that the problem under discussion is not only his but is also common to all those in the group.

(g) *Fact-finding Interview*: In this type of interview, facts are collated by meeting people individually or in groups. Teachers and guidance experts also gather facts regarding students by using this technique. It has three main objectives which are as follows.

  (i) Through this technique, psychologists gather certain facts which they otherwise cannot through other techniques.

  (ii) To corroborate the available information, fact gathering interviews are held.

  (iii) The third objective of this type of interview is to observe physical defects. Such defects cannot be found through psychological tests. During this interview, the interviewer also observes a person's movements, demeanour, appearance, mannerisms, etc.

(h) *Clinical or Treatment Interview*: Clinical interview is done after diagnostic interview. Its objective is to treat an individual. In this interview, a person is engaged in conversation in such a way that he gets rid of his worries. By giving vent to his suppressed desires and emotions he unburdens his mind.

Purpose of Interview

An interview has the following objectives.

(a) The main objective of an interview is to gather different types of information and particulars from an individual.

(b) Helping an individual to solve his educational, vocational, social and personal problems, and adjustment.
(c) It helps in choosing suitable candidates for various posts.
(d) Candidates are admitted into various courses through interview.
(e) Certain physical defects in individuals, that cannot be found through psychological tests, can be ascertained through interview.
(f) Interview elicits information on an individual's mannerisms, aptitudes and views.
(g) Psycho-analytical interview helps in curing mentally sick individuals.
(h) Interview helps in removing probable causes of various problems.
(i) Helps in finding the psycho-social impact of media on individuals.

Steps or Components of an Interview

Success of an interview depends on the ability of the interviewer. But a good interviewer adopts certain specified steps to conduct a successful and effective interview. These steps are called *essential components* of an interview. The nature of an interview depends on these steps. These steps are as follows.

(a) *Preparation or Start of an Interview*: Before starting an interview it is necessary to make suitable preparation keeping in view its objectives. The following preparatory steps are necessary for interview.

(i) During the interview, the first interviewer should establish a friendly rapport with the candidate, element of intimacy in this rapport helps a candidate in answering questions without hesitation and fear.

For striking a friendly rapport, Davison and Robinson have made the following suggestions:

- *Compassion*: For generating a friendly atmosphere you must show compassion towards the candidate so that he has the confidence that the interviewer is his well wisher.
- *Confidence*: A candidate comes to the interviewer with various hopes. Hence, the interviewer should inspire confidence in him.
- *Approval*: The interviewer either agrees with the candidate or approves his actions. This approval is given to encourage the candidate to express his feelings unhesitatingly before the interviewer.
- *Humour*: Humour is necessary to create a tension-free atmosphere.

(ii) *Personal reference*: To clarify his points, the interviewer should give instances of his personal experience.

- *Asking Questions*: To inspire the candidate the interviewer should ask questions in such a way that the candidate comes out with maximum information he carries.
- *Threat*: Sometimes the interviewer may warn the candidate of the dangers of presenting dubious information.
- *Surprise*: At the time of interview, the interviewer should also express surprise so that the candidate gets the feeling that his information is influencing the interviewer by his views. This helps the candidate to correct his statement or behaviour.
- *Informal Start*: Interview should begin by putting aside the formal working document. It should be spontaneous, without referring to the main purpose of the interview.

- *Permissiveness*: It means that the interviewer allows a free flow of conversation, without passing any judgment on his statements. This helps to case the candidate's tension.
- *Equal Time for Conversation*: In an interview both the interviewer and the interviewee should get equal time to talk, otherwise the purposefulness of the interview will be compromised.

(b) *The Body of the Interview*: The middle part of the interview is very important because it is only here that the desired information is gathered. To make the middle part more useful, attention should be paid to the following suggestions:

(i) *Use Motivating Questions*: Motivating questions should be asked in the interview by the interviewer so that the candidate feels comfortable in answering them. Questions having monosyllabic answers should not be asked. Otherwise it will be difficult to get relevant information from the candidate.

(ii) *Proper Use of Silence*: Silence should be understood in its correct perspective. While answering, if a candidate becomes silent it should not be misconstrued as his ignorance or arrogance.

(iii) *Limited Information*: The interviewer should not attempt to gather too much information in one sitting due to time boundation.

(iv) *Understanding Candidate's Attitude*: The interviewer should understand the candidate's emotions, his negative and positive reactions, and respond clearly by saying 'good', 'OK', 'yes', etc.

(v) *Control Over Interview*: The candidate should be free to express his views. However, if the interviewer does not conduct the interview in a controlled manner he might fail to obtain necessary information. After the initial liberal approach, the interviewer should draw the candidate into discussion on the main subject by putting direct questions.

(c) *Closing the Interview*: Sometimes an interviewer, propelled by his own interest, drags on the interview to such a length that the candidate starts feeling bored. Hence, during an interview care must be taken to ensure as to how to end the interview. If a process is brought to an end judiciously it leaves a healthy effect on its results. Interview can end in two ways:

(i) Round-off the interview in a way that the candidate goes back satisfied;

(ii) Or end the interview in a way that it does not take much time to start the next interview.

If a candidate is to be called again, then at the end of the interview he must be politely informed that the current interview is being ended and that he may come again when convenient for further discussion.

It is necessary for the interviewer to learn the art of interview. Bingham has given the following suggestions for a successful interview.

(i) Objective of the interview should be precisely determined before the interview.

(ii) Whatever facts are to be gathered during an interview their checklist should be prepared in advance.

(iii) The interviewer should ensure that the place, time and date of interview are fixed in advance according to mutual convenience.

(iv) There should be no partiality at the time of interview.

(v) The interviewer should prepare, in advance, a cumulative record card for recording relevant information regarding a candidate.

(vi) It is essential to follow the principle of secrecy during an interview. Only after a candidate has been assured secrecy that he will come forward with clear and exact facts.

Suggestions for Interviewing

For making an interview successful the following suggestions should be kept in mind:

(a) The interviewer should be in full control of the interview. During the interview, the interviewer should keep reminding the interviewee about the object of the interview so that his answers are suited to meet the objective which they are looking for.
(b) It is an important element of the process to gain the interviewee's confidence. This confidence can be induced in the interviewee by showing interest and trust in him.
(c) The interviewer should listen intently and with patience to all that the candidate says.
(d) While interviewing, it should be ensured that the interviewee feels at home and is comfortably seated. His emotions should not be hurt.
(e) During the interview, the interviewer and the candidate should cooperate with each other and the interviewer should exhibit goodwill towards the candidate.
(f) To make the interview successful adequate time should be given to the interview.

Qualities of a Good Interviewer

For achieving success in an interview, the interviewer should have the following qualities mentioned below.

(a) *Frankness*: For making an interview successful, the interviewer should place all the facts clearly before the candidate. Indirect talk makes the candidate feel unsure and nervous.
(b) *Humour*: To make the atmosphere tension free, the interviewer must look cheerful and witty.
(c) *Limited Information*: During the interview, talk should be on pre-determined lines and strictly objective-oriented.
(d) *No Dominance*: The candidate should be given an equal opportunity to speak. Further, the interviewer should not arrogate to himself all the right to speak. In other words, the interviewer should not interrupt the candidate while expressing his opinion.
(e) *Good Listener*: The interviewer should listen to the candidate candidly and with patience.
(f) *No Exclamatory Gestures*: The interviewer should not make any exclamatory gestures or express disapproval of any of the candidate's shortcomings or drawbacks. He should listen to the interviewee patiently.
(g) *Exhibiting Confidence*: A successful interviewer manages to retain an element of confidence and trust till the end. Secrecy of the interview should in no case be violated.
(h) *Emotional Maturity*: An interviewer should be emotionally mature and a person of balanced views, otherwise he will not be able to impress the candidate with his personality. According to Ruth Strang, 'The success of interview depends upon the personality of the interviewer'.

A successful interviewer, apart from having the above attributes, should be well-read, well-trained, adequately experienced, friendly, intelligent, and with the ability to solve problems and take quick decisions.

Advantages of Interviews

Process of guidance is also incomplete without interview. It is widely used in individual, social, educational and vocational spheres of guidance.

The method of interview has the following uses.

(a) This method is more focused on problems and attainment of objectives.
(b) It is easy to use.
(c) It helps in promoting introspection in a candidate.
(d) Interview helps in comprehensive understanding of the candidate, studying his instinctive behaviour, emotions and views.
(e) It can be used on any individual.
(f) Interview also helps in obtaining detailed information about past happenings.
(g) The method of interview can be made flexible to suit different conditions and situations.
(h) During an interview, the interviewer and the interviewee get an opportunity to exchange their views.

Limitations of Interview

This method has certain limitations also which are as follows.

(a) It is a subjective method.
(b) At times it becomes difficult to elaborate the outcome of interview.
(c) Sometimes, because of differences of social background, beliefs and views, the interviewer, fails to properly comprehend the information shared and views expressed by the candidate.
(d) Qualified specialists are needed to conduct an interview.
(e) Being susceptible to influence by personal views and considerations, this method suffers from lack of reliability and validity.

Cumulative Record

For providing suitable guidance and counselling to youngsters, it is essential to procure full particulars about them. The form in which this information is stored is called the 'cumulative record'. This cumulative record is the prime requisite for the study of a student or an individual. Without this documentation, no guide or teacher will have adequate information about a student or an individual's personality, his behavioural pattern, his aptitudes and abilities. The term 'cumulative record' or 'compilation' was first used in 1930.

Meaning of Cumulative Record Card

The term cumulative record is used to denote all those formal documents that contain useful and reliable information about the student that may enable providing educational, vocational and socio-personal guidance and assistance to the student during the period of his stay in the school. Scholars have defined cumulative record variously.

In the words of Thomas Moore: 'A cumulative record is defined as information gathered students for longer period of time'. According to Jones: 'A cumulative record is a permanent record of a student which is kept up to date by the school. It is his educational history with information about his school achievements, attendance, health, test scores and similar pertinent data'.

MC Allen has defined the cumulative record as, 'a record of information concerned with appraisal of the individual pupil—usually kept on a card—kept in one place'.

According to Jane Warters: 'Periodically the significant information gathered on students, through the use of various techniques—test inventories, questionnaire, observation, interview, case study and the like should be assembled in cumulative record'.

From the above definitions, it becomes clear that information concerning a student's life, such as physical, mental, social, psychological, his character, etc. is written in the cumulative record. Immediately after a child is admitted to the primary school his cumulative record gets maintained. This record speaks about his progress, abilities, weaknesses and achievements starting from the initial stages.

Types of Cumulative Record

Cumulative records are of three types mentioned as follows.

(a) *Single-Card Record*: It is a 9″ × 11½″ single sheet information recorded on both sides. This card cannot hold the enough information. For more information, another card has to be appended.
(b) *Pocket-Folder Record*: It is a folder with a number of pockets pasted inside. Different information can be kept in different pockets. It is easy to retrieve information from a pocket folder.
(c) *Cumulative Folder*: It has a number of pages on both sides of which facts are recorded in ruled boxes. There is provision for writing detailed information as well on the pages. This folder can keep maximum information.

Characteristics of Cumulative Record

Guidance is provided to students on the basis of accumulated information only. In other words, these cumulative records are extremely useful in providing significant information about students. Hence, it is necessary that they should have the following characteristics.

(a) *Simple and Complete Information*: A good cumulative record should contain complete information about a student's progress as incomplete information does not give a clear picture for proper guidance. Hence, to present a clear picture about a student, there should be a brief account of all the various situations of his student life written in simple language.
(b) *Factual Information*: To ensure the validity of a cumulative record, it is essential that it should contain factual information only. Hence, only the observed facts should be recorded.
(c) *Secrecy*: It is essential to maintain secrecy of information contained in the cumulative records. New information should not be influenced by previous information.
(d) *Re-evaluation*: It is essential to carry out timely evaluation of the cumulative record. On the basis of re-evaluations, necessary changes can be made and new information can be incorporated in the records.
(e) *Continuity*: Continuity is of prime importance in an ideal cumulative record, so that it is easy for anybody to peruse it. Continuity means updating information regularly.
(f) *Group-based Evaluation*: In order to make cumulative record more reliable and valid, facts should be entered after evaluation or verification by a number of different teachers.
(g) *Usefulness*: Information contained in the cumulative record should lend itself to easy retrieval and interpretation for more meaningful and extensive use.

Objectives of Cumulative Record

While cumulative records are useful for guidance and counselling, they also help in achieving certain specific objectives which are as follows.

(a) *Objective Record*: The main objective of a cumulative record is to make available to the teacher or the counsellor accurate and useful information about a child. However, only a trained person can make proper use of this information. Before teaching or counselling, the teacher or a counsellor obtains information about a child's abilities, achievements and weak areas by perusing his cumulative record.

(b) *Instant Information*: A teacher can get instant information about a new child.

(c) *Child's Problems*: Cumulative record gives the teacher or the counsellor information about a child's different problems.

(d) *Guidance*: Proper guidance can be given after understanding the problems on the basis of information gleaned from the cumulative record.

(e) *Better Evaluation*: Cumulative record is also useful in evaluating a child. It supplies data for an objective evaluation. This evaluation is more reliable than a teacher's subjective observation.

(f) *Progress*: Evaluation, done on the basis of cumulative record, helps the counsellor in charting a better course for the child's rapid progress.

(g) *Identification*: Identification information includes child's name, sex, date of birth, place of birth, community, place of residence, admission number, date of admission, class, section, permanent address, etc.

(h) *Family*: Family information includes Father's name, birthplace, educational background, occupation, dead or alive, economic and social status of family, number of brothers and sisters, mother tongue, religion, caste, father's income.

(i) *Health*: Health includes height, weight, physical defects, emotional balance, eyes, nose, ears, chest, family tradition or any disease. There should be a record of periodic medical check-ups also.

(j) *Psychological Data*: Information of various types is collected under psychological data like mental level, general mental ability, special mental ability, interests, aptitude, personality traits, emotional and social adjustment, adaptability, attitude, etc.

(k) *Personal Qualities*: Five-point scale should be used to measure personal qualities like honesty, hard work, courtesy, self-confidence, sociability, cooperativeness, initiative, emotional stability, leadership and sense of responsibility.

(l) *Educational Data*: The following details are included in the educational data.

 (i) *Previous School Record*: Achievements in the field of study, marks obtained in different classes, attendance record.

 (ii) *Current Academic Record*: Marks obtained in different subjects, interest in studies, place in the class, particulars of failures, learning ability, crafts, skills, etc.

 (iii) *Student's Attitude Towards Teachers*: Cooperative or otherwise, participation in various events.

 (iv) *Vocational Planning*: What are the child's educational and vocational plans.

 (v) *Co-curricular Activities*: Student's participation in sports, literary, cultural and social service activities.

 (vi) *Principal's View*: At the end of the year, the principal gives his comments on the student's progress. If needed, he takes the teachers' help.

Student's cumulative record can be prepared in the following ways.
While preparing cumulative record card, the following points should be kept in mind.

(a) Cumulative record card should be simple and compact, capable of mirroring a student's gradual progress.

(b) Cumulative record card should be designed keeping in view the objectives of the school.

(c) For designing the cumulative record cards, the class teacher should consult, and take consent and assistance from other subject teachers as well.

(d) Cumulative record card should be flexible so that new items can be incorporated in it, if and when required, and changes effected.
(e) Cumulative record card should be kept at a secure place to enable the teacher to easily access it.
(f) There should be a set of rules for filling in the card and making use of the cumulative record card.
(g) Cumulative record card can be useful only when the information contained in it is reliable and relevant.
(h) Information written in the cumulative record card should be kept secret in deference to the confidence placed by the parents and students at the time of giving information.
(i) Teachers should know how to use the cumulative record—it being a difficult task.

Uses of the Cumulative Record Card

Cumulative record card can be made use of both in educational and professional areas. Its main uses are as follows.

(a) *Helpful in Students' Classification*: Children should be imparted education according to their mental development. Information given in the cumulative record can help in classifying students.
(b) *Helpful in Getting Introduced to a New Class*: When a teacher takes up a new class of students with whom he/she is not acquainted, then in that case cumulative record cards help him in understanding different students. When a student leaves the school and joins a new school, he must take the cumulative record with him to enable the new teachers to have adequate information about his past and guide him accordingly.
(c) *Helpful in Making Certificates*: Cumulative record helps the principal in issuing character, behaviour and sports certificates to students.
(d) *Help in Problem Solving*: Different problems can be solved with the help of cumulative record card. It gives information about a child's intelligence quotient. If a student's intelligence quotient is below average, the teacher modifies his instruction method to suit his level so that the student derives proper benefit from teaching. Certain students have behavioural problems and are difficult to handle, and cumulative record card helps in their proper handling. It also helps in understanding genuine problems of students and finding suitable solutions to them.
(e) *Helpful in Preparing Progress Report*: Cumulative record card helps in compiling a student's progress report about his educational and co-curricular activities.
(f) *Giving Information to Child Courts*: Cumulative record helps in sending juvenile criminals to child courts and providing past information about the students to them.
(g) *Helpful in Employment Exchanges*: Youth employment and counselling services have been initiated in employment exchanges. These services can be fruitful only if they have information about the youth's potential. This information can be obtained from cumulative records.
(h) *Helpful in Educational, Vocational and Personal Guidance*: On the basis of information collated in the cumulative record, students can be provided proper educational and vocational guidance.
(i) *Helpful in Self-assessment*: Information contained in the cumulative record card helps a student in evaluating his potentials and drawbacks. By acquiring knowledge of his shortcomings, a student can make suitable amendments to secure his future progress.
(j) *Personalized Attention by a Teacher*: A teacher himself prepares cumulative record. Reliable information about students can be entered into a cumulative record only if the teacher

pays personal attention to each student and takes genuine interest. In this way, cumulative record card helps a teacher in taking personal interest in children.

According to A. E. Traxler, the following are the uses of cumulative record card.

(a) Cumulative record card helps teachers and counsellors in understanding the needs and problems of a student.
(b) Cumulative record enables teachers and counsellors to understand the potential of each child and respond to him accordingly.
(c) Cumulative record helps the teacher in periodic evaluation of the trend of a student's physical, mental, social and emotional development.
(d) Cumulative record makes a teacher or a counsellor aware of adjustment-related problems of a child.
(e) Cumulative record card helps in the process of educational, vocational and personal guidance of a child.
(f) Cumulative record card also helps when a teacher plans to constitute a group of students for giving directions with a view to ensuring more personalized instruction.
(g) Cumulative record card helps the teacher in preparing a child's progress report and discussing his progress with his the parents.

According to Thorndike and Hagen: 'The important thing about records is not what is put into them but what is gotten out of them'.

This way we see that cumulative record card has wide applications. As such maintenance of cumulative record should start as soon as the child is admitted to the school. Cumulative record card should go with the child when he goes from one class to the other, and from one school to another. But the main question is as to who should be responsible for making and maintaining the card for the students. Scholars believe that this responsibility should rest with the class teacher only because it is the class teacher who spends the maximum time with the students and as such can observe them from various points of view. He or she can note down his day-to-day observations in a diary and periodically update the cumulative record. But before compiling information other subject teachers should also be consulted.

Popularizing the Concept of Cumulative Record

Despite its usefulness and significance, the practice of maintaining a cumulative record is not very popular in India. The number of students in a class being huge in India and time allotted to teaching too being only 36 hours per week, the teacher is not in a position to establish adequate personal with rapport each student. Hence, it is treated as something apart from teaching.

Refresher courses, talks and workshops should be organized for acquainting teachers to the uses and benefits of cumulative record. The school management should realize the importance and significance of the practice of maintaining cumulative record. It is the management that can motivate teachers and initiate steps in this direction. Teachers shall certainly follow the directives issued by the management in consultation with the principal. The Board of Secondary Education has suggested that making of cumulative record should be a part of the syllabus in teacher training institutes.

Summary

The cornerstone of all methods of study of human behaviour is observation. For studying an individual, the guide gathers information by different means and collates it. The form in which this information is stored is called a 'cumulative record'. This cumulative record is the prime requisite in the process of guiding a student or an individual.

For effective guidance's, information should be as complete and comprehensive as possible. Contact should be established with the student's teachers, classmates, playmates and peer group. Questionnaire method is also widely used for gathering information about a student. Interview is by far the most prevalent technique.

Rating scale is used to measure personality and its consummation. For evaluating information, testing and non-testing methods occupy a significant place. Testing techniques are impartial and objective while non-testing techniques are subjective.

4

Knowing the Environment

Success of guidance depends on two types of information. One type of information concerns the individual and the other his environment.

Importance of Knowing the Environment

It is important to understand the environment under which the problems arise. Constant change in different spheres of modern life has made an individual's life very complex. In the current conditions, old standards of thinking and methods of working are proving incompatible and inadequate guidance. Under these circumstances, it has become very important to gain knowledge of the environmental factors responsible for influencing new knowledge. In this age of competition, different means of communication, a plethora of subjects and diversity of occupations, we are facing a virtual starvation of knowledge in different spheres of life. As a consequence, need is increasingly felt for services that may provide us necessary information about education, vocations and social needs. This information is called an *environmental information*.

In India, parents' choice of occupations for their children is limited to medicine, engineering and other prestigious occupations. The main factor responsible is the lack of adequate information about different available educational and occupational opportunities. With the help of proper dissemination and use of vocational information, the gap between capability and attainment can be bridged. This also opens the highway to the unfolding of his real personality.

The need for environmental information has gone up because of economic and social changes.

Nature and Objectives of Information Service

Information service is an essential component of guidance programme, and it is useful for a student in many ways. Whenever an individual takes a new step, whether the step is for a new educational programme or the choice of a vocation, he needs certain information. Before taking any significant decision, properly compiled information related to the new situation should be available.

Information service provides information on different vocations, essential qualifications and financial aspects of entrance into vocational courses, chances of progress and situations vacant. It provides information on different syllabi, opportunities, formal and informal teaching facilities, and systems of education. For personal guidance, the information on an individual's family and social circumstances, and other particulars is needed.

But the nature of information keeps on changing. It is essential to keep the track of these changes in the knowledge so that guidance is given in the light of the latest situation. The counsellor should have adequate information on new vocations and job opportunities so that he can give successful guidance to the individuals.

An information service should be organized to enable a student to make use of his educational opportunities for choosing the right vocation.

Objectives of Information Service

An information service is an essential and a significant component of guidance programme. Therefore, it is important to note its main objectives.

(a) Channelizing students' interests into different vocations to ensure their livelihood by making an appropriate choice for vocation.
(b) Providing information on different educational and vocational opportunities, simultaneously, through a single window without any cost.
(c) Assistance in providing objective and scientific angle to guidance.
(d) Regular evaluation of information by specialists and consultants.
(e) Helping students in taking correct decision instead of resorting to trial and error method leading to frustration.
(f) Developing the ability in students of exercising their own discretion and making their own decisions.
(g) Collecting reliable and accurate information.
(h) Helping in classifying information according to its nature and use.

Collection and Organization of Information

The first step in providing personal, educational or vocational guidance to an individual is to collect and organize information about him. It is on the basis of this information that the guide or a counsellor guides an individual.

In short, compiling information regarding an individual is called his *study*.

(a) For compiling information, personal data record is used. This record contains a student's personal information such as his/her name, residential address, sex, age, date of birth, place of birth, telephone number, etc. General information contains those facts which are necessary for establishing contact with the student.
(b) Standardized and non-standardized tests are used to compile information about a student's interests and capabilities for a proper guidance.
(c) Information about a student's family and his social life is equally important as psychological studies have proved that family and his social environment influence a student's mental and physical development. An adequate information on a student's neighbourhood environment, his/her friends, his/her rapport with his neighbours and peer group is essential for providing personal guidance.
(d) It is important to know about a person's physical as well as mental health also for providing educational and vocational guidance.

However, one must assess the importance and objective of information which information is more important and what is the objective of compiling it?

(a) While compiling the information its veracity must be ensured by updating information regularly.
(b) Information should be extensive in nature so as to answer all the educational and the vocational queries of a student.
(c) The compiled information should be complete. Success of guidance depends on the completeness of information.
(d) Information, so collated, should be in keeping with the level of the students.

Organization of Information

It is important to organize the available information. Thus, we come to know which information is incomplete and not commensurate to meet the objectives. A guide, therefore, must have sufficient information regarding a vocation.

Methods of Collection and Dissemination of Information

The following are the two methods primarily used for collecting information about jobs.

(a) Job Analysis
(b) Survey Method

(a) *Job Analysis*: Job analysis has been described by Blum (1942), as an accurate study of various components of a job. It is concerned not only with an analysis of the duties and conditions of work but is also concerned with the individual qualifications of the worker. Thus, an analysis gives a clear picture about the functions, conditions of work and special qualifications required for jobs.

In Hacket's words: 'Job analysis involves a determination of the essential elements in the job and qualifications a worker should have for its successful performance'.

It becomes apparent that there are two aspects of job analysis:

(a) An analysis of functions and work conditions of a job.
(b) An analysis of the requisite qualifications in a worker.

The different business houses make use of job analysis in different ways which are as follows.

(a) It is used for determining qualifications of workers and deciding upon the type of training required for a particular job.
(b) Organizations are categorized on the basis of job analysis.
(c) Job analysis improves efficiency and promotes goodwill among workers bagging an appropriate job they get mental satisfaction.
(d) It is also used to decide a worker's remuneration in acceptance to the job type.
(e) Through this method, factors responsible for work fatigue can be identified and remedial measures taken.
(f) Conditions of work can be analyzed and workers motivated to perform better.

Job analysis requires information on different components of a job. They are grouped as under.

(a) Identification of job
(b) Number of employees
(c) Statement of duties

(d) Machines used for job
(e) Analysis of operations
(f) Pay and incentives
(g) Relation to other allied jobs
(h) Opportunities for transfer and promotion
(i) Period and nature of training
(j) Personal requirements
   (i) General (age, sex, nationality, marital status, etc.)
   (ii) Physical
   (iii) Educational
   (iv) Previous experience
   (v) General and special abilities
   (vi) Temperament and character requirements

Methods of Job Analysis: Some of the methods of job analysis are as follows.

(a) *Individual Psychograph Method*: In this method of job analysis, those individuals are studied who have attained significant success in a particular job. Information pertaining to these individuals is collected through interviews, surveys and tests. Results obtained are depicted through a graph called '*individual psychograph*'. This graph helps in choosing people for that particular job in future.
(b) *Questionnaire Method*: This method was first used by Lippman in 1961. In this method, an inventory of questions on work-related personality traits is compiled. This inventory is distributed among people working on that job. On the basis of the answers given in the questionnaire, a list of necessary qualifications for this job is prepared. This list helps while making future appointments.
(c) *Job Psychographic Method*: Viteles has mentioned the following job requirements in this method:
   (i) Easy categorization of special mental abilities.
   (ii) Standardized evaluation technique.
   (iii) Scrutiny of people by qualified inspectors.

   In this method, in order to determine the ability required for each level in the assigned job, each quality is measured on a five-point scale. These points are as follows.

   - Negligible
   - Namesake
   - Significant
   - Very significant
   - Most significant.

   Psychograph is then made on the basis of necessary abilities and their level required for each job.
(d) *Objective Tests Method*: A job is analyzed in detail and abilities required for it determined; standardized tests are designed on their basis. Only those persons who successfully meet the requirement of abilities fixed for it are selected for the job.
(e) *Time-Motion Study Method*: According to this method, every job is divided into work units and the time taken by each unit is studied. To this is later added motion study. In motion study, motions required in each process are studied. This way a worker's motion and time

taken by them are studied. Thereafter, a comparison is done with other workers. This time and motion study helps in job analysis and selection of workers.

(b) *Survey Method*: Surveys that are done from the point of view of gathering job information are of two types.

(a) *Questionnaire Survey Method*: In this method, the surveyor distributes a questionnaire containing job-related questions among an organization's workers. Workers answer the questions. Success of the questionnaire survey method depends on workers answering for all the questions without inhibition. Questions should be brief and lucid. There should be two or three options for answers so that scoring is easy.

(b) *Personal Survey Method*: The surveyor has to collect information by personally meeting people working in an organization—technicians, inspectors, supervisors and managers. The number of questions asked by the surveyor depends on his requirement; the surveyor can write down the answers. The genuine and intimate gathering of job-related information, possible through this method, is unmatchable when compared to other methods. Opportunities of employment, incumbent remuneration, mental satisfaction and peace, positive attitude towards work, encouragement, team spirit, etc. can be easily assessed.

Dissemination of Information

There are two methods of disseminating job-related information to students as well as to those seeking vocational guidance:

(a) *Personal Method*: The communication between the interviewer and the interviewee is the personal way of providing job information. Job information should be provided to the candidate only for the jobs in which he shows interest. But it is important to find out whether the jobs in which a candidate shows interest are in consonance with his competence and interests.

Personal contact is more effective than group method. In the personal method, a candidate can be offered solution by understanding his problem personally.

(b) *Group Method*: An Interview and a personal contact are a good means of providing job information, but keeping in view the large number of candidates, the limited number of counsellors, and constraints of time and funds, personal contact should be established only with those candidates who cannot be approached through group method. There are different ways of providing job information through group technique.

(i) *Job Information as a Regular Subject*: For acquainting students with the real state of job market, job information should be imparted as a subject. As a subject, job information can be organized more scientifically. Those students who study job information as a subject are better placed to choose their job. One should also develop an interest for the subject.

(ii) *Career Seminars*: Career seminars play an important role in the dissemination of job information. These seminars can be organized at the beginning of the session, on the eve of annual function or at the end of the session. In these seminars, experienced and prominent persons in different fields can be invited. The theme and outline of the seminar must be decided in advance so that students make themselves absorbent enough to receive and ingest the material to be discussed in the seminar. There should be a provision for asking questions at the end of the papers and the desirous students should be given a chance for interviews with the experts.

(iii) *Display of Career Information Through Posters and Newspaper Clippings*: This can be done on the institution's notice boards, in the library and outside classrooms.
(iv) *Display of Charts and Other Published Material*: This can be done in the classroom as well as in the library.
(v) *Through Special Subject Teachers*: Special subject teachers can organize lectures and presentations to disseminate career information.
(vi) *Screening of Films on Technical Subjects and Career Information*: Career information can be given to groups by screening films on relevant subjects.
(vii) *Through radio and TV*: Career-related announcements can be broadcasted from radio and TV.
(viii) *Plant and Establishment Visits*: Counsellors can take students around factories and business establishments for an on-site career information.
(ix) *Libraries*: Library is an important source of career information. A vocational information received from different sources can be organized and processed for easy reference and use by students. A special cell can be created in the library for this purpose.

Sources of Career Information

A vocational counsellor should remain alert to equip a student with the latest career information.

Occupational information can be found at three levels—National source level, State source level and Local source level.

National level sources for collecting information are mentioned below.

(a) Directorate General Employment & Training, Shram Shakti Bhavan, New Delhi.
(b) Ministry of Human Resource Development, New Delhi.
(c) Department of Education, Psychology & Foundation of Education, NCERT, New Delhi.
(d) Council for Scientific & Industrial Research, New Delhi.
(e) Indian Council of Agriculture Research, New Delhi.
(f) Central Statistical Organization, New Delhi.
(g) Survey of India, New Delhi.
(h) Union Public Service Commission, New Delhi.
(i) Planning Commission, New Delhi.
(j) Directorate General of Health Services, New Delhi.

State level sources for collecting vocational information are as under.

(a) State Directorates of Employment & Training.
(b) Guidance wings of State Council of Educational Research & Training (SCERT).
(c) State level offices of all the national agencies.

Sources at the local level are as follows.

(a) Local employment exchange.
(b) University employment and information Bureaux.

Private agencies are as follows.

(a) Private Companies.
(b) Vocational Guidance Bureaux, YMCA and YWCA.
(c) Career Institute, 94 Baird Road, New Delhi.
(d) Mansyan, Netaji Subhas Marg, New Delhi.
(e) Various recruitment agencies.

Classification and Evaluation of Information

It is just not enough to collect information unless it is properly classified. Thereafter, it should be filed in such a manner that it can be instantly retrieved when needed. A classification can be done in the following ways.

(a) *Alphabetical Method*: According to this method, information is first arranged alphabetically, then it is sub-divided alphabetically again, for example, Dean—Lecturer, Master, Head Master, Principal, Vice Principal, Professor, Reader, Teacher, Assistant Teacher, etc.

(b) *National Classification of Occupations*: Under this classification, all Indian occupations have been divided into nine categories. These nine categories have been sub-divided into 55 classes. These 55 classes have been further broken up into 300 sub-classes. There is a file for each occupation family, which has been arranged according to guidance region code number.

(c) *Subject Wise Classification*: Classification can also be done according to career subjects, for example, commerce, science, arts, etc. Further, sub-division can be done as per requirement.

(d) *Classification According to Interests*: Division is done according to career interests. Super's (1962) interest classification is used in this method which is as under.

   (i) Science
   (ii) Social welfare
   (iii) Literature
   (iv) Technical
   (v) Business

5

Placement Service

Placement service has emerged as an integral part of guidance and counselling. It caters to the occupational needs of individuals seeking guidance.

Placement service means helping a person to get an appropriate place according to his qualifications and abilities, thus enabling him to get absorbed successfully in any occupation. In the absence of this service in Indian Universities and Institutions, many youths after passing out of Universities do not have adequate career information. Thus, youth being direction-less, keep hopping from one job to another for successful carrier.

Guidance Experts Have Defined Placement Service Differently

According to H. B. English and A. C. English (1958), 'ordinarily the term 'placement' refers to the assigning of a worker in the job for which he is judged best fitted. Fitness includes the individual's satisfaction as well as his abilities in relation to the job'.

As such two things are important in placement: (a) Ability for the task and (b) Satisfaction of the individual. According to Downing (1968), 'Placement is a service with the guidance programme designed to assist the students in selection of suitable courses or curricula, extra class activities and part time or full time employment'. In the words of Andrew and Willey (1960), 'Placement refers to all of the activities performed in assisting the student to make an adequate adjustment to the next step in his training whether that he is taking a full or part time job or making a choice of additional educational training'.

Clifford P. Froehlich (1958) has defied placement services as: 'Placement is concerned with helping pupils to take the next step, whatever it may be. Such a placement service assists pupils in finding jobs. It also helps them find their place in appropriate extra-curricular activities. In essence, it helps them make use of their opportunities'. According to Humphrey and Traxler (1960), 'One of the counsellor's primary objectives in helping a student to solve his vocational problems is to assist that student to enter the occupation that is best for him. Such assistance is commonly referred to as placement or job placement'.

From the above definitions, it is clear that counselling and placement are closely interrelated, but these cannot be described as one. Under counselling, students are assisted in making their future plans, whereas placement service helps them in implementing their plans.

Importance of Placement Service

Placement service has relevance in both the educational and the vocational spheres. Educational placement service helps students in the choice of subjects according to their abilities, interests and intelligence quotient. It also offers them opportunity for exchange of experiences in group discussions for fostering social interaction. It also inspires them to participate in extra-curricular activities and offers opportunities for the same. It helps them to overcome their fears and inhibitions.

Vocational placement service helps students in finding their appropriate place in the occupational field, albeit, in keeping with their interests, aptitude, education and other abilities. It is an educational institution's responsibility to ensure a youth's entry into the vocational field. Though it is an educational service yet there is a certain degree of uncertainty whether an educational institution will be able to perform this function successfully.

According to experts, a youth spends his formative years in an educational institution. All information concerning him is placed in the cumulative record compiled there. On the basis of this information, an educational institution can successfully provide vocational service with the cooperation of industry, administration and society. Job hunting is a turbulent period for the youth since he does not have the information on a career commensurate with his abilities. Moreover, in an institution students have limited freedom. Hence, while moving from student life to occupational life, students need help to start their career. It is placement service that can help them to become aware about the demands of their chosen vocations. Hence, with a view to making educational institutions discharge their part of the responsibility they should be made to institute placement or cell and appoint placement counsellors.

Placement service also influences society. Proper job placement has a direct impact on the economic aspect of society. When an individual finds a suitable placement it adds to a national income. Further, it also helps the youths to get happily adjusted in society.

Such individuals are more competent at their jobs which affects productivity.

Placement service also helps employers, they get capable and trained workers without much bother.

Placement services will be in a position to play a significant and useful role only when employment agencies, public service survey and information concerning business and industry is made available to educational institutions in a compact form.

Aims of Placement Service

Placement service has the following aims.

(a) *Helps in Looking for Part-Time Jobs*: Many students, out of compulsion, want to eke out a living along with education—by doing a part-time job. Placement service helps them in finding a suitable job.

(b) *Providing Full-Time Jobs*: After finishing education, a youth needs a job to make a living. A placement service assists him in choosing a suitable vocation according to his skill and ability.

(c) *Encouraging Extra-Class Activities*: A student has enough energy to undertake some activities apart from classroom studies. Hence, a placement service can help locate such facilities and encourage students to participate in them. These activities include various sports and hobbies, elocution, music, dramatics, painting, etc.

(d) *Proper Selection of Curriculum*: It helps a student in choosing a suitable syllabus in keeping with his interests, capabilities and intelligence quotient.

(e) *Helps in Training Programmes*: It also helps a student in choosing the right training programme by:

- (i) making a desirable training choice,
- (ii) locating training places for them,
- (iii) drawing a realistic plan for desirable training for them,
- (iv) facilitating registration of the student in the institution of his choice.

Educational and Vocational Placement

A placement service can be of two types.

(a) *Educational Placement*: The programme of assisting an individual in making satisfactory progress in educational field is called *educational placement*.

(b) *Vocational Placement*: The programme of finding a suitable occupation for an individual is called *vocational placement*. While finding the occupation, an individual's interests, competence, educational and other abilities are kept in mind.

Educational Placement

Educational institutes have a social responsibility of helping a student in getting appropriate placement. A placement service helps a student in making a rational choice of subjects, and facilitates his entry into the training programmes. This is by providing information to the student of the potential training institute on the basis of his cumulative record, so maintained in the educational institution.

An educational placement service should be run on continuing basis because students always need help in adjusting themselves to new schools environment. For successful adjustment, it is important that information regarding a student should be sent to the new school where he sought admission. It is essential for the teacher, the principal and the counsellor to be pro-active in this process. This information helps the guidance personnel in providing guidance to the student.

The different functions of educational placement are as follows.

(a) *Placement in Regular Courses*: The purpose of guidance is not only to acquaint new students with the subjects they are to study but also to help them in choosing subjects according to their interests and abilities. As a result of the recommendations of Mudaliar Commission, different curricula have been introduced. After Class 10, a student needs his teacher and counsellor's help to make proper choice of subjects. Since information available with the teacher is not comprehensive enough, he sends the student to the counsellor for guidance. For getting acquainted with students and understanding their interests and needs, it is important for a counsellor to have a personal interview. A student should be informed about all the existing educational opportunities in keeping with his abilities, interests, needs and aims.

(b) *Placement in Co-curricular Activities*: The aim of education is to ensure all-round development of a youth, i.e. physical, social, ethical and mental. A youth has various needs that can be fulfilled by co-curricular activities, for example, some students shy away from social activities. They should be encouraged to participate in group activities which would help them in their later life.

(c) *Placement in Vocational Training*: Many students in India after completing their secondary level education want to join training institutes so that they can enter the vocational field early. But they neither have full information about training institutes nor they are in a position to decide upon the type of training needed. It is here that the placement service steps in, and can help students in vocational training placement in the following ways.

(i) By suggesting them suitable training course according to their preference.
(ii) locating training institute to help them.
(iii) By preparing a plan for desired training.
(iv) By helping them in admission to the institute of their choice

Organizing Educational Placement Service

The success and effectiveness of educational placement programme can be assured in the following manner.

(a) *Keeping Up-to-date Information*: The guide or counsellor must have the latest information about different courses and curricula to be able to give correct information to the students.
(b) *Development of Good Working Relations*: A counsellor must maintain good relations with all the staff members. This helps in procuring necessary and useful information about a student's abilities and achievements which then helps in his successful placement.
(c) *Conducting Personal Interview*: For understanding a student's needs and interests, he must be interviewed in person. It is only through a personal interview that a student's reaction towards different subjects can be easily determined by a guide or a counsellor.
(d) *Maintaining a File*: A file about different clubs and associations in a school should be maintained. This helps in getting information about the future plans of a student participating in their activities.

Holding Counselling Sessions

Counselling a student in the educational sphere has become necessary. For the purpose of counselling, a student is called in counselling sessions where examination results and other facts are discussed and analyzed. On the basis of these interpretations, a student's future plans are made. Further, a student should have realistic knowledge of various opportunities.

Vocational Placement

It is directly concerned with making it possible for students to obtain employment or preparing them for employment at the most suitable time and in accordance with individual needs.

Vocational placement service is concerned with–

- procuring part-time or full-time occupation for a student.
- assisting a student in gaining appropriate vocational training in order to prepare him for a job placement.

According to Myers (1924), however, getting a student placed in an occupation is the job of the educational institution. According to him: 'Sending a student from a school to occupational field is educational service. Hence, in the proper sense, it is the job of the educational institution'.

According to experts, a youth spends his formative years in an educational institution. All information concerning him is placed in the cumulative record compiled there. On the basis of this information an educational institution can successfully provide vocational service with the cooperation of industry, administration and society.

(a) *Placement with the Help of Society*: Before getting an individual engaged in an occupation, a school's placement service should have full information about vocational opportunities. School can procure all this information from the local placement agencies. Hence, a school must maintain active contact with these services.

(b) *Popularizing Placement Service*: In India, students do not have full knowledge neither about different occupations nor the requisite skill required. Hence, there is need for making such services popular. The placement services can be popularized through magazines, counselling services, local newspapers, by writing letters to parents, etc.

(c) *Use of Student-Related Information*: Before arranging for a student's placement, reference should be made to the information contained in his cumulative record maintained in the school. The placement service people with the help of the counsellor sift through the records for obtaining correct and reliable information about the student for their reference.

(d) *Counselling*: While arranging for a student's placement in a school, personal counselling is also needed. The main aim of placement service is to ensure effective adjustment of a youth in a vocation. For this it is necessary that a commonality should be struck between a youth's interests and capabilities on the one hand, and the conditions and requirements of an occupation on the other hand. Placement service must secure cooperation of the counsellor in the school or have their own counsellor.

Organizing Vocational Placement Service

Humphrey, Traxler and North (1960) have made the following suggestions for organizing vocational placement service.

Maintaining Card File: A card is maintained for each student seeking placement in a job. On the card, the name of the student and the vocation he wants to take up is written. Whenever vocational opportunities come, the counsellor can get in touch with the student.

Establishing Cooperative Relationship with a Prospective Employer: Placement officer must establish a cooperative relationship with an employer. These contacts can be established at personal level either through correspondence or by telephonic conversation. Job-related information obtained this way can be stored in the card file and passed on to the appropriate prospective job seekers.

Interview and Registration of Job Seekers: It is very necessary to interview individuals, desirous of training and those seeking vocational placement, to obtain complete information about them, for example, name, date and place, permanent address, interests, abilities, attainments, previous experience, plans, ambitions, etc. After this the individual's name should be registered and all information recorded on a data card.

Filing System for Registering the Name: The person handling registration should be familiarized with the technique of maintaining data cards and their filling.

Obtaining Definite Information: Statements of information about the candidate should be precise, definite and unambiguous. An indefinite and ambiguous information can lead to faulty decisions.

Checking the Accuracy of Information: An information provided by a candidate should be verified, otherwise counselling would be faulty and ineffective.

Selection of Candidates to be Recommended: Candidates whose particulars have been thoroughly screened and found meeting the requirements of the job should be recommended.

Secure Approval of Registered Persons: Before recommending any candidate, it is necessary to obtain his consent.

Send a Copy of Biodata: A copy of the candidate's biodata must reach the potential employer so that he can peruse, analyze and, if necessary, verify the particulars before calling the candidate for an interview. This gives the potential employer a fair idea about the candidate he is going to interview and enables him to frame the questions accordingly.

Feedback from The Employer: Placement manager should find out from the potential employer whether the recommended candidate has joined the employment or not.

Record the Results: Placement manager must enter on the candidate's data card the result of his applications for employment. This would help him in follow-up action.

Prepare a Summary Report: At the end of an academic session, a vocational placement service should prepare a summary report giving the number of individuals registered for employment, types of occupations, number of advertisements for employment and the number of persons placed in employment. A copy of this report should be sent to the school administrator, other members of the staff, new and old students, their guardians and daily newspapers.

Conducting Follow-up Studies: Follow-up studies evaluation and development of placement service should be done by using questionnaires.

Selection of Personnel

For running a placement service properly, it is very important to make proper selection of personnel. They should be chosen from among the teachers and counsellors.

Hatch and Dresil have made the following suggestions for the selecting personnel for a placement service.

(a) Only persons capable of establishing good rapport with students should be selected.
(b) They should have some experience other than studies.
(c) They should have training in guidance and counselling.
(d) They should be aware of different strata of society.
(e) They should have experience of working as a counsellor.

Physical Facilities

For running a placement service there should be a separate office. It is essential for this office to be near the guidance office because most of the information is readily available in the guidance office. This office should be accessible to all the students without any difficulty. There should be proper sitting arrangements and a filing rack in the room. A telephone should also be provided to facilitate communication. The room should be peaceful, airy and well lighted.

Determining Areas of Placement Service: For organizing a placement service, it is essential to define its area of operation, i.e. there should be clarity about the services it will provide. (For example, whether this service has been organized for assisting seniors, drop-outs, part-time job-seekers, full-time job-seekers, etc.)

Preparing the Required Form: A proper form should be made for recording candidates' data for placement service. Here is an outline:

FORM
(Information provided shall be kept confidential)

1) Candidate's name ______
2) Father's name ______
3) Permanent address ______
4) Candidate's age ______
5) Married/unmarried ______
6) Examination passed ______ Year ______
7) Specialization area (a) Arts (b) Science (c) Agriculture (d) Commerce (e) Typewriting (f) Machine Operation (g) Literature (h) Secretarial Practice (i) Others
8) (a) Personality traits: Excellent /Very Good /Good Satisfactory/ Poor (To be filled by the counsellor)
(b) Character ______
(c) Team spirit ______
(d) Dependability ______
(e) Ownership ______
9) Interests ______
10) Co-curricular activities ______
11) Subjects of distinction
(a) ______ (b) ______ (c) ______
12) Health: Excellent/Good/Poor
13) Counsellor's comments ______
______
______
______
______

(Signature)

When an employer contacts a placement agency to intimate about a vacant situation the placement service must note down the relevant information in a form.

Here is a sample form:

FORM

1) Employer's name and address
2) Full-time/Part-time job
3) Type of job
4) Working hours
5) Educational qualifications
6) Required training
7) Starting salary
8) Chances of future growth
9) Joining formalities
10) Other facilities

Informing Students, Teachers and Employers about Placement Service: The efficacy of all placement service depends upon making the students, teachers and others aware about its aims and objectives.

A good working relationship between employers and placement service can be ensured in the following ways.

(a) *Visits*: Placement manager must pay periodic visits to business and industrial organizations in order to establish direct contact with them.
(b) *Written Correspondence and Telephonic Contact*: With a view to saving time and money, telephonic contact is more feasible these days. Placement personnel can establish contact through written correspondence with the employers as well.
(c) *Inviting Industry Representatives*: Representatives of industrial and business organizations should be invited to schools for discussion.
(d) *Publicity*: Placement manager can advertise available talent information through newspapers for the benefit of business organizations.

Summary

Placement service means placing a person in an appropriate place in keeping with his qualifications and ability. It has relevance in both the educational and the vocational spheres. Educational placement service helps students in the choice of subjects. While vocational placement service helps students in finding their appropriate place in the occupational field.

Placement service also influences the society. The placement of youths satisfactory has a direct impact on the socio-economic health of society.

For making placement service effective it is essential to make students, teachers and others aware about its aims and objectives.

6

Follow-up Service

Follow-up service is an essential component of a guidance programme. In the absence of this service, it is not only difficult but also impossible to gauge the effectiveness of guidance programmes. Some academics treat it as a part of research and evaluation service.

Nature of Follow-up Service

According to Roeber, Smith and Erickson, 'The follow-up service committee is concerned with what happens to pupils while in school or after they have left school. It is interested in their progress in relation to total or any part of the educational programme'. In the view of Downing (1968), 'The follow-up service is a basic element of guidance programme, designed to provide information needed to assist youngsters in making a better adjustment to school or a vocational training programme or a job'.

The job of guidance service is to help students in making future plans and satisfactory adjustment in school. The teachers, principal and counsellor are constantly making efforts in this direction. But problem arises in assessing progress made by students in the achievement of their objectives. According to this point of view, counsellor's job is not only to help in the area of counselling and guidance but also endeavour to answer the following questions:

(a) Are the students making efforts to achieve his objectives?
(b) Have the students chosen the right objectives?
(c) Does he/she have the suitable opportunities for the realization of his/her objectives?
(d) Does he/she need to change his objectives?
(e) Does the school have adequate facilities for providing proper education to its students?

Through these questions we can clearly define the area and significance of follow-up services.

Uses of Follow-up Service

(a) Follow-up service designed to provide information needed to assist students ensuring ideal adjustment in educational curriculum, vocational training programme or vocation.
(b) Follow-up service provides necessary information for bringing about reforms in a school's programmes.
(c) By follow-up service, a school successfully establishes contact with its old students. It also helps in collecting information about the problems being faced in schools.
(d) The counsellor is able to evaluate the effectiveness of counselling rendered by him.

Thus, on the basis of information collected through follow-up service, a school can bring about necessary reforms in its curricula and administration.

Follow-up service also gives information about a student's performance, team spirit, adjustability and satisfaction level. Moreover, through follow-up service an attempt is also made to assess an individual strength to brave the odds in the most trying circumstances.

Sadly, despite the necessity and importance of follow-up service, there is hardly any school in India that runs this kind of services.

Aims of Follow-up Service

(a) To obtain information about a student's adjustment and progress in educational, vocational and personal areas.
(b) To assess the level and progress of a student in different classes, subjects of study and co-curricular activities.
(c) To gather vocational information that can be used to help students who are making their future plans.
(d) To find out the occupational level and progress of those students who have found a placement after finishing their studies. If the follow-up is done continuously for some years, students can be offered suggestions for change or modification of their career objectives.
(e) To find out the reasons behind a student dropping out of school.
(f) To find out the progress of those students who are studying in a college or in a training institute. This helps in gauging effectiveness of a guidance programme.
(g) To find out the factors responsible for a student's maladjustment, so that he can be offered timely help.
(h) To discover the deficiencies in school curriculum and make efforts to correct them. According to Froehlich, if as a result of follow-up we feel that the school curriculum is not up to the mark and students are facing problems on that account the curriculum should be suitably modified.

On the basis of follow-up studies, guidance programme can also be modified. Follow-up service furnishes students and teachers with useful and up-to-date information. Follow-up on behavioural pattern study projects helps bring about social harmony. It can also help in verifying the results of changes made in school programmes.

Follow-up service by its very nature is an investigative, assessment and corrective service. Its main objective is to assess students' adjustability problems in educational and vocational spheres. It also assesses the success and effectiveness of guidance and counselling provided to a student. Knowledge of techniques to be followed in follow-up service is essential for its success.

Need of Follow-up Service

After a study of the objectives of follow-up service it is clear that follow-up service is important for students studying in school or in college as well as for those who drop out and take up an occupation. Hence, follow-up service is necessary for different categories of students at every level of education.

(a) *Follow-up Service for Students Studying in School or College*: A counsellor keeps on doing follow-up study to find out whether the counselling provided to students, studying in various institutions, has proved to be useful or not. While doing follow-up study, a counsellor must keep three things in mind.

(i) How far has the subject person acted on the plan and suggestions made by the counsellor?
(ii) How far can he succeed in adjusting himself to his current situation?
(iii) Does he need help in recasting his plan, or future adjustment, in the context of new changes?

There should be a provision for re-interviewing the subject person if he faces any difficulty in between the interview. The counsellor should be willing to offer his services any time of the day.

(b) *Follow-up Service for Students Leaving an Institution Before Graduation*: First of all the counsellor should figure out the possibilities of the student continuing his studies. He should find out the reasons that compelled the student to quit studies and ponder over the current situation and plans, if any. If the student's decision to quit studies is unavoidable, an exit interview should be conducted.

(c) *Follow-up Studies and Services for Former Students*: An institution should undertake follow-up service for former students also. Ordinarily, there can be difficulties in undertaking this task. Humphreys and Traxler have justified the use of follow-up service for three reasons:

(i) Feedback from former students throws light on the institution's usefulness and its achievements.
(ii) Review of achievements and standing of former students help in understanding the usefulness of education. A follow-up service can be helpful in evaluating effectiveness, justification and desirability of the institution's curricula. On the basis of this evaluation, the institution can suitably modify its curricula.
(iii) A counsellor can bring about changes in his working on the basis of feedback from former students. Cue can be taken from former students' experience to solve many problems of the present students.

(d) *Devices for Follow-up of Former Students*: Different techniques are adopted for the follow-up study of former students. These are as follows.

(i) Questionnaire Method
(ii) Exchange of Letters
(iii) Telephonic Conversation
(iv) Across-the-table Dialogues
(v) Interview
(vi) Discussion with other employees of institutions and organizations with which former students are connected.

The completed questionnaire or information received by post must contain the name of the respondent, years of study in the institution, classes, etc. The objective of the questionnaire or correspondence must be clearly explained to the respondent. While doing follow-up study through interview, a list of the questions to be asked and the subject of discussion must be prepared in advance. If needed, the information received must be documented. It can later be summarized and categorized.

While seeking information from former students through correspondence permission of the appointing authority or the employer must be obtained. The medium of information must be determined according to its need.

(e) *Follow-up method for guidance and counselling services*: This method is used for evaluating the effectiveness of the counselling programme. Students decide upon their educational, vocational and adjustment goals with the help of the counsellor.

Life is a dynamic process. A student in the course of his study gains many experiences. As a result many new opportunities, and knowledge gained in the process, influence the attainment of his objectives. Hence, a student might feel the need to revise his previously determined objectives or the method of attaining them. Such needs of a student can be determined only through follow-up study.

The counsellor must adopt a well-organized method to do follow-up study. Time, place and date must be decided beforehand so that there is no problem in establishing contact with students. In this exercise, the counsellor may need assistance from teachers, principal and other associates.

The effectiveness of follow-up study depends on its continuity. It is not enough to study a student at one go. This study should be done every year, as it enables to gauge a student's response.

Procedures of Follow-up Activity

Downing has made the following suggestions regarding the methods of follow-up study which can be modified according to the needs and circumstances of an institution—

(a) *Survey of Youngsters Studying in the Institution*: Data about the educational level of each youngster studying in an institution should be gathered. On the basis of this data, the curriculum and the co-curricular activities can be determined for the student.

(b) *Survey of Former Students*: Feedback received from former students can be instrumental in bringing about suitable modifications in school programmes it will also enable the counsellor in finding out the reasons or factors which compelled them to leave their studies unfinished.

By effecting suitable changes and providing necessary facilities in response to these findings, the number of drop-outs can be reduced.

(c) *Organizing Group Sessions*: Students get a chance to frankly express their views and experiences about school programmes. By developing a friendly atmosphere group sessions invite suggestion and criticion from students.These sessions also help students in formulating their future plans.

(d) *Staff Meetings*: It is essential to organize staff meetings to discuss the problem emerging from group discussion. These meetings can help in solving present problems as well as encourages joint efforts to introduce necessary changes in the programme.

At least two teacher meetings should be organized every year in connection with follow-up service.

(e) *Organization of Workshops*: Workshops should be organized for teachers and counsellors. These workshops provide a platform for threadbare discussion on different viewpoints and suggestions. They often act, as a catalyst, in bringing about desirable changes.

Techniques of Follow-up Process

(a) *Interview*: Interview is a useful tool in a follow-up programmes. In a personal interview, a candidate can freely express his views on different institutional programmes, teachers and curricula. It helps in determining attitude of a youth. It also helps in evaluating the educational and vocational progress made by the present students. Nuggets of aduice, for achieving efficiency can be offered during on interview.
(b) *Questionnaire*: Questionnaire is an inventory of questions through which specific information is collected. They help in establishing contact with eliciting students for educational and vocational attainments, students' educational and vocational attainments. Information received through questionnaire can become the basis for modifying different school programmes.
(c) *Checklists*: Cantrary to a questionnaire, a checklist contain only possible answers. The student has to tick one of them according to his judgment. A checklist is simpler than a questionnaire and takes less time. It is used for understanding views, evaluating propensities and gathering facts.
(d) *Group Discussion*: A group discussion promotes personal contact and creates interest in a student.
(e) *Other Sources*: Apart from the above techniques, some other techniques are also used in a follow-up study, for examle, correspondence with an individual, expressing one's views about school programmes in writing, visiting placement sites, etc.

Summary

Follow-up service is an essential component of guidance programme. It is needed to gauge the effectiveness of guidance programme. On the basis of follow-up studies, guidance programme can be suitably modified. By its very nature it is an investigative, assessment and a corrective service. If the follow-up is done continuously for some years students can be offered suggestions about their career objectives.

An institution should undertake follow-up service for former students also. Ordinarily, there can be difficulties in undertaking this task. The system of follow-up in an institution should be according to the situation prenatent

The techniques used for follow-up study are interview, questionnaire, checklists, group discussion, etc.

7

Evaluation and Research

Guidance programmes are aimed at achieving certain objectives. Once it is done timely evaluation of the progress made becomes a burning necessity. An evaluation helps in assessing the pros and cons of the programmes instituted.

While providing guidance to a youngster, we have various posers before us, for example,

(a) What has the youngster to realize according to his objective?
(b) What are the possible reasons for the shortfall in the realization of objectives?
(c) What correct measurer should be taken to the real objectives and make them useful?

Need for Evaluation and Research, and Its Aims

Evaluation is necessary for the success and development of guidance programmes.

The needs and objectives of evaluating a guidance programme can be described as follows.

(a) An institution should have full information about its guidance programmes. There is always the need to know whether the various educational and co-curricular activities are benefiting students, or do they require modifications. This knowledge can be gained only through research and evaluation.
(b) Guidance is an inseparable part of education, but the effectiveness of a guidance programme can be find out only through evaluation. A proper evaluation helps to know whether the objectives of guidance are in consonance with those of education or do they need modification.
(c) Evaluation and research help in understanding the success achieved and progress made by students.
(d) By evaluating the success, progress and satisfaction level achieved by former students, an institution can gauge the utility of its guidance services and make suitable changes, if necessary.
(e) By understanding the progress made by him and the pace of his progress as revealed by the findings of evaluation and research, a youngster constantly strives for progress.

(f) Research and evaluation make people aware about the different activities being undertaken by an institution.
(g) With the help of research and evaluation, usefulness of vocational information service, counselling service, follow-up service and other areas of guidance can be enhanced.
(h) Research and evaluation enhance the efficiency of the guidance service

In brief, the objective of research and evaluation service is to bring about improvement in guidance service, aid in the discharge of educational and vocational obligations, promote individual's educational and vocational growth, and help them in discovering new systems and methodologies.

Research also helps in making individual data collection, preparatory, counselling, placement, follow-up and evaluation services more effective and useful. But the effectiveness of all these services depends on their evaluation. Apart from this, research augments new techniques for dealing with new situations.

Systems and Techniques of Evaluation

Evaluation of guidance programmes can be done by using different systems, techniques and research. But it has to be preceded by agreeing upon certain criteria. Some of them are as follows.

(a) *Failure Due to Waste and Disruption*: Evaluation of guidance programmes can be done by measuring the extent of waste, disruption and failure in students. If the graph of waste, disruption and failure among students drops significantly, then we can term the guidance programme as successful. Otherwise it needs to be corrected.
(b) Discipline in the institution is an indication of good guidance service because a disciplined atmosphere results from relaxation, high morale and balanced personality development.
(c) *Change in Guidance Programmes*: Frequency and the quantum of change introduced in a guidance programme helps in evaluating the service.
(d) *Use of Guidance Service*: Widespread use of guidance service by students and their guardians signifies its success.
(e) *Rate of Placement and Job Satisfaction*: Placement of former students in renowned organizations and the level of their satisfaction is another pointer towards the success of guidance programmes.
(f) Only after analyzing the criteria, the guidance service should be evaluated.

Systems for Evaluating Guidance Programmes

There are mainly two systems which are used for evaluation of guidance programmes.

- Experimental Method
- Survey Method

Experimental method

In this method of evaluation, we make a comparative study of changes in a student's behaviour as a result of guidance programme juxtaposed with his earlier behaviour.

(a) It gives an idea about the development of personality.
(b) It finds out the factors responsible for change in student's behaviour.
(c) It evaluates the success of guidance programme.

Experimental method also helps in finding out whether the results of methods being used in the guidance programme, directed at a student's personality development and enhancing his achievement level, are positive or negative. It gathers facts and evidence regarding notions about youth behaviour.

Experimental method is a scientific method. Hence, it is possible to do meaningful study of problems using this method. Since the conclusions reached are not influenced by earlier beliefs, partiality, views and emotions, etc. These are largely realistic, reliable and valid, and with the help of these conclusions, it is possible to evaluate the youth's behaviour realistically. Relationship between cause and effect can also be studied through this method.

However, experimental method is very cumbersome. The investigator has to, as per need, create simulative conditions in the laboratory, which is both time consuming and cost-intensive. Therefore, this method has not found much acceptance in institutions.

Survey Method

Survey method is widely used in the field of research and evaluation. With the help of survey method, we study the current status of guidance services and programmes. Attempts are also made to realign activities if the situation demands so. This method does not lend itself to comparative study, the way experimental method does.

Given below is a brief account about the evaluation of these services.

(a) *Counselling Service*: Reference to the records maintained by the counsellor can help in the evaluation of an institution's counselling service. This is possible only if there is a qualified counsellor who maintains a detailed record of his daily work, the number of students who come for interview, efforts made by them to solve their problems, success achieved by the student, failures, difficulties encountered, etc. From this record not only the counsellor himself but also other officials and guardians can do a fair evaluation of the counselling service. The concerned officials can find out about the problems which brought the students to the counsellor, the counsellor give to them and the benefits of counselling.

While evaluating counselling service, the counsellor's qualification, personality level, experience and his knowledge of different occupations must be ascertained. This will help in understanding the competence and credibility and audibility of the counseller. *Information Service Success* of a guidance programme depends on information about students' educational and vocational areas. This information should be very precise, reliable, valuable and complete. Information service should also reach this information to students according to their needs through field trips, career sessions, conferences and group guidance activities. This could enable them to choose their career judiciously. Its function is also to give appropriate information to guidance personnel and disseminate it among all students, teachers and school administrators through various means available.

Evaluation of information service hinges on the success benefiting it, caution must be exercised in evaluating these services as local condition may inject certain peculiarities in the school's information service. Thus, it would be wrong to judge the services vis-a-vis national standards.

(b) *Placement Service*: In an educational or a vocational institution, placement service is very significant. But educational institute must have complete information about a student as well as different vocational sectors so that a student after completing his education can choose a vocation according to his ability. A placement service should continuously update its data bank of job opportunities in different sectors, and abilities and talent required for each job.

Evaluation of a placement service is based on the quantum of jobs successfully provided in a given period vis-a-vis other placement service agencies in the same period. Reliability and validity of methods of employment used by an appointing authority determines the usefulness of placement service.

(c) *Follow-up Service*: Follow-up service is a very important component of guidance programme. It helps in ganging efficacy of a guidance programme. It analyzes the pace and progress of a student's adjustment in an institution or in a particular job.

Some of the observations, while assessing a students adjustment in an institution are as follows.

- What kind of adjustment has the student, at present studying in an institution, made?
- Does their performance in their chose in subjects reflect the same?
- Is there a need for change in curricula?
- What behavioural changes were observed in the students after counselling?
- How has their adjustment been after counselling?

All this can be studied only through follow-up service.

In a similar vein, follow-up service studies and evaluates the adjustment level of ex-students in relation to their new environment, their success rate in striking adjustment, the problems faced by them and specific sphere in which counselling in needed.

Follow-up service helps us to know the quantum of change needed in guidance programmes, how can they be improved, projects to be initiated, etc.

Guidance-Related Research in India

It is through research that various difficulties encountered by a counsellor, while evaluating guidance programmes, can be understood and addressed.

Research and evaluation are needed to enhance the usefulness and effectiveness of guidance programmes. Research helps in developing new techniques in the context of new situations.

Research projects can be undertaken only when there are adequate facilities, funds and personnel available in the institution.

In a developing country like India despite the major need for guidance programmes, the movement has not made much headway for various reasons. The main reasons are financial constraints and lack of knowledge about the usefulness of guidance. Even where guidance programmes are being implemented, they fall short of being comprehensive and all-pervasive.

First of all, it is imperative to draw the government's attention towards the need for guidance programmes. Guidance is an inseparable part of education. The aim of education is to ensure all-round development of a student with a view to building an economically strong and socially developed nation. But this task would remain unachieved without proper guidance and counselling.

There is a need to find out the number of private and government schools that run guidance programmes. It helps to evaluate their penetration, comprehensiveness and conduct necessary research. There is a need to popularize the usefulness of guidance movement at the national level. It can be done by the Ministry of Education by asking various universities to introduce it as an essential component of educational programme at school level and college level.

Such problems must be identified and evaluated, and efforts should be made to overcome them. In schools where full-fledged guidance programmes cannot be run in view of resource constraints, students' problems can be studied by doing sector wise research.

Summary

Through guidance programmes, we want to achieve certain objectives. After realizing the objectives, we feel the need to evaluate the progress of our efforts. The objective of research and evaluation service is to improve the guidance service. Apart from this, research is also needed to encourage new techniques for dealing with new situations.

Evaluation can be done by using different techniques after agreeing upon various criteria. Mainly two systems are used for the evaluation of guidance programmes: (a) Experimental method and (b) Survey method.

Experimental method is a scientific method. But this method is very cumbersome and hypherate. Survey method is used to study the current status of guidance programmes and attempts are made to realign activities if the situation demands so. This method does not lend itself to comparative study the way experimental method does.

While evaluating counselling service, the counsellor's qualification, personality level, experience and his knowledge of different occupations must be ascertained. In short, the entire spectrum of services involved in guidance, such as counselling, information, placement and follow-up, need to be evaluated and reassessed with a view to modifying the entire process in the light of emerging realities.

There is a need to carry out research and periodic surveys to evolve new techniques and revise strategies for counselling and guidance in the light of changing social equations, society, frog leaps in technology, shrinking geographical barriers, hitherto unforeseen needs and futuristic expectations of GeneX.

8

Educational Guidance

Educational guidance is an important segment of guidance programmes. It is an inseparable part of education. Hence, it has a special significance. As one graduates from primary to secondary schools and then to the university level, education also becomes tough and complex, this may give rise to several problems, thus creating a need for guidance. The main aim of educational guidance is to develop in a student the ability of establishing coordination at different levels, and create in him awareness and sensitivity to make wise choice of his objectives.

Apart from this, in the light of increasing unemployment, a diversity in educational sphere, fall in the standards of education and lack of practical education, the need for educational guidance naturally becomes increasingly significant.

What is Education?

The dictionary meaning of education is 'to educate'. In other words, the knowledge imparted to a student by a teacher in a classroom is education. But an individual is a social animal who has to adjust himself to his social circumstances. Social development, however, is impossible without education and the basis of social development is the wisdom embedded in him. It is this that sets him apart from other animals.

According to T. Raymont: 'Education is defined as a process of development which consists of the passage of human being from infancy to maturity, the process by which he adapts himself gradually in various ways to his physical, social and spiritual environment'. In this definition, precedence has been given to the environment. But according to an eminent scholar Dewey: 'Education is the development of all those capacities in the individual which enable him to control his environment'.

Thus, education can be defined as that process by which an individual becomes capable of striking adjustment with his environment.

Relationship Between Education and Guidance

There is a close relationship between education and guidance, but to be able to comprehend this relationship, it is necessary to understand the following facets of education.

(a) *The Process of Changes within the Individual*: Education is the process through which necessary changes can be brought about in an individual so that he can adjust himself to society. From this point of view, education is an individualist process. If education is understood in this context, there is no need for any guidance. But to bring about changes through education, a student needs guidance.
(b) *Education is Instruction*: Teacher is the agent of society. The efficient teacher is continually trying to help the students find the method that is best suited to him, when the teacher select the method, there is teaching but no guidance but when he assists the learner to choose a method, guidance is present.
(c) *Education as Social Task*: Man is a social being. It is society's responsibility to shape him as such and guide him in his emotional, physical and mental development. In these areas of development, guidance is needed. The main objective of education is the all-round development of a youngster, which is not possible without knowing his interests, abilities and potential. This task can be achieved only through guidance.

Educational Guidance

Educational guidance has been defined variously by different scholars.

According to Brewer (1918), educational guidance is as follows. 'Educational guidance may be defined as conscious effort to assist in the intellectual growth of an individual. Anything that has to do with instruction or with learning may come under the term educational guidance'. According to Myers (1906), 'educational guidance is a process concerned with bringing about between an individual pupil with his distinctive characteristics on the one hand and differing groups of opportunities and requirement on the other, a favourable setting for the individual development of education'.

Jones (1951) too has described educational guidance as an assistance provided to students so that they can make adjustment with schools, curricula and school life. According to him: 'Educational guidance is concerned with assistance given to pupils in their choices and adjustments with relation to schools, curriculum, courses and school life'.

According to Ruth Strang (1935), 'educational guidance is intended to help the individual in choosing an appropriate programme and in making progress in it'.

Traxler (1957) has described educational guidance as an extensive process. In his view: 'Educational guidance is vitally related to every aspect of the school, the curriculum, the methods of instruction, disciplinary procedures, attendance, problems of scheduling, the extra curricular, the health and physical fitness programme and home and community relations'.

Difference Between Education and Educational Guidance

The relationship between education and educational guidance is not clear to many people. Some scholars believe that complete education is a form of guidance. A few educationists are of the view that education is guidance and guidance is education. There is as such confusion about the precise meaning and spheres of application of education and educational guidance.

In education, an educationist prepares such an inspiring atmosphere in which a student develops his inherent potential and abilities leading to his physical, mental, intellectual, emotional and social development. But educational guidance is such a process in which assistance is provided to an individual to relate the educational curriculum to his life.

According to Myers (1941), 'Indeed, the confusion between educational guidance and education itself seems to arise out of failure to differentiate between the powers, which is educational guidance (course, curriculum and school guidance) and certain methods or techniques, by which the process of education itself is carried forward'.

By analyzing the above definitions, the following characteristics of educational guidance emerge.

(a) Educational guidance is a comprehensive process.
(b) In educational guidance, many problems related to education can be discussed, such as how to study, or choosing techniques of education, fixing time, coordination of school life with other activities, regular attendance in school, doing home work on time, use of library, ability to take decisions in life, etc.
(c) It is a process of solving problems encountered at the different levels of education.
(d) It helps in providing assistance to a student in the event of his not making desired educational achievements.
(e) It provides assistance in quitting undesirable habits, and making proper adjustment and resolving problems cropping up at different levels of education.
(f) It tries to overcome difficulties in the choice of subjects and curricula at different levels of education.

Importance of Guidance at Various Stages of Education

There are so many levels of education and at each level, a student comes across different problems. A student needs educational guidance for overcoming problems faced at each stage. That is why we talk about the significance of educational guidance throughout the process of education and regard it as being its important part.

It is clear from the above description that educational guidance should start from primary school itself.

Educational Guidance at the Primary School Stage

Primary school students stand more in need of guidance because the main function of education at this stage is to help in the development of a child. A child leaves the liberal atmosphere of his home and enters a realm where there are different kinds of restrictions on his activities. In this new atmosphere, the child has to perform certain tasks at fixed times. Here, he is a member of a group that consists of a number of others of his age.

When a child leaves the much familiar atmosphere of his home and enters the school's new atmosphere, he finds certain difficulties in adjusting himself. Many children become victims of maladjustment. As a result of maladjustment, their mental development suffers, they become irritable and non-conforming. Hence, in order to provide a right direction to the child save him from maladjustment, to cultivate good habits in him and to solve learning problems, educational guidance is required. Guidance at this stage should lay stress on continuous development, controlled behaviour and mental health.

It is said that the early five-six years of a child's life determine his future. Hence, the teacher in charge of guidance should pay special attention to a child's needs in order to ensure his proper mental health.

In primary schools, a teacher's role as a guide is most important whereas a counsellor is an outsider. Teacher functions as a guide amongst groups of students and their guardians, and within his/her limitations make suggestions to the guardians for the development of their wards. A counsellor is responsible for those guidance activities which are either beyond the competence of the teacher or cannot be performed due to lack of time.

At the primary level, a counsellor provides organized guidance to students keeping in mind their special needs and interests. Apart from this, a counsellor trains teachers at primary level in the skill of data collection, compilation of cumulative records and testing methods. At the primary level, most important condition for the success of guidance programme is teamwork, that is, it can be done only with the collective efforts of the principal, the teachers, the counsellor and the guardians.

The following things come under guidance at this stage.

(a) Placing students in separate categories, classes and experience groups according to their needs.
(b) Limiting the number of students in a class so that each student can be understood properly and his needs fulfilled.
(c) Providing dull and intelligent students equal opportunities for necessary development.
(d) Selecting curricula according to the mental level of students.
(e) Paying special attention to the needs of maladjusted and physically handicapped students.
(f) Deciding upon necessary corrective steps according to the progress of students in different areas.

Educational Guidance at the Secondary and Senior Secondary Stage

When a child goes from primary level to secondary level his relationship with education starts undergoing change. At this stage, there is an upsurge in a student's friendships and relationships. His way of thinking changes and new curiosities develop. These curiosities need to be tackled wisely otherwise he will develop a rebellious attitude. He starts forming opinions about teachers' behaviour and their way of teaching. Certain interests and traits become deep rooted, for studies at the primary level. Intellect and abilities at this stage are fully developed. Those children who do not get right opportunities, they lag behind in development. A child is more dependent on his parents. But when the child reaches the secondary level, he should be encouraged to study on his own in order to inculcate self-confidence and the ability to find out and evaluate ways of studying according to his own genius. Sometimes because of the difficulty in grasping a subject, a child develops aversion for that subject. Educational guidance helps a child in overcoming such difficulties. Apart from this, educational guidance also comes forward to help a child in dealing with other factors that hinder his educational progress. At secondary level, inspiration to study is very important because it is at this stage that a youngster's interests and way of working begin assuming a definite form.

At the senior secondary level (10 + 2), the field of educational guidance becomes wider. A strong need is felt for specialists at this stage for the following reason.

(a) There is difference between the curricula of secondary and the senior secondary levels. At the senior secondary level, there is diversity in the curriculum. In view of this diversity, when a student passes class 10th examination and joins class 11th, the guidance expert or a counsellor should help him in choosing subjects according to his abilities, interests, aptitude and personality traits. This will help him in making the optimum use of his potential.

Efforts should be made from class 8th itself for encouraging students to take interest in choosing subjects and curricula. The time given for this type of guidance is called 'delta class'. Organizational work that is undertaken in delta classes has the following (main) functions.

(i) Acquainting students with the characteristics and objectives of the senior secondary school's currcula.

(ii) Helping students in evaluating abilities, aptitudes and interests and relating the same to curricula and study discussions.

(iii) Acquainting them with the vocational applications of different curriculum.

(iv) Proper dissemination of information about university education and educational institutions.

(b) There is a difference even in the constitution of staff councils of primary schools and those of secondary schools. In primary schools, there is a system of class teacher but in senior secondary schools, teachers with special skills teach different subjects. In primary schools, it is the class teacher who is answerable for the pupils' performance but in the senior secondary schools no single teacher is answerable for the same. Hence, at this stage there is a need for organized guidance service to understand the students' problems.

Pupils enter secondary school at the adolescence stage. At this age, there is a rapid physical, mental, social and emotional change and development. Even the youngster himself is not conscious about these changes. Hence, he faces different adjustment problems. Health services should also be instituted to monitor students' physical and mental health. All this underlines the need for guidance service at this stage.

Educational guidance helps in cultivating healthy practices and removing subject-related problems. At secondary level, healthy habits like studying independently should be inculcated in students to promote feelings of self-sufficiency and confidence.

Educational institutions, whether primary, secondary or senior secondary, perform three vital functions—teaching, administration and guidance. In educational institutions, pupils do not only go to acquire knowledge but also prepare themselves for future because the main function of education is to ensure a student's all-round development.

In an educational institution, both internal and external hurdles influence a student. To overcome these hurdles, it is necessary that there should be guidance service in the school. In order to successfully run a guidance programme it is necessary to organize it along professional lines. Guidance plays an important role in educational and vocational areas.

In this regard, Jones says: 'Guidance is not something that can be completely separated from the general life of the school by tucking it away in the office of the counsellor or the principal. Because it is the duty and responsibility in some measure of every member of school staff, it is a function that must be shared by all and should be so administered'. The success of guidance process depends on the initiative, foresight and skill of the people involved in it.

The form of guidance depends on the following.

(a) *Level of School*: Guidance programmes at primary level would be different from those at senior secondary level. At the primary school level needs and problems are fewer. Therefore, an expert is not needed at this stage. Class teacher himself/herself can take care of guidance programme. In contrast, at secondary and higher secondary levels guidance programme has a well organized form to address the diverse needs and problems of adolescents.

(b) *Size of School*: The character of guidance service also depends on the size of a school. In schools with a negligible student strength it is the class teacher who with the help of the principal can tackle their problems.

In bigger schools, guidance service is well organized and the work of guidance is performed by a counsellor with the help of teachers. Moreover, the work of guidance also depends on the facilities available in the school. Guidance work can be done in an effective manner in schools with proper infrastructure.

Functions and Responsibilities of Guidance Personnel: At Primary, Secondary and Senior Secondary Levels

Guidance is a specialized function. Its success depends on its personnel. For the operation of this programme in schools, a special group of workers and organizers, depending on the needs and problems of students is required.

(a) At primary level, guidance work is in the hands of school management since the problems of students are less and not much serious. Class teacher does counselling at this level because he/she is more in contact with his students and is better acquainted with their problems. But imparting complete guidance, a class teacher can seek cooperation of the principal, parents, social organizations, the physician and other teachers.

At primary level, class teacher endeavours to achieve the following objectives with the joint efforts of others concerned.

(i) Survey of individual needs, problems and characteristics of students.
(ii) Writing survey findings in cumulative record cards.
(iii) On the basis of survey findings identifying children with adjustment problems. For instance:
- Identifying those children who are unable to make social or emotional adjustment.
- Some children being either dull or over intelligent cannot adjust themselves in the regular school curriculum.
- Some students face adjustment problems due to ill health.

(iv) Establishing cordial relations with parents for obtaining detailed information about students.
(v) Obtaining information about a student's attendance to study reasons for absenteeism.
(vi) Doing regular evaluation of a student's progress.

(b) At the secondary level, guidance starts assuming an organized form because at this level students' problems become more serious than at the primary level. At this level, there being different subject teachers, class teacher does not get adequate chance to scrutinize the students. Therefore, the principal seeks the help of a counsellor to solve students' problems. The counsellor, in his turn, establishes contact with different subject teachers, guardians and other social organizations to collect information about a student.

(c) At the senior higher secondary level, students need maximum guidance. With the onset of adolescence, youngsters are in a cauldron of emotional adjustment problems, they simultaneously face the problems acquiring, choice of subjects knowledge about vocational opportunities and training facilities as well as information about universities and available courses. Due to the diversity of problems faced by a youngster at this stage, adolescence has been rightly termed as the age of stress and storm. Hence, youngsters stand in a critical need of guidance and counselling at this stage, which can be undertaken by experts alone. At this stage, even the principal is hardly able to spare time for this activity. Hence, he passed to a professionals guidance specialist or a counsellor who implements it with the active cooperation of class teacher, other subjects teacher and guardians. Specialists play a special role at this stage.

Generalists + Specialists

Personnel taking part in guidance service can be divided into two categories: (a) Generalists school principal and (b) other teachers shoulder the general responsibilities of guidance. Hence, they are generalists. The role of generalists cannot be underrated. The reason for their being treated as generalists is that their primary function being that of a teacher or an administrator, their role in guidance is secondary. In contrast, specialists being trained in this discipline are well versed in the finer nuances of guidance. Those who perform guidance activities for which training or specialized knowledge is needed are called specialists, for example, counsellor, psychologist, physician and career master.

Role of Generalists: The role and responsibilities of generalists in a school guidance programme can be distributed between the principal and the teacher.

Role and Responsibility of The Principal: Principal is the chief person in a school. Hence, he is responsible for the successful implementation of all the school's activities and programmes. Guidance being an inseparable part of education ultimate responsibility for its successful implementation lies on his shoulders.

Principal's responsibility towards guidance work can be described as follows.

(a) The principal is supposed to lead the guidance programme.
(b) He can help the concerned teachers by informing them about the importance, organization and problems of guidance.
(c) The principal is also responsible for appointing guidance personnel and farming out duties according to their abilities and capacities.
(d) Scrutiny of guidance programme is the first step towards mapping its progress. The principal can discharge his obligation by ensuring that guidance programme keeps marching ahead.
(e) The principal is also supposed to take out adequate time for guidance programmes.
(f) The principal has got financial powers. Hence, it is his responsibility to provide funds for guidance programmes.
    (i) The principal can lead guidance programme only when he has done adequate study of guidance literature, and is well conversant with the nature of work. Hence, it is incumbent on a principal to keep himself abreast of latest developments in guidance programme and have discussions with guidance experts.
    (ii) The principal should convene a guidance council in the school and become its convener. All members of this council should jointly decide about guidance programmes. But members of the council should be chosen very wisely.
    (iii) The principal can call meetings of guardians and students, discuss students' problems and affect necessary changes and modifications in guidance programmes, in the light of the discussions held.
    (iv) It is the responsibility of the principal to make available all facilities for the smooth running of guidance and counselling, for example, guidance office, furniture and other items of use.
    (v) The principal should, from time to time, re-evaluate and re-design guidance programmes with the help of the guidance council. The principal should assume the responsibility to implement all recommendations of the guidance council for modifying guidance programmes.

Responsibilities of the Teacher: In a school, the teacher is the person closest to the students. He studies them in various situations. Hence, the responsibility of guiding students and completing the guidance programme to a large extent lies on his shoulders. In countries like India where trained counsellors are only a handful, teachers can perform the job of providing guidance to students.

Teacher's role in guidance programme can be outlined as under.

(a) *Establishing Personal Contact with Students*: Teacher, by virtue of remaining in constant touch with the students, is personally acquainted with them. He can gather adequate knowledge about a student's environment, his activities and friend circle through his guardian. This information enables the teacher to learn about problems giving rise to inferiority complex, frustration and unhealthy attitude among students. It also affects their studies and relations with their class fellows and teachers. Those teachers who take interest in guidance can bring about improvement in the behavioural problems of students through sympathy, love, compassion, encouragement and kind behaviour. How far the teacher succeeds depends on his capability and experience.

(b) *Understanding Students*: All students are not equal, they differ at individual level. To be able to understand these differences and individual characteristics a teacher should be conversant with psychological tests. The teacher should also refer students to the counsellor.

(c) *Making Available Vocational Information*: When a teacher accepts the responsibility of doing guidance work then his job is not only to teach but also to scrutinize all the various activities of a student, for example his areas of interest, type of work he is capable of doing etc. He should also make available to students the information about essential educational qualifications and skills for taking up a particular occupation and discuss of future growth.

(d) *Identifying Maladjusted Youngsters*: A teacher by identifying maladjusted and backward youngsters can help them in making adjustment and progress by personally counselling them. Class teacher can also provide help to students in their health-related problems and personal problems.

(e) *Serving as a Link*: Class teacher can also act as a link between guidance experts, guardians and youngsters.

(f) *Use of Library*: A teacher can also guide students in making proper use of school library and reference facilities available for them.

(g) *Moral Uplift*: A teacher can work towards moral uplift of youngsters by inculcating virtues of honesty and encouraging them to speak unambiguously.

(h) *Promoting Healthy Environment*: Class teacher must create healthy environment in his class, so that students feel free to express themselves.

(i) *Extending Cooperation*: Teachers should extend their full cooperation to the principal and the counsellor to run the guidance programme successful.

Specialists taking part in guidance: The counsellor, the psychologist and the physician fall under the category of specialists.

The role, responsibilities and functions of a counsellor in school guidance programme:

The counsellor is a specialist in guidance and counselling programme. Being a trained person he is supposed to be the ideal person to implement a guidance programme. Financial constraints in India have led schools to engage a counsellor either on a full-time, part-time or visit basis.

Elucidating the significance of a counsellor, Ruth Strang says: 'The counsellor is like a gardener who prepares the soil and does everything he can to help each plant grow in its own best way'.

A counsellor has the following functions.

(a) A counsellor is the lead person in a guidance programme. He imparts to class teacher and other school personnel knowledge of guidance work.

(b) He assists teachers in solving students' difficulties and problems.

(c) He collects and organizes data for use by guidance workers and takes care of the technical aspects of guidance.

(d) The counsellor steps in to assist him where the class teacher experiences difficulty in carrying out guidance service.

(e) He works towards bringing about close liaison between the school, home and society.

(f) The counsellor assists in revising teaching methods according to the guidance-specific needs of students.
(g) The counsellor assists in organizing and coordinating various guidance services in the school, such as maintaining a record of a student's interest in various activities, providing employment and evaluation service, curriculum information, follow-up service, etc.
(h) Assisting students in understanding themselves and making plans for the future.
(i) Evaluating students' abilities, interests, capabilities and providing them with educational and vocational guidance.
(j) Organizing group guidance programmes with a view to encouraging social adjustment among youngsters.
(k) The counsellor can help in bringing together guardians and teachers.

Career Masters

Career Master is the second level guidance worker and his responsibilities are restricted in a scope as compared to a counsellor's. He works in close collaboration with the counsellor and his major responsibilities centre around information service and its allied fields.

The role, responsibilities and functions of a psychologist in school guidance programme: In a school guidance programme, the psychologist too has a very significant role. For making a school guidance programme successful, the psychologist can assist in the following ways.

(a) For analyzing a student's personality through psychological tests and other means, nobody can play a better role than a psychologist. A psychologist can scientifically gather information about a student's abilities, interests, aptitudes and personality.
(b) A psychologist can properly interpret findings of psychological tests.
(c) It is only the psychologist who assists talented students and those with inferiority complex in understanding and resolving their problems.

The Role, Functions and Responsibilities of the Doctor in School Guidance Programme: It is said that only in a healthy body does reside a healthy mind. Hence, to keep students physically and mentally healthy and to provide them with health-related guidance, health check-ups should be carried out from time to time. It is the responsibility of the school doctor to communicate the students' health problems to their parents or guardians.

(a) It is the responsibility of the school doctor to prepare programmes for improving students' health.
(b) It is necessary for the doctor to carry out regular check-ups to monitor the effect and results of his service.
(c) Physical illness and weakness hampers students' studies. Hence, the doctor should, from time to time, counsel students about the importance of healthy food, balanced diet, exercise and sports.
(d) Record of students' physical check-ups should be maintained in the school, so that parents and guardians also can be made aware of their wards' physical problems and advised to arrange for necessary treatment.

An important function of guidance, at the secondary level, is to understand the adolescents' abilities and interests, and to accordingly provide guidance. This helps the teenagers to stay abreast about the existing educational and vocational opportunities befitting their abilities, interests and talents, and there by choose their goal.

Another objective of guidance service is to enable the principal and the teachers to individually understand their students and create conducive environment for their learning.

Following Mudaliar Committee's recommendations, Ministry of Education, Government of India, established the Central Bureau of Educational and Vocational Guidance in 1954. Its primary task was to assist in guidance programmes, that is, at the secondary level, and provide technical consultancy. During the third Five-Year Plan 'guidance' was recognized as a centrally administered subject following guidance services was initiated in schools by the trained counsellors and career masters with assistance from school teachers.

By the end of the third Five-Year Plan, the number of schools providing guidance service in one form or the other was 3,000. But these schools housed only a career master whose job was simply to provide vocational information. As such, even as of now, very few schools have got either a full-time counsellor or a part-time counsellor to provide meaningful counselling or guidance.

Hence, it is clear that despite there being an organized movement to provide guidance service there has been a negligible progress. Our end objective should be to implement adequate guidance service in all the existing 10 + 2 schools. In the light of limited means and scant financial resources, we should launch small guidance programmes.

For each 10 schools located, in close proximity, there should be a visiting school counsellor and simple guidance work should be assigned to teachers.

Also, to understand as to what type of a service is guidance and what can be achieved through it, at least one school in each district should have a full-fledged guidance service. After seeing this model guidance service, guidance personnel would be encouraged to place this service in a wider perspective.

Qualified inspection officials should be appointed in the State Bureaux of guidance to scrutinize the work of guidance personnel in schools and to give them necessary counselling. Adequate arrangement should also be made for imparting professional training to guidance personnel. Earlier, at the central level, National Council for Educational Research and Training (NCERT) was professional training. But later, when different divisions of NCERT were re-organized, the guidance division was amalgamated with the psychology division. This division was training personnel for educational and vocational training. Research work on guidance was also done here. Now this department is known as the Department of Educational Psychology and Foundation of Education.

Central Bureau of Educational and Vocational Guidance is a centrally administered institution. Its objective is to promote guidance by creating adequate awareness about the nature and philosophy of guidance among students. Its other objective is to develop and strengthen the guidance movement in India.

With effect from the year 2000, the Central Bureau has delegated the work of guidance professionals' training to the regional institutes of guidance at Ajmer, Bhopal, Bhuvaneswar and Mysore. The main objective of the State Educational and Vocational Guidance Bureaux is to assist students in the choice of suitable educational curricula and career options.

In the State Bureaux of guidance, inspection officials should be appointed to scrutinize and counsel the work of guidance personnel in schools.

The committee has emphasized the need of incorporating the essentials and the techniques of guidance in the course content of teachers training programme for secondary schools. There should also be a provision for special course for those trainees who are desirous of doing detailed course in guidance. For lecturers and professors, there should be provision for in-service training in guidance and counselling.

Earlier, there was a national level research and training programme for the professional training of guidance personnel under which, after post-graduation in psychology, educational and general psychology, individual and group evaluation, personality psychology, social psychology and occupational organization were taught. Along with the knowledge of these subjects, a counsellor should have excellent vocabulary to be able to strike the right chord with the subject.

A counsellor has been trained to successfully solve the problems. These counsellors interpret problems on the basis of psychological tests. They choose counselling as a special area of their training. The counsellors with post-graduate qualification can design and administer the property counselling programmes properly. But the scope in schools and colleges in India is limited due to financial constraints and lack of infrastructure.

Under these programmes, there are short-term courses in which emphasis is laid on providing vocational information and guidance. In some institutes, these are termed as Career Master courses. The State Bureaux of Guidance and National Employment Service run training programme for vocational counsellors, career master's job is to collect vocational information from different sources through different means, and to categorize it according to different criteria and keep it up to date. This information helps a career master in setting up a 'career corner' in a school or in a college. He provides the students with information on employment and self-employment opportunities in keeping with their capabilities, interests and aptitudes. Career conferences, field visits and career talks are organized for this purpose.

For gathering information about local career opportunities, a career master seeks cooperation from the local employment office and maintains liaison with different business, industrial, semi-government and government organizations.

Summary

As the process of education goes on becoming tougher and tougher at successive levels, the need for educational guidance becomes imperative. It is important to understand the meaning of education, its relationship with guidance and how it is different from guidance.

The main objective of education is all-round development of a youngster, which is not possible without knowing his interests, abilities and potential. In education, an educationist prepares such an inspiring atmosphere in which a student develops his/her inherent potential and abilities leading to his physical, mental, intellectual, emotional and social development. But through educational guidance, assistance is provided to an individual to relate the educational curriculum to his life.

The nature of educational guidance differs at the different levels of education since the problems encountered at different stages are different. Educational guidance helps in cultivating healthy practices and removing subject-related problems. Many a time a student when confronted with difficulty in some subject develops aversion for it. Guidance helps in overcoming these difficulties.

The success of educational guidance depends on the initiative, foresight and skill of the persons involved in it. Personnel taking part in guidance service can be divided into two categories as generalists and specialists.

The school principal and other teachers who shoulder the general responsibilities of guidance are kept in the category of generalists. Those who perform guidance activities for which training or specialized knowledge is needed are called specialists, for example, counsellor, psychologist and physician.

An important function of guidance at the secondary or 10 + 2 level is to keep the students informed about educational and vocational opportunities befitting their abilities, interests and talents to enable them to choose their vocational goal. This function is performed by trained career masters who maintain liaison with different employment agencies.

9

Vocational Guidance

Man derives personal satisfaction from his vocation. One's vocation, apart from influencing his social life, also distinctly influences his thinking, emotions and personality. Thus, choosing a proper vocation is very important for an individual. Vocational guidances often the need of the hour. The significance of vocational guidance cannot be realized without understanding its meaning.

Meaning and Definition of Vocational Guidance

Frank Parsons first used the term 'vocational guidance' in 1908. But he never gave a substantive definition of the term vocation guidance. Ordinarily by vocational guidance people understand the choice of a right person for a job, or the choice of a right job for a person. But in today's environment of industrial development and competition it is not practically possible.

Vocations or openings are not created from the point of view of availability of personnel and their ability. Also, it is not possible for everybody to find an opening in keeping with his ability, skill and potential. Generally, an individual has got flexible potential by virtue of which if he does not find a cherished job he can fix himself into another job. Hence, vocational guidance helps individuals in adjusting themselves to different vocations.

National Vocational Guidance Association gave the first substantive definition of vocational guidance in its report in 1924. According to this definition: 'Vocational guidance is the giving of information, experience and advice in regard to choosing an occupation, preparing for it, entering in and progress in it'. Even this is not a properly evolved definition. Hence, it cannot be accepted on its face value. It was only on the grounds of its infirmity that this association put forward another definition in 1937: 'Vocational guidance is the process of assisting the individual to choose an occupation, prepare for it, enter upon and progress in it. It is concerned primarily with helping individuals make decisions and choices involved in planning a future and building a career—decisions and choices necessary in effecting satisfactory vocational adjustment'.

Despite both the definitions having been evolved by the same institution, they are different. According to one definition, guidance is a system while according to the other it is a process. In the second definition, something is imparted while in the first one just assistance is provided. The association has, however, adopted the definition evolved in 1937.

In 1949, International Labour Organization (ILO) while elucidating the meaning of vocational guidance said: 'Vocational guidance is the assistance given to individual in solving problems related to occupational choice and progress with due regard for the individual characteristics and their relation to occupational opportunity'.

Super (1962), while clarifying the meaning of vocational guidance in his book '*Appraising Vocational Fitness*' says: 'Vocational guidance is helping the individual so that he may adjust in the occupation and may make effective use of human power and to provide facilities for economic development of the society'. If we analyze Super's definition, we come face to face with three aspects of vocational guidance. The first aspect is that an individual should be able to give adequate information about his ability, potential and emotional state, and should be prepared to accept his potential and limitations. The second aspect is the choice of vocation by an individual from among those existing, after weighing his potential and limitations. The third aspect is that he should be able to derive maximum satisfaction from the chosen vocation so that both the society and he himself can benefit at large.

To ensure that all the three aspects are realized, an individual needs vocational guidance. Super has clarified vocational guidance with another elaborate definition: 'Vocational guidance is the process of helping the person to develop and accept an integrated and adequate picture of himself and of his role in the world of work, to test this concept against reality, and to convert it into reality with satisfaction to himself and benefit to society'.

The objective of vocational guidance is to organize and conserve human resources. From this point of view Myers (1941), while defining vocational guidance, says: 'Vocational guidance is fundamentally an effort to conserve the priceless native capacities of youth and the costly training provided for youth in the schools. It seeks to conserve these richest of all human resources by aiding the individual to invest and use them where they will bring greatest satisfaction and success to himself and greatest to society'.

From a study and analysis of definitions given by these scholars the following characteristics of vocational guidance emerge.

(a) Vocational guidance is a process, not an incident. It must be understood in that context.
(b) The function of vocational guidance is to help persons with appropriate potential, interests and abilities in choosing vocations, in keeping with their potential.
(c) The function of vocational guidance is not only to help in choosing suitable vocation but also to help in entering into it and progress in it.
(d) All individuals are not equally endowed with potential and capabilities. If that were the case, all individuals would have been suitable for all vocations.
(e) In vocational guidance, information can also be gathered from individuals engaged in different vocations.
(f) In this process, an individual evaluates his role in a real situation.
(g) Vocational guidance is that process which helps an individual in realizing his vocational objective.

Process of Vocational Guidance

The process of vocational guidance is very difficult and tough. Its toughness arises from the following factors.

(a) Vocation for an individual cannot be chosen without understanding his personality. It takes time to understand and analyze it.

(b) There is the need for abilities, interests, aptitudes, education and experience in keeping with the diversity of professions and rapidly changing areas of work.
(c) The third major factor accounting for the toughness of vocational guidance is taking decision about the appropriateness of the vocation and the progressive and changing nature of vocations.
(d) At times, parents' attitude and social conditions also make vocational guidance difficult.

Hence, keeping in view the above difficulties it is necessary to carry out the process of vocational guidance in different stages. This process can be elaborated as under.

(a) *Requirements for an Occupation*: For each occupation or vocation, there are some essential qualifications. Without these qualifications, an individual cannot adjust in that occupation. Hence, only after preparing an inventory of essential qualifications the next stage can be entered upon. Each guidance personnel should be adequately equipped with this information.
(b) *Study of the Individual*: For understanding an individual it is essential to carry out his study. An individual can be studied in different ways.

(i) *Initial Interview*: For collating information about an individual, the counsellor conducts an initial interview. Through this interview, he gets to know:

- The youngster's name
- Date of birth and age
- His parents' names, caste and religion
- His parents' occupations
- Brothers and sisters, if any
- His place among his siblings
- Total family income and sources of income
- Hereditary diseases
- Physical problems
- Schools in which he studied
- His friends
- Interest in sports
- Hobbies
- Other details

(ii) *Measurement of Intelligence Level*: Measuring intelligence level is essential for vocational guidance. There are two factors of intelligence: (1) General intelligence or 'G' Factor and (2) Specific intelligence or 'S' Factor. Guidance expert must measure both factors separately. They can measure the G factor by using different tests, for example, oral test, written test, verbal test, force or speed test, performance test, etc. For measuring S factor, guidance expert should use the following tests:

- *Mechanical Ability*: For measuring mechanical ability the following tests are used.
  - Minnesota Mechanical Assembly Test
  - Detroit Mechanical Aptitude Test
  - Paper and Pencil Test of Mechanical Aptitude
  - Stenquist Test for Mechanical Aptitude
  - O'Rourke Mechanical Aptitude Test

- *Clerical Ability*: For measuring clerical ability the following tests are used.
  - Minnesota Vocational Test for Clerical Workers
  - Thurston Examination in Clerical Work
  - Kiran Gupta Clerical Aptitude Test
- *Musical Ability*: For measuring musical ability the following test is used.
  - Seashore Musical Test
- *Art Ability*: For measuring art ability the following test is used.
  - The McAdory Art Test

After measuring these specific abilities, a guidance expert can find out the specific field in which an individual's intelligence lies.

(iii) *Assessment of Personality*: For assessing an individual's personality the following methods are used:

- *Personality Inventories*
- *Projective Techniques*
  - Rorshach's Ink Blot Test
  - Thematic Apperception Test
  - Psychodrama
  - Situational Tests
  - Word Association Test, etc.
- *Other Methods, e.g.,*
  - Case History Method
  - Questionnaire
  - Interview
  - Observation
  - Autobiography
  - Sociometry
  - Handwriting Test

(iv) *Measurement of Interests*: For carrying out vocational guidance work, guidance expert should have the knowledge about an individual's interest areas, apart from intelligence and personality. For measuring an individual's interests, various interest tests are used. These are as follows.

- Strong's Vocational Interest Inventory
- Hapner's Vocational Inventory Record
- Kuder's Preference Record
- Lee Thorpe's Schedule

(v) *Final Interview*: After measuring an individual's different aspects and preparing their report, it is essential to do a final interview. Only on the basis of this measurement report, an individual should be counseled for his choice of a job. During this interview both the sides can clarify their doubts, if any.

(vi) *Report Writing*: At the end, the guidance expert should prepare a report on the basis of all the test results, information received during the final interview and the guidance provided.

(vii) *Placement Work*: The guidance expert, after choosing the vocation, should help the individual in procuring a job. For this he should maintain contact with employment offices and employers.

(viii) *Follow-up Work*: The guidance expert, providing vocational guidance, must also ensure that the individual who has been placed in a job is making satisfactory progress and adjustment. If he is not making satisfactory progress, then probable factors for this situation should be probed and guidance should be given in the light of these factors.

Vocational Counselling

Vocational counselling is an integral part of educational process. Counselling in educational setting cannot be purposefully attained without including counselling towards vocational development. It helps students in their choice of curriculum. Hence, both school and college students should be given educational and vocational guidance.

Choosing a vocation is a crucial decision in an individual's life. But while making vocational choice, an individual is confronted with a perplexing situation as to which vocation to choose. There are diverse and compelling factors that influence his decision. Hence, it must be ensured that the desired vocation is in tandem with the individual's abilities, interests, potential and needs, and whether the conditions under which he shall have to work are conducive or not.

According to Super (1962), vocation is not just a means of livelihood, but a path of life, it is a social role. Counselling is a necessity. 'Vocational counselling' is that process in which an individual is assisted to prepare himself for a suitable vocation. According to English and English (1958), 'vocational counselling' is concerned with those processes which are undertaken by an individual towards finding a vocation and overcoming the problems of making preparation for it.

The nature of decision-making for a job is a very serious matter. Hence, it needs special attention. Otherwise it could result in maladjustment and unhappiness.

Occupational Information—Collection and Dissemination

Occupational information includes all those facts that are related to an occupation, like qualifications for entry, opportunities and means for growth, occupational and health hazards and related compensation, conditions prevailing in special occupations and occupation groups, etc. Apart from this, all printed literature like journals and books, cassettes, CDs, etc. containing occupational information fall under this category.

Occupational information can be gathered from various private, public and professional sources. To ensure its reliability, vocational information should be procured from original sources as far as possible. In India, we do have sources for gathering occupational information. Direct sources incorporate analyzes, surveys and systematization done by them, while indirect sources consist of written literature. Occupational information can also be disseminated through printed as well as audio-visual media like films, film strips, documentaries, television, radio, posters, charts, etc.

Agencies of Occupational Information

(a) In India, occupational information is released by different organizations. At the national level, Directorate General of Resettlement and Employment as well as Directorate of Audio

Visual Publicity undertake the task of publishing employment related information. Information published by Directorate General of Resettlement and Employment comes under the following four categories:.

(i) *Career Guides*: These are booklets of 8–12 pages and contain general information about different occupations in simple language.

(ii) *Occupational Field Reviews*: The details about an occupation and its related fields are given and this literature is used by career masters. It is selected on the basis of National Classification of Occupations (NCO).

(iii) *National Classification of Occupations*: All small and big occupations in the country have been classified into nine classes. These have been divided into 55 sub-classes and these sub-classes are further split into 300 sections.

(iv) *Handbook on Training Facilities*: These books are published at state level. They contain information regarding training facilities available in that particular state.

(b) *Vocational Guidance Bureaux*: In India, Vocational Guidance Bureaux too have proved quite popular and useful. They also have brought out some vocational publications. These mainly contain information about job opportunities, vocational training facilities, etc.

(c) *Defence Ministry Publications*: Ministry of Defence brings out regular publications about job opportunities in the army, air force and navy wings as well as in the engineering services. Similarly, Publications Division, Ministry of Information & Broadcasting, brings out publications like 'Our Merchant Navy', 'Our Police', 'India's Forests', etc.

(d) *Employment Exchanges*: District employment exchanges have been set up throughout the country. Even Guidance Bureaux work in coordination with these employment exchanges. The person seeking employment has to register his name in the exchange. From time to time the exchange brings out information about job availability. It also sends intimation to the registered persons regarding jobs available according to their qualifications and ability.

(e) *Rotary Club*: Rotary Club brings out career pamphlets from time to time. But the information contained in these is about limited professions and not in an easy-to-understand format.

(f) *YMCA, Calcutta*: YMCA, Calcutta, too brings out 'Vocational Guidance Series' that gives useful vocational information.

(g) *Central Bureau of Educational and Vocational Guidance*: Functioning under the Ministry of Education, Government of India, it has brought out a number of vocational publications and also made some short films on the subject.

(h) *Visits to Places of Industrial Importance*: An effective means of vocational information is visits to places of industrial importance. By visiting such places, a student can directly seek (a) relevant information, (b) remove his doubts and (c) learn about the practical aspects of an industry. Information received this way is more reliable.

(i) *Films and Film Strips*: Films and film strips play an important role in providing vocational information. Through these films detailed information about various aspects of an industry or a profession can be gained. This information gets registered on a candidate's mental screen and is retained there for a long time.

(j) *Publications and Advertisements*: Vocational information can also be procured from different types of publications, such as daily newspapers, magazines, journals and industrial publications. The best information can be had from daily newspapers also. In this age of advertising, serious employers advertise their manpower requirements through classified columns and display advertisements 'Employment News', published weekly in

Hindi, English and Urdu languages by the Ministry of Information & Broadcasting, New Delhi, provide rich and detailed information about jobs, training, etc. currently available in India at all levels. Various states also publish such weeklies or fortnightlies. 'University News', also a weekly, is a good source of information for jobs and opportunities in higher education.

Dissemination of Occupational Information: There are two ways of disseminating occupational information to students and individuals desirous of vocational guidance.

(a) *Providing Vocational Information at Individual Level*: Vocational information at individual level can be provided through interview between the candidate and the counsellor. The candidate should be provided vocational guidance only about the vocation in which he shows interest. But care should be taken to ascertain that his choice of vocations should match his capability, qualification and interests.

(b) *Group Method*: Interview or personal contact is a good medium of disseminating vocational information. But in view of the limited number of the counsellors, constraints of time and funds and very large number of candidates, personal contact should be made only when information cannot be provided through group method. Providing vocational information to groups can be done in various ways.

(i) *Occupational Information as a Regular Subject*: In order to familiarize students with the real state of occupational field, vocational information should be taught as a subject. As a subject, occupational information can be compiled in a more organized way to enable students to make a better vocational choice. Moreover, they will receive inspiration for further education.

(ii) *Career Conferences*: Career fairs and seminars play a significant role in disseminating vocational information. These conferences are organized at the beginning of the session, on the eve of annual days or at the end of the session. Experienced and working professionals are invited to address these conferences. The theme of the conference and the subjects to be discussed must be decided in advance so that students are mentally prepared to receive the relevant information. At the end of the discussion, time should be given to the students for asking questions. Interested and motivated students should be given an opportunity to interview the visiting professionals to receive further information and seek clarifications.

(iii) *Display of Posters and Advertisement Clippings*: Vocational information can also be disseminated by display of posters and newspaper advertisement clippings on the school notice boards, in the library, inside and outside classrooms.

(iv) *Display of Charts and Other Printed Material*: Charts, pamphlets and other printed material can be displayed in classrooms and library.

(v) *Through Special Subject Teachers*: Teachers connected with vocational guidance can also disseminate vocational information.

(vi) *Through Movies and Documentaries*: Movies and documentaries are proven and effective means of providing occupational information to groups.

(vii) *Through Radio and Television*: Announcements of vocational information can be made through radio and television, which people can receive sitting at home.

(viii) *Visits to Industrial and Commercial Establishments*: Vocational information can be provided to students in a more practical way by conducting tours of commercial and industrial establishments.

(ix) *Library*: Library is a very important platform for providing vocational information. A special cell can be created in the library to gather, classify and distribute vocational information.

(x) Group method of disseminating vocational information can be widely used in order to save time and money.

Theory of Vocational Choice

Why an individual gets attracted to a particular vocation and selects it for his life? How does one achieve vocational growth? What are the main factors behind the choice of a vocation? In the absence of an answer to these questions, a guidance expert cannot provide successful vocational guidance to the students.

It is, therefore, essential for a guidance expert to have the knowledge of vocational principles. The underlying fact behind all principles of vocational choice has been that vocational development is a long-term process. The credit goes to Eli Ginzberg and his associates for adopting an organized approach towards vocational development in their book titled 'Occupational Choice'. It was in 1951 that Ginzberg for the first time published a study in the field of principles of vocational choice. According to Ginzberg, vocational choice is a process divided into three stages, as described below.

(a) *Fantasy Period or Stage*: According to Ginzberg, the process of occupational development starts with the birth of a child and continues throughout his life. Occupational development in a child can be studied from his seventh year onwards.

The process of occupational choice prior to the age of 11 years is the fantasy stage. During this period, a child undergoes various fantasies about his occupational choice.

(b) *The Tentative Period or Stage*: After the fantasy stage, the stage from the age of 11–17 is called the tentative stage. During this stage, a youngster visualizes various possibilities about his future vocation. According to Ginzberg, a tentative stage can be further sub-divided into three sub-stages as follows.

(i) *Interest Stage*: At this stage, a youngster develops his interests.

(ii) *Capacity Stage*: At this stage, a youngster's choice is based on the abilities and capabilities acquired by him.

(iii) *Value Stage*: At this stage, a youngster becomes capable of apportioning value to his choice and is able to decide what is important for him from the point of view of his choice of future vocation. He can now analyze choices.

(c) *Realistic Period or Stage*: This stage starts from the age of 17 years and continues till such time as he joins some vocation. Like the tentative stage, Ginzberg has sub-divided the realistic period or stage also into three sub-stages as under:

(i) *Exploration Stage*: During this phase, a youngster looks around for vocations.

(ii) *Crystallization Stage*: During this phase the youngster precipitates his choice. In other words, having tried various choices the youngster zeroes in on his direction.

(iii) *Specification Stage*: At the end, the youngster narrows down his choice to a specific area of a vocational activity.

In accordance with the principle of gradual development, the above stratification is extremely useful because it helps in understanding how a youngster graduates to maturity.

Super's Theory of Vocational Development

Super (1953), however, has severely criticized Ginzberg's theory. He has formulated 10 propositions which comprise his theory of development as follows.

(a) Individuals differ with regard to their abilities, interests and personality attributes.
(b) They are capable of entering a number of occupations by virtue of their abilities, interests, etc.
(c) Different types of occupations require different patterns of abilities, interests and traits.
(d) Peoples' preferences for different vocations change with their self-concepts which get modified with time and experience. This makes choice and adjustment a continuous process.
(e) The process of adjustment involves a series of life stages which are identified as growth, exploration, establishment, maintenance and decline. In each of these stages, there can be periods corresponding to fantasy, tentative and realistic aspects and the trial and stable phases which make up the establishment change.
(f) The career pattern of the individual is determined by several factors, the important factors among which are parents, socio-economic conditions, intelligence, personality and available opportunities.
(g) Vocational development can be guided by assisting in the maturation of abilities and interests and providing for reality testing.
(h) Vocational development helps in implementing self-concept which develops as a result of the interaction between the subjective factors and the environmental conditions.
(i) The process of compromise involves role playing either in imaginary situations or in real life situations.
(j) Satisfaction from work is dependent on the extent to which the individual is able to find expression for his abilities, interests, personality traits and values. Work satisfaction also depends on work situation.

Super's theory helps in understanding the developmental concerns of young people.

According to Super, it is the constructive aspect of self-concept that forms the basis of vocational choice. Finding satisfaction in a job and being satisfied with life depends on whether a person can make full use of his abilities, interests, personality traits, values and beliefs or not.

Anne Roe's Theory of Career Development

Anne Roe's (1956) theory of career development is very closely related to Maslow's (1954) personality theory. The theory is stated in a set of propositions as under.

(a) Genetic inheritance is important. It sets limits to potential development.
(b) The development of inherited characteristics is affected by unique experiences, cultural background and socio-economic factors.
(c) The pattern of development of interests, attitudes and personality is determined by the individual's experience. The mode and degree of satisfaction of individual needs determine which of the needs become the strongest motivating factors and which do not. The pattern of psychic energies is the major determinant of interests. The intensity of the needs and their satisfaction determines the degree of motivation.

Holland's Theory of Vocational Choice

John Holland (1952), criticizing Ginzberg's and Super's theories of vocational choice, by saying that it is very difficult to take any decision on vocational choice on the basis of these theories.

According to Holland, an individual's vocational choice is the result of combined influence of his inheritance, civilization, culture, guardians, peer group, elders, family's socio-economic level and physical environment.

An individual, on the basis of various experiences, learns to react and adjust in a typical way with his environment. Thereafter, he chooses a vocation that gives him maximum satisfaction. An individual divides vocations in certain groups. Holland has described these groups as 'occupational environment'. He has divided different occupations into six groups as follows.

(a) *Intellectual Environment*: It includes professions like doctor, chemist, physicist, mathematician, physician, etc.
(b) *Aesthetic Environment*: It includes artists, poets, writers, sculptors, musicians, etc.
(c) *Conventional Environment*: It includes bank clerks, secretaries, filing clerks, booksellers, etc.
(d) *Realistic Environment*: It includes workers, machinists, farmers, drivers, carpenters, artisans, counsellor etc.
(e) *Enterprising Environment*: It includes salesmen, politicians, managers, etc.
(f) *Social Environment*: It includes social workers, teachers, consultants, guides, interviewers, etc.

According to Holland, a particular lifestyle is needed for each type of occupation. If an individual's lifestyle is in conformity with the characteristics of a particular occupation, then he would derive satisfaction from his job and have a balanced personal. Believes that intellectuals have more thinking power than working prowess. Individuals with artistic personality attach utmost significance to self-expression. Individuals belonging to conventional environment attach more significance to vocations with status, respect, power, authority, etc. Individuals belonging to enterprising environment impress people with their communication skills. Those from social environment have a knack for maintaining good relations and are endowed with a humanitarian outlook.

In accordance with the above theory, Holland has described the under-mentioned process by which an individual makes his occupational choice:

(a) First of all an individual chooses his occupational environment in accordance with his lifestyle.
(b) On the basis of his abilities (especially mental), an individual chooses an occupation from among the main occupational environments or groups.
(c) The above-mentioned processes are influenced by an individual's knowledge, vocational information, suggestions from family and friends and socio-economic circumstances.

Apart from the above three main premises, Holland also enumerates the following sub-premises:

(a) If the development of an individual's lifestyle is unidirectional, then vocational choice does not take much time.
(b) If an individual's interests coincide with the vocational environment, then vocational choice becomes easier.
(c) Self-knowledge helps in deciding vocational choice.
(d) In the absence of self-knowledge, individuals are not able to determine their vocational direction and level.
(e) For making vocational choice it is very necessary to have correct knowledge of vocational environment or group.
(f) Age also influences one's vocational choice.
(g) For making vocational choice, it is important to take into account external elements like the state and the level of unemployment, available jobs, competition, social values and prestige attached to a vocation.

Thus, we may conclude that like or dislike for an occupation depends on a number of factors. Principles of vocational choice can be implemented only where the full occupational opportunities are available.

In India, due to rampant unemployment, an individual has to sacrifice his likes and interests before the available job opportunity and make it the object of his life.

Essential Aspects of an Occupation

Before choosing an occupation it is necessary to study it because each occupation has different aspects. For providing vocational guidance it becomes imperative to determine the relevant aspects of an occupation and its suitability vis-à-vis an individual and his needs.

Thus, studying the different aspects of an occupation is an essential need of the guidance process. The following are the essential aspects of an occupation:

(a) *Importance of an Occupation*: Some of the questions to be analyzed are: How useful is the occupation from the point of view of the student, society and nation? How many people can find employment from it? Whether it is a developing occupation or a developed one.

(b) *Nature of Work*: What is an individual's nature of work in a particular occupation?

(i) Whether it is a desk job?
(ii) Does the occupation involve much travelling?
(iii) Does it involve fieldwork?

This enables to make correct vocational choice.

(c) *Working Conditions*: It is important to know working conditions and whether those conditions are congenial or not.

(i) Whether there is adequate arrangement for light, air, water, etc. and is humidity under control?
(ii) How arduous is the work?
(iii) How many hours has one to work, and is it a day shift or a night shift?
(iv) Is there any rest time between work or not?

(d) *Requisite Abilities*: What type of abilities are required in the occupation, whether these are physical abilities or mental abilities, or both? In certain occupations physical abilities are required. If the job requires physical ability, does it involve the entire body or specific parts of body like mouth, hands, eyes, feet, etc.? If mental ability is required, what mental level is needed? Mental ability includes visualization, creativity, logic, memory, etc. In certain occupations along with mental and physical abilities, psychological abilities are also needed, for example, the level of emotional maturity, patience, courage, stability, personality, etc.

(e) *Entry into Occupation*: The mode of joining each occupation is different. Hence, it is necessary to know the mode of joining an occupation. Is it through employment exchange, an application to the employer and a subsequent interview, or through passing an entrance test?

In the case of self-employment the following must be ascertained:

(i) How much investment is needed at the onset?
(ii) Is any licence or certificate needed for the occupation?
(iii) Is previous experience needed?
(iv) Is any legal formality to be fulfilled, and if so how much time does it take?

(f) *Training Needed*: The type of training needed for an occupation has to be ascertained? Where is the training available and what is its duration? How much experience does the employer need or can the experience be done away with?

(g) *Salary*: What is the pay scale in the occupation? What is the annual increment? What is the highest salary in the scale? Are the wages given daily, weekly or monthly? Facilities other than salary, for example, free medical aid, housing facility, servant, telephone, pension, bonus, productivity bonus, gratuity, etc. How much is paid for over time? What facilities are provided in case of working till late?
(h) *Chances of Promotion*: Are there chances of promotion in the occupation? After what length of service does promotion become due? What are the extra qualifications, other than experience, required for promotion? The tenure of service?
(i) *History of Occupation*: Prior to studying any occupation it is necessary to know its brief history. History of an occupation gives information about its beginning, growth, stability and future progress.
(j) *Regularity of Work*: Does work continue through the year? Or does it last for only some months of a year?
(k) *Place of Posting*: Among all aspects of employment this aspect is most important. An individual must know the possible places where he can be posted, the climatic conditions, temperature, availability and quality of water, language and geographic location.

If while choosing an occupation, an individual considers all the above aspects he will not face any problem in his vocation.

Summary

Vocational choice is the most crucial decision in an individual's life. Since all individuals are not equally endowed with potential and capabilities, choice of vocation, therefore, assumes an added significance. Hence, vocational guidance is needed while choosing a vocation. Significance of vocational guidance cannot be realized unless its meaning is clearly understood.

An individual, on the basis of various experiences, learns to react in a typical way with his environment. Thereafter, he selects a vocation that offers him the maximum satisfaction. Vocational guidance is a process which helps an individual in realizing his vocational objective. Its function is to help an individual with appropriate potential, interests and abilities in choosing his vocation, entering in it and then progressing in it. In this process, an individual evaluates his role in a real life situation.

Before choosing an occupation it is necessary to study it because each occupation has its peculiar aspects. For providing vocational guidance it becomes imperative to determine, by analyzing the relevant aspects of an occupation, whether the incumbent individual fits into the requirements of that occupation, or whether the occupation adequately answers his needs, interests and potential.

It is essential for a guidance expert to have full knowledge of vocational principles. The underlying fact behind all principles of vocational choice has been that vocational development is a long-term process.

10

Personal Social Guidance

There are four aspects of an individual's personal life—social, family, physical and mental. An individual is constantly trying to fulfill his needs through means at his disposal. Yet it is not possible to fulfill all his needs. The state of non-fulfillment of these needs gives rise to different kinds of problems in an individual's personal life. The help that is rendered for resolving these problems is called *personal guidance*.

Personal guidance is concerned with an individual's personal and social adjustment problems because its main aim is to assist in his physical, emotional, social, moral and spiritual development and adjustment.

From the view point of discipline, social behaviour and work, guidance is an adjustment because guidance facilitates personality development through its adjustment service. Hence, it is very important to understand the nature of adjustment.

Meaning of Adjustment: An individual reacts differently in different environments. Change in reaction, behaviour or feeling, according to the change in environment, is called adjustment. According to Lawrance F. Shaffer (1956), 'Adjustment is the process by which a living organism maintains a balance between its needs and the circumstances that influence the satisfaction of these needs'. In this definition two things that stand out are (i) individual's needs and (ii) circumstances influencing the needs.

In other words, we can say that an individual's behaviour is prompted by different kinds of internal needs and desires. An individual's behaviour, therefore, inspired by different kinds of desires and needs. However, one cannot negate the role of external influences like social mores, traditions, etc. and internal influences like physical and mental states, means, aptitude, attitude, etc. in shaping one's behaviour.

In the process of adjustment, an individual has to strike balance between situations and inspirations. For instance, a student desires to pass B.A. in first division. For the fulfillment of his desire, he works hard but is unable to fulfill the desire to get first division because he is either not so intelligent or there are some other reasons hindering his desire. As a result, he transforms his desire from first division to second division. Through this transformation he is able to satisfy his desire. Hence, he solves the adjustment problem by striking a balance between his need and situation. Thus, adjustment is a continual process by which a person varies his behaviour to produce a more harmonious relationship between himself and his environment.

Adjustment Process

Man is an intelligent being. He himself is aware of his needs and accordingly he relates himself to his environment. By the process of adjustment, we mean 'achieving an effective and appropriate interaction between an individual and his environment'.

There are three main elements in the process of adjustment.

(a) *Motive*: The process of adjustment begins with some inspiration or need present in an individual.

(b) *Thwarting Conditions*: If environmental factors do not hinder the fulfillment of needs, adjustment probably comes about and there are no problems. But thwarting circumstances steer forward the process of adjustment.

(c) *Varied Responses*: In the event of non-fulfillment of needs, an individual reacts in many ways. These responses can be normal as well as abnormal. As a result of these reactions, the individual makes an adjustment with his environment.

The process of adjustment begins with inspiration. Inspiration is objective-oriented. As a result, the individual performs activities aimed at the objective. Many a time obstructions confront these activities. These obstructions evoke different responses in different individuals, the response may vary for trying work harder to giving it up to thinking an alternative plan to meet the objective.

Evaluation of an individual's personality adjustment can be done as per the following criteria.

(a) *Balance of Personality*: Personality is the sum total of many characteristics. The main criterion of personality adjustment is the formulation of personality. All the mental faculties like intelligence, emotions, desires and determination are fully involved in it and these function in unison. A well-developed personality is flexible, determined and cohesive. The ability to adjust is proportionate to the integration of personality. An individual with well-adjusted personality is balanced and realistic. He is not easily upset by failures and disappointments, and his emotions, needs, thoughts and other mental activities are also balanced. On the other hand, a maladjusted individual's personality is imbalanced. His life is devoid of peace and he deprives others too of their peace.

(b) *Minimal Tension*: Another sign of well-adjusted personality is minimal tension. Non-fulfillment of needs gives rise to tension. This tension lasts till needs are fulfilled. In other words, the adjustment of an individual can be gauged from the amount of tension he has.

(c) *Harmony Between Needs and Environment*: The amount of harmony is directly proportionate to the amount of adjustment. An individual with a well-adjusted personality keeps his needs and desires in consonance with the state of his environment and alters his environment according to the demand of his needs. Thus, achieving mutual adjustment from both the sides accounts for more success. For instance, some people with ordinary financial means manage their affairs very well and look content. On the other hand, some people with very good financial means are seen complaining of shortage of money, and are never content because their expenses outstrip their income. As a result, personality adjustment goes haywire. For good adjustment of personality it is necessary to modify both the needs and the environment, and strike an ideal balance between the two of them.

Motivation, Conflict and Frustration

Motivation: Motivation is an individual's internal urge which directs an individual's action. It inspires an individual to achieve his objective. Thus, the inspired propelling force is called motivation. The process of adjustment starts with some sort of motivation.

In the process of adjustment, social motivations are more significant. They develop in the cultural milieu. Different social modifications are observed in individuals hailing from different cultures. One can observe motivations of self-respect, security, love and compassion in our culture. In the process of adjustment, powerful motivations dominate over weaker motivations. Powerful motivations once aroused do not lay content till they are satisfied. Their non-satisfaction creates tension, conflict and frustration

Conflicts: According to fraud's words, an individual is made up of a series of conflict situations. By passing through conflicts that an individual leaders the great lessons of life because easy going person does not learn anything, when two or more contradictory motives arise in an individual, the fulfillment of one obstructs the realization of other by an individual's fear of failure and his indecisiveness. Conflict is less severe in an individual's conscious state than in his sub-conscious state.

Types of Conflict: Conflict is mainly of three types.

(a) *Approach—Approach Conflict*: When two attractive desires sprout simultaneously and are equally attractive, then conflict comes into play. When they are not equally attractive there is no any conflict and fulfillment of one does not create hurdle in the other's way.

$$+G \longleftarrow P \longrightarrow G+$$ Positive individual aim attraction

(b) *Avoidance—Avoidance Conflict*: When two unattractive desires sprout simultaneously and are equally unattractive, the individual does not want the fulfillment of either. But a situation arises where one of the two has to be chosen. When avoidance—avoidance conflict becomes too severe, it gives rise to adjustment problems.

$$-G \longrightarrow P \longleftarrow G-$$ Negative

(c) *Approach—Avoidance Conflict*: In this conflict situation, an individual has only one aim which has both positive and negative attractions inherent in it. The individual is in a fix. He desires to achieve it as well as run away from it.

$$P \longrightarrow G\pm$$

Frustration: Frustration arises from an individual's failure and is felt especially when an objective is not realized. In other words, when a hurdle or obstruction comes in between an individual's need and the means of its fulfillment or the objective, or when there is no solid objective before an individual, frustration arises.

The main cause of dissatisfaction and frustration among today's youth is the prospect of a bleak future after their education. Finding an occupation is not only difficult but also almost impossible due to stiff competition, the cult of recommendation, bribery and nepotism. Frustration has two forms—defeat and struggle. When faced with defeat, an individual adopts aggressive behaviour towards individuals or objects he considers responsible for his defeat. This aggressive posture can be manifest as well as veiled.

In boys and people of younger age aggressiveness is in a manifest form. In mature people and those with developed personality, it assumes a veiled form. If a boy is punished for this type of aggressive behaviour his aggressiveness outwardly vanishes but he feels oppressed and exhibits signs of fear and insecurity. Different reactions for making adjustment gradually turn into habits. Hence, in adults well-defined individual difference, in the levels of adjustment, can be observed.

Extent of frustration mainly depends on two factors as (i) strength of motivation and (ii) distance from the goal.

High Ambition Level: When an individual is deficient in abilities and his ambitions are high he gets engulfed by disappointments.

Exceptional Children and Problems of Guidance

Those children who are significantly different from average and normal children and need educational guidance are called exceptional children. These children's, whether they are extraordinarily intelligent or backward, are not able to make their own future plans. So, in order to successfully implement the plans, educational guidance is needed. For successful learning, it is necessary that children's education should go in the right direction. Before guiding exceptional children it is necessary to know who exactly is an exceptional child.

According to Hunt (1960), 'An exceptional child is one who deviates from the normal or average child in mental, physical, emotional and social characteristics to such an extent that he requires a modification of school practices or special education services in order to develop to his maximum capacity'. Cruickshank and Orville (1958) have defined an exceptional children one who deviates intellectually, physically, socially or emotionally so markedly from what is considered to be normal growth and development that he cannot receive maximum benefit from a regular school programme and requires a special class or supplementary instruction and services.

According to this definition, exceptional children are different from normal children in the following respects.

(a) Physical differences:

(i) Externally disabled, like maimed, lame, deaf, dumb, etc.
(ii) Internally disabled, heart problem, lungs problem, etc.

(b) Mental differences:

(i) Talent, affluence
(ii) Dullness, deficiency

(c) Personality imbalance:

(i) Emotional imbalance
(ii) Social imbalance

Gifted Children with Adjustment Problems

Till now a student with 130+ IQ was believed to be talented. But according to the current point of view, IQ is not the sole criterion for being talented. If a student with 130+ IQ is not successful in behavioural sphere, he cannot be called talented.

Talented children are nation and society's assets. Hence, it is the teachers' and guidance personnel's duty to identify talented students for providing guidance.

About talented children, Kolesnic writes: 'The term gifted has been applied to every child who, in the age group, is superior in some ability which may make him an understanding contributor to the welfare and quality of living in our society'.

According to National Society for the Study of Education—'The talented or gifted child is one who shows consistently remarkable performance in any worthwhile line or endeavour'.

It is clear from the above definitions that giftedness does not depend on intelligence quotient. It is generally the sum total of ordinary intelligence and specific intelligence. A gifted child performs ordinary chores successfully and by working successfully in a specific sphere he achieves excellence. In other words, a gifted child cannot exhibit his excellence in every field. He achieves excellence only in that field in which he has special ability which, in turn, is correlated to ordinary intelligence at a higher level.

Talented students cannot be provided suitable guidance till they are clearly identified in a reliable and valid manner. This helps in creating a stimulating environment for promoting their talents.

Such children complete their work satisfactorily, in less time, without being given much attention by the teacher.

Talented students can also be identified on the following basis.

(a) *Mental Ability*: Talented students' mental ability is 130 and more. But according to some educationists it is 140 and above.

(b) *Intangible Thinking*: Talented students' superior thinking process enables them to take comparatively less time to understand and solve difficult problems. They have sharp discerning ability, good memory, instant repartee, clarity of knowledge, thought and values, logical communication of ideas, vast vocabulary, and can express themselves eloquently.

(c) *Physical Prowess*: Talented children are physically also better developed than normal children. They learn walking and speaking earlier than normal children.

(d) *Social and Emotional Firmness*: They are more sociable and emotionally stable than normal children. They are good at making friends, are well-disciplined, obedient and humble. They perform well in jobs involving responsibility and do shy away from ownership.

(e) *Leadership Quality*: These children are good leaders and win others' respect for their leadership.

(f) *Vigilance*: Talented children are more vigilant than normal children and do challenging jobs more carefully. They learn new things quickly and have better mental retention.

(g) *Interest in Knowledge*: Talented children show interest in world affairs and are keen to know about them.

(h) *Creative Interest*: They evince creative interest in one or the other subject like music, art, sports, instrumentation, literature, etc.

(i) *Alertness*: These kids are wonderfully alert and successfully deal with difficult situations.

(j) *Problem-solving Ability*: Talented children can easily correlate two events and therefore can easily find solution to resultant problem.

(k) *Less Need for Guidance*: Need for guidance is less because of better intellectual and physical abilities. On the basis of their intelligence and experience they are able to solve their own problems.

(l) *Better Behaved*: They are better behaved than the normal children. Hence, they are more successful in educational and vocational fields.

From the characteristics of talented children it is evident that they are superior in almost every field than normal children. Even their needs are qualitatively better than normal children's. Non-fulfillment of these needs gives rise to adjustment problems. Hence, these children need special kind of education and guidance in order to achieve optimum growth of their personality. Limitations of school in different areas also give rise to their special needs. The child seeks fulfillment of his superior needs within the school, but due to lack of resource, funds and opportunities whatever he wants to learn properly and their intellectual growth does not receive adequate fillip.

Talented children and guidance services are as follows.

(a) Gifted children should be identified through reliable and recognized guidance services. Thereafter, appropriate information should be passed on to schools with a view to suitably modifying teaching methods and course content.
(b) The second main function of guidance services is to assist these children in developing their talent further, according to their abilities, potential and interests.
(c) Curricula and teaching methods should be so designed as to promote their normal and specific abilities along with powers of logic, thinking and creativity to the maximum extent.
(d) Special teachers are needed to teach such students. Hence, guidance service should arrange for special teachers and analysts to devise and use special teaching methods to meet these students' requirements.
(e) Some talented children, for the reason of not being identified, keep receiving ordinary education which hardly benefits them. Special teaching techniques need to be used to impart both intensive and extensive knowledge. Such students take special interest in studies, hence there should be adequate availability of relevant books in the library.
(f) Students can be assisted in the development of their talents by paying special attention to them, praising them for their performance and aiding them in their endeavours.
(g) Guidance service should not only encourage these students in doing self-evaluation and self-analysis but should also assist them in such efforts.

In the absence of proper guidance, a talented child can go astray and adopt anti-social way of life. Hence, a teacher should keep talented students busy in activities replete with basic values, excitement, complexity, etc.

Mentally-Retarded Children

In the field of education certain children do not make as much progress in studies as do other children of their age. In other words, those children whose IQ is below normal, or below 75, are called mentally retarded children. Their mental age is less than their physical age. Mentally retarded children can be identified through intelligence tests and other methods.

Children are categorized on the basis of intelligence tests. Those with IQ between 75 and 90 are called dullards, though they are not mentally retarded, their progress is comparatively slow. They cannot make as much progress as normal children can make. Hence, they need special attention. No child should be declared a dullard merely on the basis of intelligence tests. Other means should be used to identify dull children.

Through ordinary training, mentally retarded children can be made to perform ordinary chores for livelihood. They can be made self-dependent to some extent.

Guidance for Mentally-retarded Children: There are many individuals in society whose IQ is below normal. Their problems are different from those of normal individuals. In this context, two facts that surface are as follows.

First, such individuals because of their low intelligence cannot make as much progress as normal individuals. Secondly, because of low intelligence they face discrimination in society leading to adjustment problems. Therefore, there should be special guidance programmes for such individuals. It is equally important to organize special diagnostic classes for mentally retarded children.

The main aim of guidance programme should be to identify the causes of their low intelligence and take rehabilitative measures. These measures could be establishment and provision of special schools, special classes, special curricula, special teaching methods and special teachers.

(a) *Provision of Special Schools*: There should be a provision of special schools for mentally retarded children where their development can be taken care of better than in ordinary schools. There are separate schools for mentally retarded, deaf, dumb and blind children, established by the Government.

(b) *Provision of Special Classes*: Special classes should be held for mentally retarded children. Students should be of the same mental level their number should be limited and speed of teaching should be slow. Teachers should be specially trained, experienced and qualified. Periods should not be long, and for different subjects there should be different classes. Classes should be based on syllabus and there should be arrangement for physical and creative activities as well in the school. Special classes will have a cushioning effect on mentally retarded children who would feel themselves secure in these classes.

(c) *Special Syllabus*: For mentally retarded children, a special syllabus should be designed according to their intelligence quotient. They should be provided vocational education like painting, carpet weaving, chair seat and back weaving, gardening, etc.

(d) *Special Teaching Methods*: For such children, special teaching techniques should be used.

  (i) Teaching should be slow and there should be frequent revision.
  (ii) Teachers should simplify teaching by using teaching aids so that children enjoy learning.
  (iii) Instead of giving bookish knowledge, they should be given practical knowledge to foster their personality development.

(e) *Special Teachers*: For mentally retarded children, there should be specially qualified teachers.

  (i) Teachers should be trained with complete knowledge of child psychology and behavioural psychology.
  (ii) Teacher's behaviour should be free from bias and full of compassion.
  (iii) Teacher should have knowledge about the problems and weaknesses of mentally retarded children.

The counsellor should very carefully find out these children's interests and aptitudes so as to provide them educational and vocational guidance commensurate with their interests and aptitudes.

Mentally retarded children need vocational education. Hence, their education should be closely related to their life.

While providing educational, vocational, personal and family guidance to mentally retarded children, care must be taken to ensure that their maladjustment does not increase because of special guidance programme. Special care is needed in this area. Self-confidence should be aroused in mentally retarded individuals so that they are able to cope with the pressures of mainstream life.

Handicapped Children and Problems of Adjustment

There is a segment of society that is called handicapped because of various physical defects either from birth or incurred through accidents or disease. There is a large number of such people in our society. This area came into focus in 1981 when the International Handicapped Year was observed.

Handicapped people find it difficult to establish themselves in a society. For this reason, they fall in a special social category. It is, however, unfortunate that instead of being encouraged and motivated, sympathy is expressed towards them for not being like other normal individuals. As a result of sympathy, they become victims of inferiority complex and despondence.

Crow and Crow have defined physically disabled as 'The youngster whose physical handicap prevents him or imposes limitations on him from participating in normal activities will be called a physically handicapped youngster'.

From the point of view of providing guidance to the physically handicapped individuals, it is essential to classify them into:

(a) those who are suffering from hearing problems;
(b) those who are suffering from impaired eyesight;
(c) those who cannot speak;
(d) spastics.

Hearing Defects

Youngsters suffering from hearing problems can be divided into two categories.

(i) Those who are completely deaf.
(ii) Those who are hard of hearing.

Those who are completely deaf cannot hear anything. Some are born deaf. Others lose their hearing power because of ear diseases or accidents. Generally, those who are deaf from birth and are dumb too.

Those who are hard of hearing fall into different categories depending on their degree of deafness. Those who are simply hard of hearing can overcome their problem with the help of hearing aids. They can be educated regular by the teacher. The itinerant teacher helps in the use of hearing aids and imparts auditory training in lip reading and language development.

Those who cannot be cured through surgery or with the help of hearing aids need guidance. They can neither hear anything nor they can speak anything by copying lip and other vocal movements. They express their feelings through indistinguishable voice.

A teacher can organize lip-reading classes where she can deliver lecture slowly in well-punctuated words and clear cut accent with the help of aids. In these classes, students should be encouraged to watch their teacher's lip movement and speak out the words uttered by him. These lip-reading classes should be small so that each student can cope easily. Thus, trained teachers with adequate knowledge of language signs are needed.

Eyesight Defects

Eyesight defects too are of many kinds, like inability to see clearly, near-sight weakness, distance-sight weakness, inability to see in bright light, colour blindness, complete blindness. Individuals who are completely blind do not face that many problems as do individuals with other eyesight defects.

Completely blind persons simply believe what they hear but youngsters with other eyesight defects give their own interpretation to what they hear. They, often, stand the chance of misrepresenting a thing. Defective eyesight affects a student's performance, adjustment, personality and interests which give rise to many problems.

For completely blind students, there are separate classes, while those with defective eyesight study in the normal class along with other students. Because of defective eyesight they find difficulty in reading words in their books, hence they cannot study properly. They should be taught through recorded cassettes and at the time of examinations they should be provided writers.

Needless to say, youngsters suffering from eyesight defects need guidance. But the guidance personnel will have to study and understand their eye defects before working out a guidance programme.

Writing paper should be of light cream texture with thick black lining. There should be a provision for an eye doctor also, who would do routine checking recommend and give information about appropriate diet necessary and useful for eyes. For completely blind students, there should be separate classes and there should not be more than 15–20 students in a class. Education for them should be through the braille system.

Apart from this, while dealing with such students never give them the impression that they are suffering from some disability or defect. They should rather be encouraged to determine goals for their life and achieve them, so as to instil self-confidence and self-reliance in them.

Speech Defects

Defects to do with speaking are called speech defects. These are of many kinds, such as stammering, lisping, stuttering, suppressed speech, indistinct speech, uncontrolled speech, dumbness. Some of these defects are related to speech organs, some to emotional problems and work environment, and still others develop as an aftermath of diseases or drug addiction.

Defects related to speech organs or emotional problems can be minimized or cured through treatment but imbibed defects are acquired through copying the elders, family members and neighbours accept such defects as being an individual's normal speech.

Extreme caution must be exercised while providing guidance to youngsters afflicted with speech defects. When they come to know that they are abnormal in their speech they become emotionally imbalanced and like to stay aloof. If their friends imitate them or make fun of them, they steep deeper into seclusion. Even if they want to speak something they speak the least due to inferiority complex. Herein, lies the role of a teacher. He should adopt a friendly and sympathetic approach towards them and encourage them to speak.

Further, children afflicted with speech defects should be sent to a speech therapist, who through different signs, proven techniques and voice modulation, teaches how to use tongue and lips for different letters and words.

Spastics

A permanent damage or injury to the neural centre in the brain that controls muscular movement can lead to lack of muscular coordination or muscular dysfunction in their various body organs. This hinders the proper function of the body and can also affect one's speech. The defect can be from birth, or as a result of a disease or an accident.

Spastics may lead to low esteem, inferiority complex, loneliness, etc. The guidance expert or counsellor, should instil confidence, high morale and self-reliance in them.

There is also the need to change society's attitude towards these youngsters. Instead of inflicting ridicule and reproach on them, efforts should be made to imbue them with a feeling of dignity. Those undertaking rehabilitation of such youngsters should make efforts to encourage them to use their hidden talents and skills.

Summary

The non-fulfillment of these needs gives rise to different kinds of problems. Guidance facilitates personality development through its adjustment service. The process of adjustment involves achieving an effective and appropriate interaction between an individual and his environment.

An individual's circumstances influence his desires, needs as well as their fulfillment. But human behaviour is not determined solely by these desires and needs. There are other situations, both internal and external. In the process of adjustment, an individual has to strike a right balance between situations and inspirations.

Evaluation of a personality adjustment of an individual can be done on the basis of criteria like balance of personality, minimal tension, harmony between needs and environment, etc.

An individual has got certain internal urges or motivations under whose influence he acts. This motivation always keeps inspiring an individual to achieve his objective. Non-fulfillment of motivations creates tension, conflict and frustration.

Conflicts are of three types: (a) approach—approach conflict, (b) avoidance—avoidance conflict and (3) approach—avoidance conflict. Frustration arises from an individual's failure and is felt especially when an objective is not realized. For reducing conflicts and tensions, modern day psychologists have recognized the value of meditation. The practice of meditation involves constant observation of mind by detaching oneself from external physical and mental influences for a brief period.

In an educational setting, those children who are significantly different from average and normal children and need educational guidance are called exceptional children. These children, whether they are extraordinarily intelligent or backward, face adjustment problems. Hence, they stand in need of special guidance. It is important to identify them early.

In the absence of appropriate guidance, a talented child can go astray and adopt anti-social way of life.

Talented students should be kept busy in activities replete with basic values, excitement, complexity, toughness and thrill. On the other hand, mentally retarded children need vocational education. Hence, their education should be closely related to their life. Similarly, students with various physical handicaps need special education and guidance.

11

Counselling

An individual faces numerous problems during his lifetime. These problems are solved through guidance. The extent and nature of problems may, however, differ from individual to individual. For solving these problems, various services are used in a guidance programme. Counselling is one of them. Counselling has existed in human society in one form or the other since ancient times. But because of man's life being simple in the olden days, the need for counselling was not felt so much; teachers and other experienced people used to solve the problems. Modern society has, however, become very complex. Hence, teachers are unable to provide adequate guidance. Specially qualified and trained professionals are needed because in this complex society the scope, nature, extent and the very meaning of counselling has changed.

Before delving deeper into the various aspects of counselling, it is important to understand the meaning of counselling in today's context.

Meaning of Counselling

Counselling is an extremely ancient word. As a result it has been defined in many different ways. According to Webster's dictionary—'Consultation is mutual interchange of opinions or deliberating together'. But this definition is just a technical explanation of the term.

Scholars have come out with widely varying views while defining 'counselling'. One reason for these variations is the change in perceptions with the change of time.

Good in his 'Educational Dictionary' has defined counselling as an individualized and personalized assistance with personal, educational, vocational problems in which all pertinent facts are studied and analyzed, and a solution is sought, often with the assistance of specialists, school and community resources and personal interviews in which the counselee is taught to make his own decisions.

According to Robinson (1950), 'The term counselling covers all types of two-person situations in which one person, the client, is helped to adjust more effectively to himself and his environment'.

In others words, in counselling two individuals, the counsellor and the client or counselee, relate to each other.

An individual seeking counsel has certain problems and needs that he himself cannot redress and fulfill. For the resolution of these problems and the satisfaction of these needs, an individual requires scientific opinion. This scientific opinion or suggestion is called counselling.

Corroborating the above views, Hahn and MacLean (1955) say that a scientific suggestion can be given only by a counsellor who is adequately experienced and trained. According to Willy and Andrew: 'Counselling is a process of mutual learning'. In this process, there are two individuals—one seeking for help and the other trained one, who assists the first person in such a way as to ensure his optimum development.

Defining counselling, Rogers (1942) says, 'Counselling does not mean providing a service by means of which specific problem of an individual may be solved. The process should help the counselee in gaining clear insight into the problem and in achieving self-confidence'.

Brewer describes counselling as talking, conversing and carrying on a friendly dialogue. The main aim of this type of exchange of thought is to identify and develop an individual's potential.

According to Jones (1951), in the process of counselling all the relevant facts are gathered, student's experiences are studied, his capabilities are observed in a specific context and for the purpose of solving the problem, the youngster is provided direct and indirect assistance. But Jones also clarifies that a youngster's problems cannot be solved through counselling; he is rather enabled to solve them.

Erickson (1962), however, believes that the process of counselling is counselee centred. 'A counselling interview is a person to person relationship in which one individual with problem and needs turns to another person for assistance'. In this process of guidance, an individual can be assisted only through an interview and a personal contact.

In the views of Humphrey and Traxler: 'Counselling is the application of personnel resources of the school or other institution to the solution of the problems that individuals have'.

According to Arbuckle (1965), 'Counselling is a "human relationship", a warm relationship, in which the counsellor, fully and completely, without any ifs or buts, accepts the client as a worthy person'.

Characteristics of Counselling

From the study and analysis of the above, the following characteristics of counselling emerge.

(a) The process of counselling is related to two individuals—the client or the counselee and the counsellor.
(b) In counselling, the counsellor and the counslee or the client have a face-to-face contact.
(c) Solution of the problems is arrived through mutual discussion.
(d) The counsellor, being a trained person, finds out the problem and its importance in his counselle's life through his skilful questioning.
(e) The counsellor, through the process of counselling, makes the student vomit facts.
(f) Counselling is the active part of the entire process of guidance.
(g) Counselling is a learning-oriented process.
(h) Counselling helps in solving individuals' behavioural problems in which emotions and motivations are the main factors.
(i) Counselling helps individuals in overcoming or removing those inabilities and weaknesses which come in the way of their learning process.
(j) Counselling is both an educational and a vocational service.
(k) Counselling focuses on an individual's problems.

(l) Counselling is based on an interview.
(m) The process of counselling is a mutual effort.
(n) Counselling is possible only by a qualified and trained person.
(o) Counselling is possible in a cordial and cooperative environment.
(p) In counselling, effort is made to provide an opportunity to the individual to understand and solve his own problem.

Different Theories, Principles, Viewpoints and Types of Counselling

From the point of view of nature and role of counselling, there are three schools of thought.

(a) *Counsellor-Oriented Counselling*: This type of counselling is referred to as Directive Counselling, Counsellor-Oriented Counselling or Perspective Counselling.
(b) *Counselee-Oriented Counselling*: This type of counselling is referred to as Non-Directive, Client Centred or Permissive Counselling.
(c) *Counselling Equally Oriented to Both the Counsellor and the Counselee*: This type of counselling is referred to as Eclectic Counselling.

Counsellor-Oriented or Directive Counselling

In this process of counselling, counsellor plays the major role. He focuses his attention more on the problem than on the individual. The main exponent of this school of thought was E.G. Williamson (1950) of Minnesota University.

Directive counsellors accept the principle that nobody can do his own study impartially. It is for the purpose of an impartial study that a counsellor is needed.

The principle of directive counselling can be clearly explained on the basis of the following points.

(a) In this process, considerable responsibility is assumed by the counsellor. He leads the interview, investigates the problem, defines it, diagnoses it and suggests remedial measures.
   (i) *Analysis*: The counsellor gathers data using different techniques and tools, and analyze them. The tools used by the counsellor are: cumulative record, interview, autobiography, anecdotal narrative, psychological tests, case history, etc. It also includes family history, entertainment interests and habits.
   (ii) *Synthesis*: Synthesis is a sort of summarized or integrated mechanical and graphic juxtaposition of data obtained through analysis are used to improve client self-understanding and to service as a wide to the counsellor.
   (iii) *Diagnosis*: A youngster's problem is diagnosed after finding its causes. Diagnosis is an important step which helps in arriving at a decision after identifying the present status of the client is ascertained, and decisions are made for curse of action.
   (iv) *Interpretation*: The counsellor interprets for the client to aid him in gaining intellectual insights and understanding from which future progress and growth cab be realized. Purposeful questions are asked by the counsellor to stimulate the thinning of the client and to gain although this is client participation but decisions reached are of the counsellor but with the approval of client.
   (v) *Follow up*: Effectiveness of counselling is evaluated and the benefits derived by the counselee assessed.

(b) The counsellor places more emphasis on the counselee's intellectual aspect than on his emotional aspect.

(c) It is the counsellor who takes all the decisions about the counselee but it involves the counselee's consent also.
(d) In directive counselling, study of the counselee's past is equally important as his present problems. Different means are used to study his past but his future is determined by the counsellor.

Counselee-Oriented or Non-Directive Counselling

The client-oriented counselling revolves round the client or the counselee. In other words, in the non-directive counselling the focus is on the activities of the counselee. Exponent of this school of counselling was Carl R. Rogers (1951).

According to this principle, an individual is adequately endowed with the prowess to solve his own problems. A counsellor's duty is only to create a suitable environment so that the counselee by recognizing himself can grow, develop and face the real life situations. According to Rogers, directive counselling is non-psychological and ineffective because the focus of guidance is the individual rather than his problem.

Rogers has pointed out some characteristics of non-directive counselling.

(a) The objective of this counselling is to make the counsellor provide such environment in which a counselee is free to grow and shape his genius according to his will.
(b) In non-directive counselling, emotional and sentimental aspects are emphasized over intellectual aspects.
(c) Importance is attached to current problems. It has nothing to do with past problems. Hence, the counsellor does not study the counselee's life history.
(d) The therapeutic experiences provide the opportunity for the client and promote growth of the client.
(e) Non-directive counselling can be further elucidated on the basis of the following concepts:
    (i) Mutual relation of the counsellor and the counselee is emphasized, and this is the essence of counselling. The progress and benefit accruing to the counselee depend on these relations. The counsellor does not suggest any specific decision. The final decision is to be taken by the counselee. The counsellor generates an environment in which the counselee endeavours to find a solution by himself.
    (ii) In non-directive counselling, the counselee is given an opportunity to express his feelings freely. He obtains exact knowledge about his feelings and aptitudes which in turn helps in finding a realistic solution to the problem. Here, significance is attached to the expression of feelings while intellectual aspect is treated as secondary.
    (iii) Such relations get established between the counsellor and the counselee that the counselee feels relieved after giving vent to his suppressed feelings. This gives him emotional strength and he feels secure. In short, the counsellor generates such an environment that the counselee takes his own decisions. He does not leave the job of taking decision to the counsellor. This way the counselee is able to know himself properly.
    (iv) In non-directive counselling, there is no place for any kind of opinion, evaluation and diagnosis. Synthesis is given more importance.

William Schneider has expressed some extremely useful views to elucidate the nature of non-directive counselling. They are as follows.

(a) The counselee is free to determine his own life goals whatever be the opinion of the counsellor.
(b) For maximum satisfaction, the counselee chooses his objectives himself.

(c) Through counselling he is able to freely take his own decisions.
(d) Emotional conflict is the biggest hurdle in the way of proper adjustment.

According to Carl Rogers, there are some steps in the process of non-directive counselling. They are as follows.

(a) The counsellor defines the helpful situations.
(b) He places the counselee in a proper environment to enable him to express his feelings freely.
(c) The counsellor reorganizes and clarifies the counselee's acceptable and negative feelings.
(d) As self-realization gradually develops in the counselee, the counsellor goes on clarifying the counselee's emotions.
(e) At the end, the counsellor believes in what he is doing and has faith in the outcome.

Eclectic Counselling

The eclectic counselling is best characterized by freedom, the counsellor is not limited to only one operational view point or method.

The chief exponent of this school of counselling is F. C. Thorne (1950). In this process, the counsellor studies the needs and personality of a counselee. After this the counsellor selects the techniques which would be more useful and helpful for the counselee. The counsellor can start counselling with any method and after some time make amends in it as per the need. Eclectic counselling includes the useful elements of both the directive counselling and non-directive counselling methods.

In eclectic counselling, the counsellor should be professionally qualified and deft enough to use all the methods and techniques of counselling. In case he has to give up one method and adopt another for achieving the objective, he should be able to justify the situation and the rationale for the switchover.

According to Thorne, eclectic counselling has the following characteristics:

(a) In this process, those coordinative methods are used which are appropriate to both the counsellor and the counselee. These methods can be changed as per the needs of the counselee.
(b) Flexibility of techniques is the main feature of the permissive counselling process.
(c) The counsellor is totally free to choose methods and express feelings for the counselee.
(d) Stress is laid on providing opportunities to the counselee so that he himself can find a solution to his problem. The counsellor likewise makes adaptations and adjustment.

Limitations and Use of Psychological Tests in Counselling

In the course of counselling interview, the counsellor obtains some information about the counselee which help in understanding the problems of the counselee. In different sessions of the counselling interview, the counsellor needs some objective information as well. In such situations, the counsellor has to use psychological tests. Along with the psychological tests, the counsellor uses certain non-standard tests like case history, study of his environment, scrutiny, cumulative record, etc. The counsellor uses this information for diagnostic purpose.

Psychological tests are the first step to know a counselee. Counselling without obtaining adequate knowledge about a counselee's background and experiences is like attempting an impossible task. Thus, there is a close association between psychological tests and counselling. These psychological tests are used for diagnosing problems in different systems of counselling. Through diagnosis, basic causes of the problem are ascertained. After identifying these causes, the counsellor suggests solutions to the counselee.

Apart from this, information obtained through non-standard tests is also useful for understanding and diagnosing problems. In counselling it is also important to understand a counselee's personal adjustment, that is, his relations with his parents, friends, teachers, neighbours, etc. and the factors influencing his adjustment.

Psychological tests serve as a facilitator in elucidating the factors influencing adjustment. Psychological tests are also used for screening. Psychological tests assist the counsellor in the procures of therapy. Although the usefulness of psychological tests is significant yet these have certain limitations. These limitations are in the areas of validity, reliability, usefulness, etc. as described below.

(a) Psychological tests are designed for a specific community for specific use. But sometimes these are used for people and purposes for which they have not been designed.
(b) Psychological tests do not give comprehensive measurement. It is therefore suggested that instead of using a single test, it is desirable to combine a number of such test to give a composite score.
(c) Psychological tests are only a measuring tool. They cannot give any judgment.
(d) Psychological tests give scores that have to be interpreted in terms of certain norms.

Maximum use of psychological tests is made, apart from diagnosing problems, for evaluating the results of counselling process.

Psychological tests are also used for mapping future plans. In educational and vocational future planning, a counsellor uses different psychological tests for providing counselling according to the abilities, interests and wishes of the counselee.

Psychological tests are also used for segregating normal children from mentally deficient children or those with low IQ because children with low IQ have scant chance of succeeding in higher education. Hence, these children are provided counselling in different work areas according to their mental ability.

Summary

Counselling is of paramount importance in guidance. It is rather the heart of the process. Scholars have come out with widely varying views while defining 'counselling'. One reason for these variations is the change in perceptions with the change of time.

In counselling, two individuals, the counsellor and the counselee, relate to each other. An individual seeking counsel has certain problems and needs, for the resolution and satisfaction of which he requires scientific counselling.

The choice of counselling techniques should be related to the characteristics and personality of the individual. It is not necessary to use only one technique. From the point of view of nature and role of counselling, there are three broad techniques: (a) counsellor-oriented counselling, (b) counselee-oriented counselling and (c) counselling equally oriented to both the counsellor and the counselee.

In the course of counselling interview, the counsellor obtains detailed information about the counselee. Along with the psychological tests, the counsellor uses certain non-standard tests like case history, study of an individual's environment, scrutiny, cumulative record, etc. The counsellor uses this information for diagnostic purposes.

In educational and vocational future planning, a counsellor uses different psychological tests for providing counselling according to the abilities, interests and wishes of the counselee.

Psychological tests are also used for segregating normal children from mentally deficient children as well as those with above average IQ.

12

Process of Counselling

Counselling is a process in which the client or the counselee exchanges views with a trained counsellor for resolution of his problems.

Elements of Counselling Process

The process of counselling has three main elements:

(a) Objective of counselling
(b) Counselee
(c) Counsellor

The objectives for which counselling is initiated are achieved only when relations between the counsellor and the counselee are cordial and warm. Relations would be good only when there is mutual trust and respect between them. The counselee would express himself before the counsellor clearly and frankly only when counselling is carried out in a cordial and cooperative environment. The counsellor, being experienced and trained, will also try to understand the counselee's feelings from his facial expressions and body language.

For obtaining requisite information from the counselee, the counsellor should ask such questions and in such a way that the counselee does not feel any difficulty or hesitation while answering his questions.

For the development of relations between the counsellor and the counselee certain techniques have been developed. Normally these techniques are based on the techniques of developing human relations. Rogers and Wallen (1946) have described some counsellor-oriented techniques as under.

(a) *Questioning*: Questions should be framed in such a way that they go deep enough to help in understanding the causes of the problem.

(b) *Praise*: The counsellor should also praise the counselee from the point of view of predicative evaluation in order to develop self-confidence and a feeling of acceptance in him.
(c) *Criticism or Negative Evaluation*: The counsellor should also do negative evaluation of the counselee.
(d) *Interpretation*: After evaluating the details furnished by the counselee, the counsellor should tell him how different aspects of behaviour are inter-related. The counselee should also be encouraged to furnish those details which he has held back.
(e) *Advice and Suggestion*: The counsellor should indicate the course to be adopted and activities to be performed by the counselee for his development.
(f) *Persuasion*: The counsellor must explain the utility of the advice and suggestion offered to him. Examples of people who have followed the advice of the counsellor should be illustrated.
(g) *Identification*: The counsellor must identify with the counselee's experience to generate self-confidence in him.

Some of the techniques followed by the counsellor are as follows.

(a) *Silence*: In certain situations simply listening to a person without reacting is more productive. While the counselee narrates his problem the counsellor becomes a silent listener. This reassures the counselee that the counsellor is listening to his narration attentively and with interest and giving it a serious thought.
(b) *Acceptance*: While the counselee is presenting his problem to the counsellor, the counsellor should from time-to-time express his approval either through words or by gestures which would reassure the counselee that the counsellor is clearly understanding his problem and accepting it. But the counsellor should utter his approval in such a way that the counselee's flow is not interrupted. These words are 'all right', 'very good', 'yes', etc. Sometimes the counsellor just nods to show his approval.
(c) *Clarification*: On certain occasions, the counsellor should express clarification on the counselee's narration but care should be taken to ensure that the counselee does not get the impression that he is being forced to accept the clarification. Otherwise he will not be able to express his problems frankly and freely.
(d) *Restatement*: In restatement, the counsellor repeats only that statement which the counselee has made. He does not, however, interpolate any kind of amendment or clarification in the statement.
(e) *Expression of Feelings*: Sometimes the counselee is unable to put across his problems before the counsellor properly. In such a situation, the counsellor should restate the main points expressed by the counselee to reassure the counselee that he has properly understood his views.
(f) *Structuring*: The counsellor should succinctly clearly explain to the counselee to the nature of his relationship with him.
(g) *Approval*: The counselee presents different views about his problem. The counsellor approves some of them. The views that have been approved impress the counselee. The counselee is also impressed by the knowledge and personality of the counsellor. If the counsellor keeps on approving his views in between, then approval becomes ineffective. This fact should be borne in mind.
(h) *Asking Questions*: In order to encourage the counselee to express more views about his problems, the counsellor should ask him some questions. These questions should be asked only after the counselee has finished his narration.

(i) *Humour*: In order to soothe the counsellee's nerve and make the environment light and friendly, the counsellor should sprinkle a few doses of humour.
(j) *Assurance*: Assurance is the most significant, effective and psychological technique of counselling. It makes the counselee hopeful of the solution to his problem. Through assurance the counsellor, while accepting the counselee's narration, also lends support to it.

Steps in Counselling Procedure

Williamson and Darley (1937) have delineated six steps of counselling.

(a) *Analysis*: It is that process in which facts are gathered for the purpose of studying the individual.
(b) *Synthesis*: In this process the gathered information is organized.
(c) *Diagnosis*: The causes of problem are diagnosed.
(d) *Prognosis*: This is a pre-statement or opinion on the use of diagnosis.
(e) *Counselling*: This is the stage at which steps are taken by the counsellor and the counselee for adjustment.
(f) *Follow-up*: This is the stage at which effectiveness of the counsellor's services is evaluated and attempt is made to assist the counselee in solving his problems.

Interview for Clinical Counselling

It was H. B. Pepinski (1948) who first used the term 'clinical counselling'. Clinical counselling is related to an individual's maladjustments and it does not focus only on the personal problems of an individual but also takes into account the whole individual.

According to English and English (1958), the word 'clinical' is used in the context of studying an individual in his unique wholeness. Through this process his special behaviour can be scrutinized and his special characteristics treated as his essence, but the aim is to understand the individual concerned.

The aim of clinical counselling is to diagnose the problems associated with maladjustment and to resolve them. In clinical counselling, the relationship between the counsellor and the counselee is that of being face to face as individuals. The method used for achieving the objective is called counselling interview. It is the finest technique of counselling a student for the purpose of educational, vocational or personal guidance in order to resolve his problems. In a clinical interview, information about an individual's family environment is sought to diagnose his problem. In simple words, in a clinical interview attempt is made to identify the probable causes of an individual's problems. For this purpose, information about an individual's history, family relations and personal adjustment problems is gathered.

(a) Before initiating an interview, its purpose must be clearly identified and an inventory of items on which information is sought by the interviewer should be prepared beforehand.
(b) Much information about the student can be obtained from his cumulative record card.
(c) Environment should be congenial, with adequate lighting, air and humidity control. Time and date of an interview should be decided according to mutual convenience.
(d) Secrecy is the special feature of an interview. Only when secrecy is assured the counselee will express his views uninhibitedly. Hence, secrecy is sacred during an interview.
(e) Before initiating an interview, the appropriate counselling method should be decided.

(f) It is essential for an interviewer to be impartial, sympathetic, patient, pragmatic, logical, encouraging and trained.

According to Dorley, the success of an interview depends on four things.

(a) During an interview, the interviewer should neither give a sermon nor attempt to suppress the interviewee.
(b) The interviewer should use simple language and give only essential information to the interviewee.
(c) The interviewee should be apprised of the interviewer's expectation so that he can prepare himself accordingly.
(d) The interviewer should know about the interviewee's feelings and attitude so that there is no difficulty during the interview. Thus, it is clear that the interview method is helpful in obtaining information about an individual. The problems of an interviewer and interviewee can be understood in the context of their entirety. To sum up, it may be said that the objective of an interview is to resolve the counselee's problems through guidance. Clinical counselling helps in analyzing and diagnosing the problem of an individual.

For conducting an interview, certain rules have been framed. They are as follows.

(a) Whenever an individual or a candidate comes to an interviewer he is full of apprehensions, inhibition and hesitation. Hence, the interviewer should first of all try to be cordial with him and put him at ease. To make the environment friendly, he should talk to him about his areas of interest and aptitude so that the subject feels free to talk and answers the questions truthfully.
(b) Thereafter, an encouraging atmosphere should be created in which the interviewer should give the candidate freedom to talk. The interviewer should restrain from making any comments. This reassures the candidate that whatever he says would be accepted. During the conversation, the interviewer should express his sympathy so that the candidate looks upon him as his a well-wisher.
(c) A candidate comes to the interviewer with certain expectations. In such a situation, the interviewer should assure the candidate that all his problems can be resolved.
(d) To keep the atmosphere free of tension, humour should be interpolated in conversation so that the candidate answers the questions without any tension.
(e) During an interview, the interviewer and the interviewee should get equal amount of time to talk or else the usefulness of the interview is compromised and the objective is not achieved fully and properly.
(f) Questions asked in an interview should be inspiring in nature so that the candidate is encouraged to answer the questions. An attempt should also be made to understand the candidate as a whole.

Here, some other points to be kept in mind are as follows.

(a) The interview should be terminated by telling the candidate, 'The interview is over. You may please go now. I'll get back to you'.
(b) The way in which an activity ends influences its outcome.
(c) Before the interview is terminated, the candidate should be made to feel satisfied.
(d) The interview should be rounded off in such a way that the next interview can commence as soon as possible.
(e) Information obtained during an interview should be recorded immediately.

Post-Interview Contact

After counselling, its success is evaluated through follow-up. In follow-up, the counsellor should find out about the counselee's current status. He should have full information about it. While doing follow-up study the counsellor should keep three things in mind:

(a) How far has the counselee acted upon the counsellor's suggestions?
(b) How far is he successful in his present situation?
(c) In the context of new changes, does he need more assistance in his existing plan or in its restructuring?

To conduct the follow-up study, the counsellor obtains information about the counselee through correspondence, telephonic conversation, an interview or by discussion with the authorities.

Summary

The process of counselling has three main elements: (a) objective of counselling, (b) counselee and (c) counsellor. The objectives of counselling are achieved only when relation between the counsellor and the counselee is cordial and warm.

There are certain well-defined techniques for fostering cordial relations between the counsellor and the counselee. Among the important steps needed in the process of counselling are analysis, synthesis, diagnosis, prognosis, counselling and follow-up.

Counselling interview is the finest technique of counselling a student for the purpose of educational, vocational or personal guidance. For this purpose, information about an individual's history, family relations and personal adjustment problems is collated. Encouragement, appreciation and reassurance ensure satisfactory conclusion of an interview. Thereafter, the success of counselling is evaluated through follow-up.

13

Skill of the Counsellor

Success of counselling depends on the skill and proficiency of the counsellor.

Nature of the Counsellor

In the beginning instead of the word 'counsellor' the term 'guidance expert' was used. But around mid-nineteenth century the word 'counsellor' came into vogue.

A counsellor guides students in establishing correlation among different factors in the guidance process. The nature of a counsellor has been vividly discussed by different scholars. According to Jones, a counsellor is the individual whose job is to give counsel. This means the counsellor's job is simply to counsel and not to do anything else. Hence, no work other than counselling should be given to the counsellor. Keeping in view the nature of counsellor and the process of counselling, Jones has clarified the duties of a counsellor. According to him, the counsellor performs the following functions.

(a) He interprets the information about an individual's problems.
(b) He enables a counselee to solve his own problems.
(c) He listens to the problem attentively, investigates its causes and then offers counsel on how to resolve it.
(d) He creates awareness about the problems which are there but are not being recognized as such.
(e) He defines those problems which have been identified but not yet understood.
(f) He assists those individuals who have become maladjusted.

Steffler and Grant define a counsellor's role as under.

(a) A counsellor's objective is to gather information about students' abilities, talents, interests and capabilities, and to assist students in modifying their behaviour.

(b) The counsellor uses various techniques to gather the information about a student and his environment. Each thread of information is a source of numerous probabilities.
(c) The counsellor sometimes asks questions with a view to clearly understanding his behaviour. These questions are also designed to accelerate the process of the subject understanding himself. Questions should be asked in such a manner that helps in arriving at the root of the problem.
(d) The counsellor while conversing with a student listens to his talk very attentively and also gives temporary consent by using words like 'yes', 'all right', 'very good', etc. These temporary consensual gestures assure the student that the counsellor clearly understands him. At times the counsellor makes necessary suggestions also. Routine suggestions are made at the start of the interview. Specific suggestions are made later.
(e) The counsellor also helps the student to understand himself by giving him information related to his personality, social values, selective psychological hints, etc.
(f) The counsellor also provides the student information about social environment such as job opportunities, schools, financial sources, community facilities and services, training programmes, guidance for progress, changing social values, various opportunities, the country and the world at large.
(g) The counsellor also functions as a consultant. He may advise the student about delaying his decision, taking a tentative decision, appearing in an exam, etc. This helps a student in taking his own decision.
(h) The counsellor can also use psychological tests for gathering information about a student. He can also obtain specific information about him through others like his parents, teachers and confidential conversation with his friends. The objective of this confidential conversation is to provide him effective counselling.
(i) Another important task of a counsellor is to gather standard data. Data obtained from any test are meaningless unless it is test compared with the data of an individual with known abilities. Many standards are available for these tests. The counsellor has to decide which standard would be appropriate for the purpose of comparison. Sometimes the appropriate standard is not available. In such a situation, the counsellor has to decide the ways to obtain the standard data. Standard data may be needed for customary indicators as well.

According to Myers, a counsellor should perform the following functions.

(a) Fixing the meeting time.
(b) Making arrangement for the meeting.
(c) Preparing for the meeting.
(d) Attending the meeting.
(e) Keeping record of the meeting.

Stewart has outlined the following functions of a counsellor.

(a) Understanding the needs and problems of the student.
(b) Assisting the student in ascertaining the value of his experiences.
(c) Gathering necessary information about the student.
(d) Meeting with the student.
(e) Striking harmony between the school and the family, and between the school and the class.
(f) With reference to education striking, harmony between progress and socialization.
(g) Providing group guidance.

Based on various research findings Cox has identified the following characteristics of a successful counsellor:

(a) Fairness
(b) Sincerity
(c) Good personality
(d) Good character and wholesome philosophy
(e) Common sense
(f) Good physical and mental health
(g) Emotional stability
(h) Approachability
(i) Ability to get along with people
(j) Sympathetic understanding
(k) Interest in people
(l) Understanding people different from self
(m) Flexibility and adaptability
(n) Intelligence and mental alertness
(o) Broader background of knowledge
(p) Leadership
(q) Awareness of one's own limitations
(r) Understanding of classroom conditions
(s) Understanding of working conditions
(t) Understanding of social and economic conditions

Professional Dedication of a Counsellor

It is essential for a counsellor to be fully dedicated to his profession only then he will be successful in his work. The sense of dedication can be identified on the basis of the following elements.

(a) Professional aptitude
(b) Professional attitude
(c) Sense of mission
(d) Loyalty and enthusiasm to the cause of education
(e) Strong sense of professional ethics
(f) Professional growth
(g) Desire to do some extra work
(h) Taking interest in counselling

A vocational counsellor can do the following six things by using his qualifications.

(a) Providing free educational and vocational counselling to students at a social centre or a community supported agency.
(b) A vocational counsellor selects suitable tests for the applicants and makes arrangement for those tests.
(c) Participates in professional seminars along with other counsellors and elucidates the conclusions arrived at.
(d) Provides counselling on the basis of interviews, results of tests and professional seminars.
(e) Identifies suitable job opportunities for the counselees interested in placement, according to their abilities, interests and capabilities, and suggests them which employment authorities to contact.

(f) With a view to assisting the counselees he sends them to social welfare and employment agencies. He also recommends the counselees to concerned agencies for financial, medical, legal and any other type of assistance.
(g) With the cooperation of other persons, he sponsors programmes for their improvement and expansion. He also participates in research projects and activities of professional bodies.
(h) Provides group guidance for vocational adjustment problems of the youth.

The counsellor while doing his work should also ensure that the counselee is making steady progress in his vocation.

(a) When the counsellor speaks to teachers, administrators or other persons about his services and experiences, he should ensure that his presentation is in conformity with the situation.
(b) He should not do anything that is beyond his competence.
(c) The counsellor is a part and parcel of the school. Hence, he should fulfill his obligations with full dedication.
(d) The counsellor should offer his services without any distinction of caste, creed, economic and social status.
(e) If the counsellor is bogged down by immense workload then he should intimate the concerned administrative authority. Till such time as assistance comes he should prioritize his duty on the basis of priority.
(f) The counsellor should continue to achieve his professional growth by actively participating in the activities of allied professional bodies.
(g) When a counsellor is associated with an educational institution he should abide by its rules and regulations.
(h) A counsellor should not take up any responsibility that may go against his professional interests and ethics.
(i) A counsellor should associate himself with such research activities which may contribute to his professional growth and development.

Preparation

Guidance and counselling are highly professional tasks, and therefore, proper professional training is required for counsellors. From the professional point of view, the counsellor should have adequate knowledge of principles of guidance and applied psychology. Along with the experience in guidance and counselling, he should have knowledge of other areas of psychology as well.

Froehlich, in his report, has detailed the psychology lessons that should be studied by the counsellors. The kind of training a counsellor ought to undergo should be determined by his nature of the job. The plan for all counselling training programmes should be prepared on the basis of this principle.

Determination of different functions of a counsellor depends on the area of his specialization. For tasks which are common to all the areas of counselling, a counsellor needs only basic training for them. But before this training, a counsellor must have a thorough knowledge of psychology.

The Counsellors' Training Committee of Guidance Psychologists Division of American Psychology Society has accepted that counsellors should have training in all of the following areas of psychology.

(a) Foundations of psychology
(b) Growth and development

(c) Nature and importance of individual differences
(d) Principles of learning and their use in other fields of psychology and education
(e) Personality development and mental hygiene
(f) Testing and non-testing techniques
(g) Procedures and principles of counselling
(h) Practice of counselling and diagnosis
(i) Research methods and statistics

Certification of Counsellor

The certificate to practise as a counsellor is granted on the basis of his qualification and training. A counsellor's job is not only to resolve educational and vocational problems but also to offer solutions to all kinds of behavioural problems. Apart from this, a counsellor's job is also to gather and disseminate educational and career information. To this end he should have a close liaison with various institutions and employment agencies for the purpose of maintaining an up to date and reliable database.

In India, a Master's degree in psychology or education is a prerequisite for getting the professional training of a counsellor. These training courses were available in the Department of Educational Psychology and Foundation of Education of NCERT, New Delhi, Institute of Vocational Guidance and Selection, Bombay, Bureau of Psychology, Allahabad, Punjab University, Chandigarh, College of Educational Psychology and Guidance, Jabalpur, and Department of Education, MS University, Vadodra. With effect from the year 2000, the NCERT has delegated the work of guidance professionals training to regional institutes of guidance at Ajmer, Bhopal, Bhuvaneshwar and Mysore.

In 1993, NCERT and IGNOU signed a Memorandum of Understanding that they will collaborate to offer diploma programmes in guidance. IGNOU has also launched a certificate course in guidance for teachers, parents and child managers.

In addition, every counsellor must possess certain personal qualities. Different scholars have given different lists—enumerating abilities for a counsellor. But Professional Standards Committee of the American College Association has furnished the best list. It has been clearly described by Andrew and Willey. According to this list, a counsellor must possess the following personal qualities:

(a) Socializing interest in people, respect for others' needs, general knowledge
(b) Leadership quality decision taking ability, self-reliance
(c) Team spirit
(d) Friendliness
(e) Warm behaviour
(f) Impressive personality
(g) Self-confidence
(h) Strong religious and moral beliefs

Attitude and Skill of a Counsellor

In the context of a counsellor's attitude and competence, Steffler and Stewart have mentioned some of the essential qualities required in him. They are as follows.

(a) *Ethical Behaviour*: A counsellor's main quality is his commitment to ethical values. Maintaining secrecy and limiting the confidential information to himself is the prime duty of a good counsellor. Unless a counselee has full faith in the counselor, he will remain shy and will be unable to establish a cooperative relationship with the counselor.

(b) *Intellectual Competence*: For the success of counselling process, it is essential for a counsellor to be intellectually competent. He should have the ability to link an individual's behaviour and present incidents. Moreover, he should have logical thinking.

(c) *Flexibility*: A counsellor should not be strict and adamant. He should keep himself aware of the changes taking place in the counselee's thought process. He should change his strategy in keeping with the changes of his counselee.

(d) *Sensitivity*: A counsellor should be sincere and sensitive towards his job. In order to be impartial in the conduct of his duties it is important that a counsellor should be honest and aware of his responsibilities. Only then he will be able to discharge his duty with devotion and justice.

(e) *Acceptance*: Accepting every statement of the counselee is the characteristic of a counsellor. When a counselee comes to a counsellor for counselling, he is a bundle of disappointments, worries, fear and suspicions. In such a situation, a counsellor should accept the counselee's narration.

(f) *Understanding*: The counsellor should try to understand the counselee at emotional and thinking level. A counsellor can relate himself to the counselee at both these levels. When the counselee begins feeling that the counsellor is accepting him, giving importance to his persona and is serious and patient towards his views, he feels free to express his hitherto deeply inhibited emotions and views before him. His hesitation evaporates. These very views and emotions can serve the basis for his adjustment. Thereafter, the counsellor can assist the counselee in understanding and accepting himself.

Summary

It is essential for a counsellor to be totally committed to his profession. Only then he will be successful in his work. The sense of dedication can be identified on the basis of the following elements.

(a) Professional aptitude, (b) professional attitude, (c) sense of mission, (d) loyalty and enthusiasm to the cause of education, (e) strong sense of professional ethics, (f) professional growth, (g) desire to do some extra work and (h) taking interest in counselling.

The counsellor while doing his work should also ensure that the counselee is making steady progress in his vocation. From the professional point of view, the counsellor should have adequate knowledge of the principles of guidance and applied psychology. Moreover, a counsellor should be deft in resolving all kinds of behavioural problems.

A counsellor must possess the following personal qualities.

(a) Socializing, interest in people, respect for others' needs, general knowledge, (b) leadership quality, decision taking ability, self-reliance, (c) team spirit, (d) friendliness, (e) warm behaviour, (f) impressive personality, (g) self-confidence and (h) strong ethical and moral beliefs.

14

Group Counselling

Man is a social animal. He is instinctively inclined to live in a group or a community. This instinctive need first manifested itself when man started living as a family for security reasons. Hence, family is one basic group that influences an individual's life. An individual's behaviour with others in society and his relations with others, to a large extent, depend on his experiences of family life.

What is a Group?

Modern man is a member of numerous social groups and communities in which he has trust and gives expression to himself. Of some groups he is an active member while in others he has a notional representation. Equally true is the fact that an individual does not behave in the same manner in all the groups. An individual behaves differently in different groups. According to psychologists, group behaviour depends on group's composition and the stability of its norms. Hence, for group counselling it is necessary to gain insight into the group's nature and type.

According to Jane Warters: 'Common purposes, satisfaction of individual needs, interaction and interdependence of members are conditions essential to the existence of a functional group'.

In the opinion of W.J.H. Sprot (1958), 'they are marked out in terms of differential social intercourse, their members have a consciousness of membership which may persist even when intercourse with co-members has ceased, as with an Englishman living abroad, they are purposive though their purposes differ from one group to another, and they have standards of conduct in some ways common to many, in some ways peculiar to each'.

If we study the definition of a group, we will find that when there is an association between two or more individuals and they are engaged in social and psychological interaction then they constitute a group. In the opinion of MacIver and Page (1961), 'A group is any collection of human beings who are brought into social relationships with one another'. Psychologist Cemp writes in his book, 'Foundations of Group Counselling': 'Persons in all walks of life sense the need for meaningful relationship and many look to it as the means of gaining new understanding regarding the significance and purpose of life itself. Hence, the interest and increase in the use of what is now known as group counselling'.

Objectives of Group Counselling

Knowing Each Member's Objectives: In group counselling, the most important thing for a counsellor is to know about each member's objective or goal. Only after acquiring this information a counsellor can make group counselling successful.

Organizational Decisions: Counselling can be made more effective only when a counsellor gives due importance to organizational decisions in the process.

Group counselling has some basic objectives which must be taken into consideration. These objectives are as follows.

Self-awareness: The main objective of group counselling is to make an individual aware of his abilities and capabilities. Many individuals are unaware of their capabilities or they know very little about them. For this reason, they cannot take advantage of the experiences of a group life. Through group counselling, the individual is made capable of recognizing his real abilities and capabilities in comparison to others and removing his shortcomings.

Recognizing Possibilities: An individual has many inherent strengths. He discovers the possibilities of their development while working in a group. An individual achieves success in future by working according to these possibilities. From this point of view, group counselling is useful.

Effect of Individual Differences: Group counselling does not mean that there is no place for individual differences in it. In certain groups, individuals' problems can be similar but still they may be different at individual level. Hence, group counselling can be useful only if the counsellor conducts it keeping individual differences in view.

Group Experience in Developmental Process: An individual is a social being and his development can be taken well care of on the basis of experience gained in group activities carried out in social environment. In a society or a group, he develops such inter-relationships which assist in his all-round development.

Identifying Students Requiring Extra Help: It is easier to identify students who need individual assistance more than others. Here, it is the duty of the counsellor to be aware about such students and invite them for individual counselling.

Promoting a Spirit of Cooperation and Teamwork: In group counselling, students get a chance to meet each other and have verbal discussions. This generates a feeling of cooperation and teamwork.

Identifying with Others: In group counselling, students get an opportunity to deliberate over their interests, emotions, desires as well as problems. While doing so they realize that most of the problems they are facing are also faced by others of their age. This kind of realization helps reinforce and enhance their self-confidence.

Counsellor's Professional Gain

Through the medium of group counselling, the counsellor comes in contact with various students. As a result, the knowledge of his students' varied needs and problems provides him the inspiration and encouragement to rehash and refine his programmes.

In an educational institution, there are a number of students with similar problems. In such a situation providing counselling to each one of them separately is certainly a waste of time and resources. Hence, the idea of providing counselling to groups was conceived.

Another reason for constituting a group for counselling is that the number of students in educational institutions is increasing day by day. It becomes well-nigh impossible for a counsellor to study all the cases individually and give his suggestions. Another reason for group counselling is the short supply of qualified and trained counsellors.

When students suffering from maladjustment are provided counselling in groups it enhances their sociability. A group also influences students' attitudes. Some students are extra sentimental. They lose their mental balance over minor remarks made by their friends. A group helps them to keep control over their sentiments and retain their mental balance. In brief, it may be said that group situations help in the development of students' personality.

Types of Groups

Types of groups studied on the basis of social equations are as follows.

(a) *Primary Group*: In a primary group, there is a close and evident relationship and cooperation between the members. In primary group, members are fewer in numbers and more of friendliness, compassion and family feeling is found in this group.

From the study of primary groups, that is, family, neighbourhood, etc. it has been found that only those groups can be treated as basic in which there is a physical proximity. In other words, members of a primary group live close to each other. Being few in number, they are successful in maintaining close relationship with each other. Relationship of members in a basic group is permanent and there is more continuity and stability among them. Being committed to same objectives, there is a firm unity. For this reason, each member tries that his relationship with the others is at an individual level. Hence, there is informality in their relationship. They try not to do anything that might hurt the family interests.

(b) *Secondary Group*: Secondary group is found in developed societies. There need not be similarity among different members. While one member enjoys a high social status another one might be of low social status. Political parties, business associations, etc. are the examples of the secondary group. They are more significant in such societies whose economies are based on big industrial and business conglomerates. In secondary groups, the number of members is large and their relations are primarily indirect and formal. Due to lack of physical proximity, relations do not grow close. In other words, when physical nearness among members decreases, closeness also decreases.

Forming a group

While forming a group the counsellor has to choose its members. Some of the criteria for choosing the members are as follows.

Age of Members: The age of members selected to form a group should be more or less the same.

Form of the Group: Consideration must be given to the form of the group which group depends on the maturity of the counselees and the nature of their problems.

How to Initiate: For initiating group counselling, the counsellor must make a clear appraisal of his as well as the members' roles. The problems to be discussed in group counselling should be related to all members of the group. They should be adequately aware of the subjects, only then they will enthusiastically participate in it. The counsellor should enthuse among all the members the spirit to actively participate in the discussion.

Developing Relations: As the group grows in number, the possibilities of a member straying away from his main goal and becoming sceptical about objectives also loom large. In such a situation it is the counsellor's responsibility to keep reminding the members of their main goal and objectives. The counsellor should be sincere and impartial towards all members in order to reassure them that he is ever ready to assist them.

Expulsion from the Group: The rate of progress among different members of a group varies. Some members achieve the objective, some others inch towards it while the rest members make adequate progress to achieve the objective. In such a situation, the counsellor has to take a decision whether only a few members would walk away or the entire group should be wound up. The counsellor's insistence on the members to remain committed to their objective is also a sort of pressure.

If some active members are separated from the group their relations with other members would cease. As a result, effectiveness of counselling would suffer. If new members are included in the group then due to the problem of mutual mistrust there is a possibility of the group's effectiveness suffering. Therefore, while sending out some members of the group or taking in new members, the counsellor would do better to take into consideration the needs of the remaining members. He should reconstitute the group only with the consent of both the old and the new members. He should also ensure that all of them can together achieve the specified objective within the stipulated time span.

Evaluation: The final step in counselling is the evaluation of its effectiveness. But it is not possible through scrutiny or through rating of their colleagues by members of the group. Hence, the counsellor should carry out appraisal of the objectives in such a way that they become measurable.

Investigating the usefulness of group counselling is very important. Hence, the role of the counsellor in group counselling is of great significance. The counsellor should be so skilled in group counselling that he creates an atmosphere in which each member of the group proves successful in the attainment of his objective.

Responsibility of Group Members

In group counselling, performance of a group depends on the members of the group and the counsellor. The development of any group takes place on the basis of its common objectives and interests. The attainment of these objectives and interests depends on the spirit of cooperation among its members. Only group in which all members participate whole heartedly with firm commitment is considered as being successful.

(a) All members in a group are different from each other but it is the oneness of the objective that unites them. Hence, inspired by this spirit of unity they are sympathetic towards each other.

(b) When a group is formed its members start determining their respective roles in conformity with the objectives of the group. All members of the group do not have to perform similar work. For the attainment of objectives determined by the group, different things need to be done. Hence, each member of a group contributes according to his ability and potential. But in the beginning, there are certain members who want to impress the group. At the same time, there are members who are eager to do something that might benefit the group.

After sometime when members of the group start expressing their views and emotions freely tension vanishes. Now they try to understand each other's point of view and strike a rapprochement. Still there remain some who are not in favour of any kind of rapprochement and like to opt out.

The spirit of cooperation among members surfaces only after the initial tension and differences have subsided. Now they want to work with each other in close harmony. Group mobility is an evidence of the fact that no group can come into its own without some tension and differences. It blossoms only from difficulties encountered in the formative period. A good counsellor should have the knowledge of the aims and direction of different members of the group. He should infuse courage, friendliness, truthfulness, the ability to take decision, discreetness and faith in them.

(c) A counsellor should have the ability to motivate members of the group and rekindle their interests.
(d) A counsellor should be quite observant to ascertain the characteristics and normal state of different groups.
(e) A counsellor should have the ability to predict the results of different groups so that he can make necessary revision.
(f) A counsellor should be skilled, flexible and alert in his work.
(g) A counsellor should be able to bring together the different members of the group.
(h) A counsellor should be endowed with the vision to identify topics for discussion.
(i) A counsellor should be committed to the welfare of the group members.
(j) A counsellor should be emotionally involved in his job.
(k) A counsellor should create such favourable conditions in the group that at the end every member achieves his objective successfully.

Thus, group counselling is like a close inter-personal activity. In group counselling, attention is paid to instant inter-personal relations between one member and the other. Group members are able to understand each other through different roles.

Group counselling is successful to the extent to which members interact with each other during exchange of views, and the degree of their self-awareness. It enables an individual to understand himself and make his place in society.

Summary

Modern man is a member of numerous social groups. In an educational institution, there are a number of students with similar problems. In such a situation providing counselling to each one of them individually looks farcical. Moreover, when students suffering from maladjustment are provided counselling in groups it enhances their sociability.

Types of groups are studied on the basis of social equations. There are two main types of groups as (a) primary groups and (b) secondary groups.

In a primary group, there is close and evident relationship and cooperation. Members are few in numbers and there more of friendliness, compassion and family feeling is found. Secondary group is found in developed societies. There need not be similarity among different members.

In group counselling, it is important for a counsellor to know about each member's objective or goal. Only after acquiring this information a counsellor can make group counselling successful. Investigating the usefulness of group counselling is also very important in order that the hurdles and problems encountered in the course of counselling may be considered.

Development of any group takes place on the basis of its common objectives and interests. The attainment of these objectives and interests depends on the spirit of cooperation among its members. The process of group counselling is successful to the extent to which members interact with each other during exchange of views.

15

Modern Trends in Counselling

Counselling is concerned with the problems related to different areas of life. The different problems of individuals require different types of counselling.

Counselling and Psychotherapy

Counselling is concerned with normal beings. Counselling helps in understanding problems related to adjustment. Whereas, psychotherapy, is concerned with individuals having serious behavioural problems and deeper emotional disturbance.

In counselling, for gathering information about an individual, testing and non-testing techniques are used. But in psychotherapy, modern techniques like ply therapy, psycho-drama, finger painting therapy, socio-drama, etc. are also used to make individuals express their suppressed emotions.

Operational area of counselling is very extensive while that of psychotherapy is deep. Psychotherapy deals with limited problems but to know their causes it goes into depth. A counsellor cannot be a psychotherapist but a psychotherapist can become a good counsellor. The counsellor sends individuals of serious nature to a psychotherapist.

In psychotherapy, a psychotherapist treats mental disorders, especially psycho-neurotic ones, through psychological techniques. The main aim of counselling is to assist an individual in solving his problems, and thereby help in the development of his personality. The objective of psychotherapy, on the other hand, is to transform an individual so that he can face not only present but can also face future problems.

According to Shaw, counselling should be related to creative assistance while psychotherapy should be related to mental disorders. On the other hand, Tyler (1953) defines counselling as a process of making an individual understand himself more clearly. But psychotherapy attempts at changing the basic developmental structure.

Psychotherapy is related to reconstructive goals while counselling is concerned with re-educative and supportive goals. It means counselling intends to make individuals more self-directed and autonomous. Concerned with psychological development of the individual which contributes to

Table 15.1 Difference Between Counselling and Psychotherapy

Counselling	Psychotherapy
(1) Counselling helps in understanding and resolving adjustment problems of normal human beings.	Psychotherapy helps in understanding and resolving behavioral problems of abnormal human beings.
(2) Counselling needs educational settings	Psychotherapy needs medical settings.
(3) Operational area of counselling is very extensive.	Operational area of psychotherapy is deep.
(4) An individual understand himself more clearly (self-directed and autonomous).	Psychotherapy attempts to change the basic developmental structure.
(5) Counselling is concerned with re-educative and supportive goals.	Psychotherapy is concerned with re-constructive goals.
(6) Counselling takes much less time.	Psychotherapy takes much more time.
(7) In counselling, more of suggestion and advising.	Psychotherapy diagnosis interpretation and treatment.
(8) Cognition and rational factors are their in treatments.	Greater distortion of reality and cognition and rational factors not much avail.

the total development here as in psychotherapy, psycho pathology was involved and clinical treatment was only the remedy counselling which is related to immediate situations. Psychotherapy is concerned with complete alteration of basic character structure.

Counselling takes much less time than psychotherapy. In counselling, psychological tests are used while in psychotherapy, case history is taken into account.

In counselling, there is more of suggestion than interference while psychotherapy diagnoses the problem.

Counselling is an assistance provided by the counsellor to the counselee. In psychotherapy, the problem is diagnosed and treated by a psychotherapist.

Acting Strategies in Counselling Psychology: In these methods, the counselee is encouraged to act out his feelings, problems and struggles under controlled stage conditions. After identifying the counselee's problems, the counsellor gives the counselee a chance to participate in an imaginary role. In the play, the counselee selects one particular role according to his own choice depicting his problems and expresses his feelings of anger, hatred, happiness, jealousy, struggle, etc. The counselee gets so engrossed in acting that he has no inhibition about making any gesture. Through this acting his suppressed emotions find an outlet and he feels relieved.

By this strategy, the counsellor obtains information about incidents in a counselee's life which otherwise cannot be ascertained in conscious state. An acting strategy can be used in individual cases as well as for groups.

In group acting, there are various roles out of which a counselee can select a role of his liking. Group acting helps the counselee to become self-confident. When the counselee participates in a group activity it promotes his individual as well as social development.

Role of a Counsellor

The role of a counsellor has been elucidated as follows.

(a) A counsellor's job is to assist an individual in solving his personal, educational and vocational problems by making him aware of himself and his environment.

(b) He assists a teacher in enhancing his sensitivity towards understanding students' development related problems.
(c) A counsellor's job is to use psychological concepts of learning for solving an individual's problems.
(d) A counsellor can give advice to higher institutes of learning for effective change in their teaching methods.
(e) Counselling service should be used for problem solving in other spheres of life also.
(f) A counsellor should pay special attention towards those children who consistently underperform in their examinations. They stand in big need of counselling.
(g) A counsellor's duty is also to assist students in bringing about change in their behaviour through learning. Students want to know more and more about their characteristics, abilities and interests, so they should be informed about the utility of knowledge in bringing about change in their total behaviour.
(h) Among the most sensitive issues of modern society is the increasing adjustment problems of old age. Here too a counsellor's help can go a long way.

A counsellor should also keep some practical aspects in view which are as follows.

(a) A counsellor should work only in his own sphere of activity.
(b) He should not impose any problem over the counselee. He should rather assist him in solving his problems with the help of various problem solving tools.
(c) Before closing the doors to education and vocation, a counsellor should open other doors for the counselee.
(d) A counsellor should not impose his views on the counselee.
(e) A counsellor should remain in control of himself. He should not express surprise, nonacceptance or formal acceptance nor should he get easily agitated. Instead of applying his own moral yardstick to the counselee, he should endeavour to assist him in understanding and accepting himself on a practical plane.
(f) He should open up all possibilities before the counselee.
(g) The final decision is to be taken by the counselee. Hence, he should look at the counselee's problems from all angles.

Keeping these facts in view, a counsellor should:

(a) Collect data regarding the counselee.
(b) Gather data about different vocations.
(c) Gather information about different types of education, educational institutions and training facilities.
(d) Organize seminars.
(e) Establish social contacts.
(f) Do follow-up.
(g) Obtain appropriate approval and implementation.
(h) Create appropriate physical conditions and services.

Apart from this, a counsellor's contribution is also significant in terms of organizing, developing and co-ordinating guidance activities.

Role of Other Members

Role of a Clinical Psychologist: From the point of view of achieving students' all-round personality development, a psychotherapist role is crucial in education. Because of individual and environmental differences, many students become problem children. For instance, a boy keeps fighting with his playmates, another boy steals his friends' goods, a third boy is very quiet and shies away from talking. A psychotherapist helps a teacher in identifying and diagnosing these cases, making the guidance programme successful.

Role of Medical Staff: In case of individual guidance, medical problems occupy an important place. Physical illness affects mental development. Thus, doctors and nurses play an important role. A physician advises children about correct diet and exercise. He also teaches them about first aid so that it can be used when needed. A doctor should carry out complete medical test of each student twice a year and its outcome should be recorded in a student's cumulative record card. Parents and guardians should be given timely intimation about their wards' health status, so that necessary preventive and therapeutic measures may be taken.

Values of Counselling

Counselling has been prevalent in human society in one form or the other ancient times immemorial. With the change of time and social values, complexity of human problems has gradually grown. This in the nature of counselling has brought about a change.

Modern age has become very complex and distressful from economic, social, religious and moral angles. Because of changing value system the sphere, nature, size and the very meaning of counselling have changed, posing new problems for counsellors.

Hence, before deciding how to do counselling, it is necessary to ascertain the meaning of counselling today, what are the social values and mores? If we look at the joint family system, we find that its character has changed. Earlier, individuals in a joint family had a feeling of financial and social security. In nuclear families, the feeling of security has given place to problems and apprehensions. As a result, we see moving bundles of tension and worry around us.

The Three-dimensional Model

In the present age, work sphere of a trained counsellor has changed according to different situations, such as individual counselling, group counselling, educational counselling, vocational counselling and marriage counselling. The type of counselling depends on the nature of the problem of the counselee. The interpretation of different theories of counselling can be done only on the basis of affirmation of correlation of events, which can be verified within specified parameters. From this it is clear that neither counselling's new concepts like group counselling, micro counselling, etc. nor counsellor's new functional areas like vocational counselling career counselling, etc. fall under any unified conceptual pattern. There is no theoretical model conceived to provide for the integration of the expanding of activities of the increasing number of counsellors within a single conceptual framework. In this context, a group of counsellors in Western Inter State Commission for Higher Education is engaged in working out one. They have arrived at significant conclusions in this respect.

Clyde Parker propounded a three-dimensional framework in 1974. This model was recognized to be of both practical as well as of heuristic value. For quite some time, it was being believed that counselling is a face-to-face contact between two individuals—the counsellor and the counselee—in which the counsellor assists the counselee in understanding himself. According to this concept, the counsellor is under pressure to save time and money but at the same time he has to ensure maximum effectiveness. This consideration led to the development of group counselling.

The first dimension is the level at which counselling is done. In the beginning, counselling was done at an individual level. Now its nature has changed and it is done in basic groups, common interest groups and at community level. Individual counselling is done to resolve personal problems. In a basic group, counselling is restricted to a family or to a group of 8–10 people in which assistance is given for achievement of specific objectives.

Sometimes the counsellor has to give counselling to a secondary group, like resolving of students' problems in a class. Apart from this, the counsellor has to help out members of a community in identifying and resolving their problems.

The second dimension, or objective of counselling done at these four levels, is solution, prevention, acquisition and development.

The third dimension of a counsellor's work is the selection of methods. These are as follows.

(a) Traditional or direct services.
(b) Consultation and training.
(c) Media approach.

In the modern age, the trained counsellors provide assistance to individuals through different techniques. The third method of providing assistance to community is through different media, like newspapers, magazines, books, films, television, etc.

Three dimensions of a counsellor's work are as follows.

(a) Who is the target of counselling?
Individual, Primary Group, Secondary or Common Interest Group, Community
(b) What are the objectives of counselling?
Solution, Prevention, Acquisition, Development
(c) What are the techniques to be used for counselling?
Direct Service, Consultation media approach

Robinson has expressed his views about the counselee in the context of these three dimensions as under.

(a) *Preparing the Counselee*: According to Robinson, a counselee does not get easily drawn to counselling. Hence, he has to be motivated. For attracting a counselee, he is to be called and a suitable environment should be created so that when he needs assistance he comes on his own without hesitation.

Occasions for talking to the counselee should be selected carefully so that he can place his views before the counsellor without any hesitation.

A counsellor's behaviour towards the counselee should be such that it instils in him an insight to understand his own nature and strike adjustment with the outer world.

(b) *Development of Insight in the Counselee*: Ordinarily, a counselee is not much aware about the different aspects of his life that he may be able to comprehend different situations and accept them. Secondly, a counselee at times is unable to develop a practical point of view. He also interprets his behaviour wrongly. Hence, a counselee needs insight from all these three points of view. The counsellor should assist the counselee in developing this insight.

(c) *Growth of the Counselee*: Inherent within every counselee is certain ability and possibility of development. Exploiting this very aspect of a counselee is called counselling. When insight gets developed a counselee becomes capable of making plans for the future and implementing them. At the end, a counselee does not need assistance any more and snaps the link.

But in the present scenario, when dramatic changes like global competition, information technology, shift from vertically integrated hierarchies to networks of specialists, are affecting the world, our value systems too are changing. This is creating problems for Guidance Psychologists and Counsellors. They have to decide the values to beheld and rules to follow. A counsellor is supposed to be a culture interpreter, culture mediator and an agent of culture change. As such he must lead the change rather than follow it. For this, he requires a break from traditional practices and focus on emerging trends.

Summary

In the present age, work sphere of a trained counsellor has changed. For quite some time, it was being believed that counselling is a face-to-face contact between two individuals—the counsellor and the counselee.

However, in 1974, Clyde Parker propounded a three-dimensional framework. According to this concept, the counsellor is under pressure to save time and money but at the same time he must ensure maximum effectiveness. This consideration led to the development of group counselling.

Three dimensions of a counsellor's work are as follows.

(a) Who is the target of counselling?
Individual, Primary Group, Secondary or Common Interest Group, Community

(b) What are the objectives of counselling?
Solution, Prevention, Acquisition, Development

(c) What are the techniques to be used for counselling?
Direct Service, Consultation and training, Media approach

Of late, psychotherapy too is being increasingly applied as an interventional technique. Normally, counselling helps in understanding and resolving adjustment problems of normal human beings; while understanding and resolving adjustment problems of abnormal individuals comes under the ambit of psychotherapy. Psychotherapy needs medical setting while counselling needs educational setting. Operational area of counselling is very extensive while that of psychotherapy is deep.

A counsellor cannot be a psychotherapist whereas a psychotherapist can become a good counsellor. While the main aim of counselling is to assist an individual in solving his problems to ensure the development of his personality, the objective of psychotherapy is to transform an individual to enable him to face his problems. Psychotherapy is related to reconstructive goals while counselling is concerned with re-educative and supportive goals.

Annexure

State Guidance Agencies in India

Educational and Vocational Guidance Bureau (Science Branch), Centre III, Plot No. 3, Link Road, Karol Bagh, New Delhi.

Educational and Vocational Guidance Bureau, State Council of Educational Research and Training, Kennelworth Road, Laitumkhrah, Shilong, Meghalaya.

Educational and Vocational Guidance Department of State Educational Research and Training, BP Wadia Road, Basawangudi, Bangalore, Karnataka.

Educational and Vocational Guidance Section, Directorate of Education, Simla, Himachal Pradesh.

Government College of Educational Psychology and Guidance, Jabalpur, Madhya Pradesh.

Guidance and Counselling Wing, State Council of Educational Research and Training, Aizawl, Mizoram.

Guidance Resource Centre, State Institute of Education, Sector 32 C, Chandigarh.

Guidance Wing, State Council of Educational Research and Training, Mahendru, Patna, Bihar.

Guidance Wing, State Council of Educational Research and Training, Alwar Road, Gurgaon, Haryana.

Guidance Wing, State Institute of Education, Poojappura, Thiruvananthapuram, Kerala.

Guidance Wing, State Institute of Educational Research and Training, Saheli Marg, Udaipur, Rajasthan.

Institute of Vocational Guidance, Government of Gujarat, Ahmedabad.

Maharashtra State Council of Educational Research and Training, Institute of Vocational Guidance and Selection, Mahapalika Marg, Mumbai, Maharashtra.

Manovigyanshala, 2 Lowther Road, Allahabad, Uttar Pradesh.

Regional Institute of Guidance, Pushkar Road, Ajmer, Rajasthan.

Regional Institute of Vocational Guidance and Selection, Sadasiv Pethe, Pune, Maharashtra.

State Bureau of Educational and Vocational Guidance, Directorate of Secondary Education, Kahilipara, Guwahati, Assam.

State Bureau of Educational and Vocational Guidance, SCO, 66–67, Sector 17-A, Chandigarh.

State Council of Educational Research and Training, Aliya School Compound, Hyderabad, Andhra Pradesh.

State Council of Educational Research and Training, PRT Training College Compound, Raikhad, Ahmedabad, Gujarat.

Vocational Guidance and Counselling Wing, Directorate of School Education, Kohima, Nagaland.

Vocational Guidance Unit, State Council of Educational Research and Training and Non-formal Education, Directorate of Education, Imphal, Manipur.

Bibliography

Allport, G. W. 1937. *Personality: A Psychological Interpretation*. New York: Henry Holt & Co., Inc., pp. xiv, 588.

Arbuckle, D. S. 1965. *Counselling Philosophy, Theory and Practice*. Allyn and Bacon, Inc., Boston, pp. 63–70.

Bell, H. M. 1934. *The Adjustment Inventory*, Stanford University. California: Stanford University Press.

Bernreuter, Robert G. 1935. *Manual for the Personality Inventory*, Stanford University. California: Stanford University Press.

Bhatia, C. M. 1955. *Manual for the Administration of Bhatia Battery of Performance Tests of Intelligence under Indian Conditions*. Oxford: Oxford University Press.

Binet, A., and Th. Simon. 1905. *Methode Nouvelles pour le Diagnostic du Nouveau Intellectual Des Anormaux* (New methods to diagnose the intellectual level of abnormals). L' Année Psychologique, 11:245–366.

Bingham, W. V. 1937. *Aptitudes and Aptitude Testing*. New York: Harper and Brothers, pp. 16–7.

Bingham, W. V. D. 1942. *Aptitude and Aptitude Testing*. New York: Harper and Brothers.

Blum, M. L. 1944. *Industrial Psychology and Its Social Foundations*. New York: Harper & Bros., p. 448.

Blum, M., and B. Balinsky. 1959. *Counselling and Psychology: Vocational Psychology and Its Relation to Educational and Personal Counseling*. New Jersey: Prentice Hall.

Brewer, J. M. 1918. *The Vocational Guidance Movement*. New York: The Macmillan Co., p. 14.

Brewer, J. M. 1955. *Education as Guidance*. New York: The Macmillan.

Brown, A., and V. Martin. 1938. 'Anecdotal Records of Pupil Behavior.' *California Journal of Secondary Education* XIII:205–8.

Burt, C. 1949. 'The structure of the mind: a review of the result of factor analysis.' *British Journal of Educational Psychology* 19:110–1; 176–99.

Butcher J. N., and C. L. Williams. 1992. *Essentials of MMPI-2 and MMPI-A Interpretation*. Minneapolis: University of Minnesota Press.

Butcher J. N., W. G. Dahlstrom, J. R. Graham, A. Tellegen, and B. Kaemmer. 1989. *Minnesota Multiphasic Personality Inventory-2 (MMPI-2) Manual for Administration and Scoring*. Minneapolis: University of Minnesota Press.

Cardinal Principles of Secondary Education 1918 U.S. Office of Education Bulletin, 35, Washington Government Printing Office. Co.

Carl, R. R. 1942. *Counselling and Psychotherapy*. Boston: Houghton Mifflin Co.

Carl, R. R. 1958. 'The characteristics of a helping relationship.' *Personnel and Guidance Journal* 37:6.

Cattell, R. B., A. K. Cattell, and H. E. Cattell. 1993. *Sixteen Personality Factor Questionnaire*, 5th ed. Champaign, Illinois: Institute for Personality and Ability Testing.

Cemp, C. G. 1970. *Foundations of Group Counselling*. New York: McGraw-Hill Book Co., p. VII.

Cleeton, G. U. 1937. *Vocational Interest Inventory*. Bloomington, IIlinois: Mcknight and Mcknight.

Crow L. D., and A. Crow. 1962. *An Introduction to Guidance, Basic Principles and Practices*, 2nd ed. New Delhi: Eurasia Publishing House.

Cruickshank, W. M., and G. O. Johnson. eds. 1958. *Education of Exceptional Children and Youth*. New Jersey: Prentice Hall.

Downing, L. N. 1968. *Guidance and Counselling Services: An Introduction*. New York: McGraw-Hill Book Co., Inc.

Downing, L. N. 1968. *Elements and Services in Guidance Program*, Chapter 10. New York: McGraw-Hill Book Co.

Dugald, A. S. 1965. *Counselling Philosophy, Theory and Practice*. Boston: Allyn and Bacon, Inc., pp. 63–75.

English, H. B., and A. C. English. 1958. *A Comprehensive Dictionary of Psychological and Psychoanalytical Terms*. New York: Longmans Green & Co.

Erickson, K. A. 1962. *Blueprint for Counselling Programmes*, vol. 43. Phi Delta Kapar, pp. 304–11.

Eysenck, H. J. 1959. *Manual of the M.P.I.* London: University of London Press.

Froehlich, C. P. 1958. *Guidance Services in Schools*, 2nd ed., Chapter 11. New York: McGraw-Hill.

Galton, E. 1879. 'Psychometric Experiments.' Brain: *A Journal of Neurology*, 2:149–62.

Galton, F. 1883. *Inquiries into Human Faculty and Its Development*. London: Macmillan Co.

Garrett, H. E. 1971. *Statistics in Psychology and Education*. Bombay: Vakils, Feffer and Simons Pvt. Ltd.

Ginzberg, E., and others. 1951. *Occupational Choice an Approach to General Theory*. New York: Columbia University Press, p. 196.

Glanz, E. C. 1994. *Foundations and Principles of Guidance*. Boston: Allyn and Bacon, Inc., pp. 176–8.

Goleman, D. 1995. *Emotional Intelligence*. New York: Bantam Books.

Gough, H. G., and P. Bradley. 1996. *CPI Manual*, 3rd ed. Polo Alto, CA: Consulting Psychological Press.

Guilford, J. P. 1969. *The Nature of Human Intelligence*. New York: McGraw-Hill.

Guilford, J. P. 1988. 'Some changes in the structure of intellect model.' *Educational and Psychological Measurement* 48:1–4.

Guilford, J. P., and R. Hoepfner. 1971. *The Analysis of Intelligence*. New York: McGraw-Hill.

Hahn, M. E., and M. S. Maclean. 1955. *Counselling Psychology*. New York: McGraw-Hill, p. 6.

Hepner, H. W. 1931. *Vocational Interest Quotient Booklets*. New York: Psychological Corporation.

Holland, J. L. 1959. A theory of vocational choice. *Journal of Counselling Psychology* 59:35–45.

Humphrey, J. A., A. E. Traxler, and North R. D. 1960. *Chicago Guidance Services*, Science Research Associates, Inc., Chapter 10.

Humphreys, L. G. 1962. The organization of human abilities. *American Psychologist* 17:475–82.

Hunt, J. T. 1960. 'Guidance and the exceptional children.' *Education* 80:344.

Husband, R. W. 1949. *Applied Psychology*. New York: Harper & Bros.

Jalota, S. S. 1954. 'The psychologists' predicament.' *Calcutta Review*, pp. 37–8.

Jones, A. J. 1934. *Principles of Guidance*, 2nd ed. New York: McGraw-Hill Book Co., Inc., pp. xxvii, 456.

Jones, A. J. 1951. *Principles of Guidance*, 4th ed. New York: McGraw-Hill Books Co.

Jones, A. J., B. Stefflre, and N. R. Stewart. 1971. *Principles of Guidance*. New York: McGraw-Hill Books Co.

Jones A. J., B. Steffler, and N. R. Stewart. 1971. *Principles of Guidance*, 6th ed. Delhi: Tata McGraw-Hill Co., Inc., p. vii.

Kelley, T. L. 1914. *'Educational Guidance', Teachers College Contributions to Education*, vol. 71. New York: Teachers College, Columbia University, p. 4.

Kelley, T. L. 1928. *Crossroads in the Mind of Man: A Study of Differentiable Mental Abilities*. Stanford, CA: Stanford University Press.

Kulshreshtha, S. P. 1970. *Manual for Vocational Interest Record*. National Psychological Corporation, Agra: UP.

MacIver, R. M., and C. H. Page. 1961. *Society*. London: Macmillan Co., p. 213.

Maslow, A. H. 1954. *Motivation and Personality*. New York: Harper and Row.

Mc Adory, M. 1929. 'The construction and validation of an art test, teachers college contributions to education,' vol. 383. New York: Teachers College, Columbia University.

Moreno, J. L. 1953. *Who Shall Survive? Foundations of Sociometry, Group Psychotherapy and Sociolarma*, 2nd ed. New York: Beacon House.

Murray, H. A. et al. 1943. *Thematic Apperception Test: Manual*. Cambridge, MA: Harvard University Press.

Myers, G. E. 1906. 'Moral training in the school.' *Pedagogical Seminary* XIII: 452.

Myers, G. E. 1924. 'A critical review of present development in vocational guidance with special reference to future prospect.' *The Vocational Guidance Magazine* (March), vol. II, p. 139.

Myers, G. E. 1941. *Principles and Techniques of Vocational Guidance*, Chapter XV. New York and London: McGraw-Hill Book Co., Inc.

O' Connor, J. 1934. *Psychometrics*. Cambridge: Harvard University Press.

Parker, C. A. 1974. 'The new scope of counseling.' *Personnel and Guidance Journal* 52: pp. 348–50.

Paterson, D. G. and others. 1930. *Minnesota Mechanical Ability Tests*. Minneapolis: University of Minnesota Press.

Pepinsky, H. B. 1948. The Selection and Use of Diagnostic Categories in Clinical Counselling Applied Psychology Monograph No. 15.

Pepinsky, H. B., and P. Pepinsky. 1954. *Counselling: Theory and Practices*. New York: The Ronald Press.

Raven, J. 1983. 'The progressive matrices and mill hill vocabulary scale in western societies,' *Human Assessment and Cultural Factors*, eds. S. H. Irvine and J. W. Berry. New York: Plenum Press, pp. 107–14.

Robinson, F. P. 1950. *Principles and Procedures in Student Counselling*. New York: Harper and Row.

Roe, A. 1956. *The Psychology of Occupations*. New York: Wiley.

Roeber, E. C., C. E. Smith, and C. E. Erickson. 1955. *Organization and Administration of Guidance Services*. New York: McGraw-Hill Book Co., Inc.

Rogers, C. R. 1942. *Counselling and Psychotherapy*. Boston: Houghton Mifflin Co.

Rogers, C. R. 1951. *Client Centered Therapy*. Boston: Houghton Mifflin Co.

Rogers, C. R., and J. L. Wallen. 1946. *Counselling with Returned Servicemen*. New York: McGraw-Hill Book Co., Inc., p. 19–21.

Rorschach, H. 1942. *Psychodiagnostic, A Diagnostic Test Based on Perception* (ed. P. Lemkau and B. Kronenberg, Trans.). Berne: Huber (I. German, ed. Published 1921; U.S. Distributors: Grune and Stratton).

Seashore, C. E. 1916. 'Vocational guidance in music,' *Monographs*, First series, vol. 2. Iowa City: University of Iowa Press.

Seashore, C. E. 1920. *The Psychology of Musical Talent*. New York: Silver, Burdett and Co., pp. xxvi, 288.

Shaffer, L. F. and J. E. Shobbeh, 1956. *The Psychology of Adjustment*. Boston: Houghton Mifflin.

Spearman, C. S. 1904. 'General Intelligence' objectively determined and measured. *American Journal of Psychology* 15:201–93.

Spearman, C. S. 1927. *The Nature of Intelligence and the Principles of Cognition*. New York: Macmillan Co., pp. 5–6, 341–3.

Sprott, W. J. H. 1958. *Human Groups*. Harmondsworth: Penguin Books Ltd., p. 15.

Stenquist, J. L. 1923. *Measurements of Mechanical Ability*, New York: Teachers College Contributions to Education, Columbia University. vol. 130.

Sternberg, R. J. 1977. *Intelligence, Information Processing, and Analogical Reasoning: The Componential Analysis of Human Abilities*. Hillsdale, NJ: Erlbaum.

Sternberg, R. J. 1985. *Beyond IQ: A Triarchic Theory of Human Intelligence*. New York: Cambridge University Press (a).

Stewart, F. J., and Brainard. 1932. *Specific Internet Inventories*. New York: Psychological Corporation.

Strang, R. 1935. *The Role of the Teacher in Personal Work*. New York: Teachers College, Columbia University.

Strang, R. 1937. *Counselling Techniques in College and Secondary School*. New York: Harper & Bros., pp. xt, 159.

Strong, E. K. Jr. 1938. *Manual for Vocational Interest Blank for Men*. Stanford, CA: Stanford University Press, p. 1.

Super, D. E. 1949. *Appraising Vocational Fitness by Means of Psychological Tests*. New York: Harper and Row.

Super, D. E. 1953. 'A theory of vocational development.' *American Psychologist* 8:185–90.

Super, D. E. 1957. *The Psychology of Vocational Careers Development: An Introduction to Counselling*. New York: Harper and brothers.

Super, D. E., and J. O. Crites. 1962. *Appraising Vocational Fitness by Means of Psychological Tests*, rev. ed. New York: Harper & Row Publishers, Inc.

Terman, L. M. 1916. *The Measurement of Intelligence*. Boston: Houghton Miffin Co.

Terman, L. M. 1921. 'Intelligence and its measurement,' *Journal of Educational Psychology* XII: 128.

Terman, L. M., and M. A. Merrill. 1937. *Measuring Intelligence*. Boston: Houghton Merrill Co.

Terman, L. M., and M. A. Merrill. 1973. *Stanford-Binet Intelligence Scale*. Boston: Houghton Miffin Co.

The Principles and Practices of Educational and Vocational Guidance Report of the committee of the National Vocational Guidance Association, Occupations. 1950. *The Vocational Guidance* magazine, May 1937, pp. 772–8.

Thorne, F. C. 1950. 'Principles of personality counselling.' *Journal of Clinical Psychology* 301–2.

Thurstone, L. I. 1935. 'Factorial analysis of vocational interest,' paper presented at a meeting of the American Psychological Association.

Thurstone, L. L. 1938. 'Primary mental abilities.' *Psychometric Monographs* 1.

Traxler, A. E. 1957. *Techniques of Guidance*, rev. ed., New York: Harper and Bros.

Traxler, A. E., and D. N. Robert 1966. *Techniques of Guidance*. New York: Harper Row Publishers, Inc.

Tyler, L. E. 1961. *The Work of the Counsellor*, 3rd ed. New York: Appleton.

United States Employment Service. 1965. *Dictionary of Occupational Titles*, 3rd ed., Washington, D.C.: Government Printing Office.

Vernon, P. E. 1960. *The Structure of Human Abilities*, Rev. ed. London: Methuen.

Wechsler, D. 1939. *The Measurement of Adult Intelligence*. Baltimore: Williams and Wilkins.

Willey, R. De Verl, and D. C. Andrew. 1955. *Modern Methods and Techniques in Guidance*. New York: Harper and Row, Inc.

Williamson, E. G. 1950. *Counselling Adolescent*. New York: McGraw-Hill Book Co.

Williamson, E. G., and J. G. Darley. 1937. *Student Personnel Work*. New York: McGraw-Hill Book Co., Inc.

Woodworth, R. S. 1958. *Dynamic Psychology*. New York: Henry Holt & Co., Inc.

Index

P

Q

R

S